DARK DAYS
OF THE
REBELLION

Other books by Steve Meyer:
IOWA VALOR
IOWAN'S CALLED TO VALOR
DISCOVERING YOUR IOWA CIVIL WAR ANCESTRY

Dark Days
OF THE
Rebellion

Life in Southern Military Prisons

Benjamin F. Booth
& Steve Meyer

Meyer
Publishing

DARK DAYS OF THE REBELLION

Printed in the United States of America
First printing of revised edition: May 1996

Published by
Meyer Publishing
304 East Maple, Garrison, IA 52229

Meyer
Publishing

ISBN 0-9630284-5-6

Library of Congress Catalogue Number: 95-094880

To the Widows,
Children, Fathers, Mothers,
Brothers, Sisters, Friends
and Surviving Comrades

OF THE

THOUSANDS OF BRAVE MEN

Who left the pleasures and comforts
of home, abandoned cherished
enterprises and business schemes....

FOR THE PURPOSE OF

SERVING THEIR COUNTRY,

AND WHO HAVE BEEN CAPTURED BY THE
ENEMY WHILE IN THE FAITHFUL PER-
FORMANCE OF THEIR DUTY,

AND GONE DOWN TO

UNTIMELY GRAVES THROUGH UNPARALLELED
SUFFERINGS,

Is this Volume Most Respectfully Dedicated by

THE AUTHOR,
[B.F. BOOTH (1897)]

PREFACE

Nearly a century after the ink dried from Benjamin F. Booth's revelation of prison life at Libby, and more poignantly Salisbury, his words now deserve re-visitation and re-publication. For reasons known only to time, Salisbury Prison–a place synonymous with that of Andersonville in the agony it caused Union soldiers, has historically received only token notice alongside the more prominent accounts of Andersonville and other Confederate prisons such as Florence and Libby. Save for one comprehensive study–*The Salisbury Prison: A Case Study of Confederate Military Prisons: 1861-1865*, by Louis A. Brown, which served as an invaluable reference for my editorializing of this reproduction; nothing more has been written about Salisbury Prison.

Acknowledged in Brown's study of Salisbury Prison as the most complete account of Salisbury ever published was Benjamin F. Booth's *Dark Days of the Rebellion or Life in Southern Military Prisons*. Booth was known as "reporter" among his comrades at Salisbury. He strove to write daily a record of events that occurred in Salisbury Prison throughout his incarceration. No small task, given the conditions endured by the men imprisoned there. The difficulties he encountered in even finding paper (often scraps) to write upon, and in preserving these cherished notes through his life at Salisbury and his life afterward can but be imagined. Thirty years following his release from Salisbury these notes and observations were formulated into *Dark Days of the Rebellion or Life in Southern Military Prisons*. Family history reveals that Booth's book, when originally self-published, was not popular. Its unpopularity was not because of any particular literary style, but because of its stark revelation of the exacting toll taken upon Union soldiers at Salisbury, and Booth's prejudice and bitterness towards the southern people for the hardships he endured during his imprisonment. Few copies were sold, and family folklore has it that in later years Booth used many of his unsold books for fuel in his wood stove.

In Booth's words, the carnage inflicted by Americans on fellow Americans once again surfaces to reveal another microcosm of the great conflict which refined and defined our great nation during its trial from 1861 to 1865. To Booth's original text I have added my own introduction to the four principal parts of this book, and throughout the original text I have added some commentary and background information as well as photos. When needed I have also modified the original text to add clarity. Where this was done, diligence was paid to preserving Booth's intent. As was typical of the age, Booth used commas more frequently than contemporary writers and readers prefer, and thus created sentences of paragraph length. These I broke up to make a more readable text. Booth also had the somewhat annoying habit of abruptly changing from first to third person and past to present tense abruptly and seemingly without purpose. This problem I have also endeavored to smooth out by various means.

I must mention one error in Booth's statements from his Foreword, wherein he states that more Union soldiers died in Salisbury than in any other prison during the Civil War. Though there is no doubt that Salisbury Prison was a bad place, the distinction of harboring the greatest number of deaths goes to the infamous Andersonville. Lest the reader assume that the South was alone in indecent treatment of its prisoners during the war, research has found conditions were not any better in the North, and an equal amount of suffering was inflicted upon Confederate prisoners by the Union.

For first making me aware of Benjamin F. Booth's book, and for making a transcript available to me, I would like to recognize O. J. Fargo. I would also like to thank a descendent of Booth; Carol Floyd Gross, for providing me with some biographical and family information. Others who were of considerable assistance in were Louis A. Brown, a Salisbury Prison historian; W. Clark Kenyon, the foremost historian I know of the 22nd Iowa Infantry; Edwin C. Bearrs, William J. Miller, and James A. Percocco, who took the time to review *Dark Days of the Rebellion* and provide testimonial of its worth. Without the assistance of these individuals this book would not have been possible.

Steve Meyer
1995

BENJAMIN F. BOOTH

Photo possibly taken at about the time he wrote *Dark Days of the Rebellion or Life in Southern Military Prisons.*

FOREWORD

By B. F. Booth
(1897)

The following pages are offered to inquiring minds with the hope that they may throw some light upon the inhuman treatment we received in Southern prisons.

The multiplied woes of the battle-field, the suffering of the sick and wounded in hospitals which the federal government had established, might almost be considered the enjoyments of Paradise, when compared with the heart-rending and prolonged agonies of captives in rebel stockades.

For thirty-one years I have waited and watched for some one to publish a history of Salisbury, N.C., Prison, but I have waited in vain. I am egotistic enough to believe that the reason why such a history has not appeared is because no other man brought out from that place of inhuman torture has the data from which to compile such a history. It is a singular fact that Libby, Andersonville, Belle Isle, and other Southern prisons have had such a large place in the published records of the war, that they have become household names in Northern homes; while I am convinced that thousands of our loyal people do not know that such a place as Salisbury Prison ever existed. And yet, in this prison pen more of our brave and noble soldiers were killed, died from starvation, and from numerous loathsome diseases and conditions, than in any other prison in the Southern Confederacy during the dark days of the war. My only purpose in writing this book is to give a true record of life and conditions as I experienced and observed them during my imprisonment in Libby and Salisbury prisons. Every day of the time, beginning with my capture October 19, 1864, to my return home, March 19, 1865 (except during my long sickness after reaching home), I kept a true and faithful record of all that was experienced by me or that passed under my eyes. To what straits I was often put to get material on which to write the daily record–the scraps of paper, books, in fact, anything and everything that would show a pencil mark, the careful treasuring of bits of pencils, often less than an inch in length; the many narrow escapes I ran of losing my precious records, and the many ways which I took to hide them from the eyes of prison authorities, who would never have allowed me to take them out of the prison if they had known I had them; of these and many other interesting things connected with the making and preservation of this journal, I can not now write.

I am aware it would be an unpardonable presumption for me to pretend to claim that this is a complete history of Salisbury Prison. No; no tongue nor pen can tell the whole, dreadful story of this awful place. I do claim that it is a correct history so far as the experience, observation, study and conscientious preservation of written facts one man can make of it. My claim of accuracy is strengthened by endorsements received from officers of the Confederate army who were familiar with the prison, and from hundreds of comrades who were sad participants with me in the events and experiences of which I have written. For reasons stated at the proper place, the schedule of the daily deathlist, found in Chapter XXII, who were taken out and buried in the trenches was made by my own hands from the records of the dead-house the day I went out of the prison, and is the only record of the Salisbury Prison dead in existence. It is absolutely correct as I have still in my possession the original record made by me in that dead-house.

Some there are who will say; why publish such books? Why not let bygones be bygones? Why not let the dead past stay where it belongs? Instead of arousing animosity, and perpetuating the bitterness of those sad days, we ought to do all we can to blot out the dark memories and perpetuate peace and good-will among all men.

That is true. We rejoice that the war is over; that peace reigns over all the land; that nature and the advance of enterprise are slowly, but surely, blotting out all traces of Southern prison pens; that our glorious flag waves over a united nation. I rejoice in all this, while at the same time I am sure that the story of our great conflict for the preservation of the Union, and the defense of our flag, will never cease to be of interest and importance to those who were either directly or indirectly engaged in the mighty conflict. This Nation can not afford to forget the men who fought its battles from 1861 to 1865. It cannot afford to forget the deeds of daring and suffering on battlefields and in prison pens which make these years the most memorable in American history.

I do not ask for vengeance or retribution for the thousands of heroic men who died from murder, starvation, cruelty and disease in these prison pens of the Confederacy. I only ask that the great sacrifices of my dead comrades shall not be suffered to pass into oblivion. I ask that the example of this noble heroism and loyalty to their country and their flag shall not be forgotten or treated as a mere trifle. Let their deeds be treasured and handed down to the generations yet to come, that they too may be as ready to do, and dare, and die for right, honor and good government, when these are assailed by the enemies of the Nation, whether at home or abroad, as were the men of 1861-1865. It seems to me that in order to show our appreciation of their virtue, and reap the reward of their sowing of tears and blood, we must hold up to some the crime of those who made their sacrifices necessary. I can not understand what good examples of such heroic sacrifice can accomplish if they are to be followed by such a maudlin confusion of moral ideas as now threaten to obliterate all distinction between the men who fought, and suffered, and died for the right, and those who resisted, killed and tortured them for the wrong.

I am conscious that, from a literary standpoint, this book is open to severe criticism. I do not claim literary accuracy for it. I have endeavored to give, as nearly as I could, the facts as they were originally constructed. Therefore, I get the leniency of critics, bearing in mind that my only purpose is to give a plain, honest, impartial history of life in Salisbury Prison–the only work of the kind now in existence.

B. F. BOOTH,
Company I, 22d Iowa Infantry.
(1897)

CONTENTS

PART 1

THE 22ND IOWA INFANTRY

On August 18, 1862, twenty-five year old Benjamin F. Booth became a member of the 22nd Iowa Infantry and the growing legion of men from a state which distinguished itself above all others in its patriotism to the Union cause. Though the blood-letting of such battles as Shiloh, which had exacted a heavy toll on Iowa troops, had touched every living soul of the Hawkeye State, the aura of patriotism continued to inspire Iowa men from all walks of life to answer the Union's call.

Originally the 22nd Iowa Infantry set out to be the Johnson County Regiment, with all one-thousand of its men coming from Johnson County, home to the first capitol of Iowa–Iowa City. The recruiting effort for this endeavor fell short of its goal, and three companies, with one each from Jasper, Monroe and Wapello counties, were added to the seven hundred recruits from Johnson County to complete the regiment's roster. Company I was the lot to which Booth was assigned. At the time of his enlistment he lived in the now long forgotten town of Foote, Iowa, in southeastern Iowa County, which bordered Johnson County. The town is listed as having a post office from 1863 to 1900. Now the streets of Foote where Booth and others walked are part of Iowa's cornfield landscape.

Like many others enlisting, Booth had little idea of, and perhaps little cared to think of, what lay ahead over the next three years. He went into the camp of instruction with the 22nd Iowa Infantry and the 28th Iowa Infantry at Camp Pope, one of Iowa's wartime "Camps of Instruction." Camp Pope was located on the outskirts of Iowa City and was overlooked by Governor Samuel Kirkwood's home. At Camp Pope the rudimentary training required of all recruits was imparted to them, and on September 15, 1862, the regiment departed for Benton Barracks in St. Louis, where it remained until its dispatch for duty southward only one week later on the 22nd of September.

Under command of Colonel William M. Stone, the 22nd Iowa first tasted combat during Grant's Vicksburg Campaign in such memorable action as the Battle of Port Gibson, the Battle of Champion Hill, and the Engagement at Big Black River Bridge. At Big Black River Bridge the 22nd Iowa had its first opportunity to display its valiant fighting character. The 22nd was brigaded together with the 21st and 23rd Iowa Infantry Regiments, the 1st Iowa Battery of Light Artillery and the 11th Wisconsin Infantry. This brigade was commanded by Colonel Stone. At

William M. Stone: First Colonel of the 22nd Iowa Infantry and Iowa's Second "War Governor."

Champion Hill on May 16, the 22nd was held in reserve, but on the following day its brigade carried the front of an assault on Big Black River Bridge where the brigade succeeded in overpowering a reinforced Confederate position. In that assault 221 of the 279 Union casualties were born by this brigade–Colonel William H. Kinsman of the 23rd Iowa was killed, and Colonel Samuel Merrill of the 21st Iowa was severely wounded.

The fighting character of the 22nd was again, and probably never more aptly, displayed on the 22nd of May, 1863, during Grant's second assault on Vicksburg. It was on this day that the 22nd Iowa, leading a charge upon Vicksburg, gained the distinction of being the only Union troops to actually gain the works of Vicksburg during the long period of combat action that city was subjected to. On this day, fifteen members of the 22nd Iowa under the leadership of Sergeant Joseph E. Griffith of Company I, succeeded in planting the flag of the 22nd Iowa on top of Railroad Redoubt ("Fort Beauregard") at Vicksburg. They entered the fort, were unable to be reinforced, but did manage to send out thirteen captives and maintain their position until the end of the day. Of those who actually entered the fort, only Sergeant Griffith and David Trine, also of Company I, retreated to safety at the end of the day.

In the valiant charge and effort on May 22, Colonel Stone and Major John B. Atherton were wounded, Lieutenant Colonel Harvey Graham was captured, and nearly one half of the men engaged from the 22nd Iowa were casualties. Sergeant Leonidas Godley of Company E was wounded severely three times. After he lay wounded in the sun all day he was taken prisoner and had his leg amputated without anesthetics. He survived in spite of these injuries, and was later awarded the Medal of Honor. In 1868, Joseph Griffith, who was promoted to 2nd Lieutenant of Company I on the 22nd of May, wrote the following description of that memorable day:

The 22d Iowa belonged to the 2d Brigade, 14th Division, 13th Army Corps, according to the re-organization of the Army of the Tennessee in the March preceding the Vicksburg Campaign. History records the events of the march through Louisiana to Hard Times Landing, the passage of the Mississippi below Grand Gulf in the face of the enemy, the eighteen days' campaign, the brilliant affairs of Port Gibson, Champion Hills, and Black River Bridge.

In the march towards the river from the rear, after the severing of the armies of Johnston and Pemberton, the 13th Army Corps occupied the left of the line, and was led by McClernand. The impetuosity of the movements from Champion Hills over the Black River gave the enemy no time to rally his men until the walls of Vicksburg formed a barrier to give them shelter. On the 18th of May the Union lines enveloped the fated fortress, from Haines' Bluffs to within a short distance of Warrenton. In this victorious array and along the line of the Jackson

Railroad, was posted the 22d Iowa. Forming but a small integral part of the heroic band which so fearlessly bearded the lion in his den, it still made itself heard and seen in the transactions of the envelopment, prior to the last charge. Men who had accustomed themselves to be regarded as invincible, who had been victorious on every field, following in the trail of the fortuitous events which Grant had dictated, clamorously begged to be led on to those ominous-looking earth-works. Do those now living of that number present, remember the feelings experienced on the night of the 21st of May, when towards dark the word came from headquarters that, at ten o'clock the next day, our wishes were to be gratified? They certainly must, for such thoughts come but once in a life time.

Our troops were then on the line of hills nearest, and parallel to the commanding heights occupied by the rebel works. After dark, about 11 o'clock, we moved over the hill, carrying the ammunition and the necessaries of a battlefield on our shoulders. The remainder of the night we slept in the ravine under the guns of the forts. The rebel picket on the side and crest of the hill must have had a forewarning of the events of the coming day, for how restlessly did he gaze and peer into the darkness below him! Our boys now realized, in the few unexcited hours which separated us from the Johnnies, that we had an affair on hand which would cost us much blood; and yet how jokingly the men talked of eating dinner at the Washington Hotel; and many a one who had hopes of a furlough to go home, at the close of "to-morrow," had received his final furlough—lay stretched in death. The men, wearied with their labors and vigils of the three previous weeks, stretched their limbs for a few hours' rest, preparatory to the work before them. How merrily, in the silent hours of the night even, did the light-heartedness of our soldiers compare with the well-known sang froid of the followers of Napoleon's eagles, thinking only of certain victory. The bed picked out, the watchful sentinel alone showed signs of life.

Promptly at daybreak of the 22d of May, to prevent a surprise, the regiment is up, cooking their breakfast; the knapsacks and extra equipment's are piled up, each company by itself, and a man detailed to guard them. Early in the morning a detail is sent up to the crest of the hill to skirmish with the enemy. Company "A" is afterwards sent out on the same duty. The balance of the regiment is variously occupied. No signs of trepidation, no anxieties shown to avoid the unequal contest which is felt to be coming on; and yet many, acting under the admonitions of a presentiment, prepare their worldly affairs and seek peace with their Maker.

The ground in front of the rebel fort which we are to assault is in part a level plateau, the rest small ravines, intersected by ruts and hollows; all exposed to a direct enfilading and in part a reverse fire from the enemy. We are happily ignorant of the locality until the moment had come where we are to cross it, or I imagine the men would not possess the firm appearance of victory and success which they do. The numbers of the enemy are also unknown to us. It is imagined that the rebels dare not make a very strong defense.

About a half an hour before ten, the regiment is called to "Attention!" in two lines, the right wing in front. The 21st Iowa is on our left, the 19th Kentucky and 77th Illinois are to support us. The lines move forward, up the hill—a difficult operation, too, in line of battle; the ground being so cut up, we are sheltered from fire until near the crest. We know that Grant, McClernand, Carr and Lawler are watching our movements; but we little know of the warm reception which we are to receive in a few moments. Our color bearer is in the front rank—the same flag which we carried from Camp Pope eight months ago is inciting us to victory. Stone, Graham, Robertson, are exhorting us to do our duty; it is unnecessary—each one of that column feels that his beloved Iowa is looking for good news from her sons.

The 22nd Iowa Infantry planting its flag upon Railroad Redoubt
(Photo courtesy Mason & Eddy–San Francisco)

Quietly and in good order the regiment advances to the summit, outstripping the troops on the right and left in the race for glory; but how soon does the devoted hand discover the true position of affairs, when with a yell of defiance it starts over the intervening ground which separated it from the front of Fort Beauregard! Leaving their comrades by the scores, the remainder dauntlessly close on the enemy, who from the moment a head was visible over the crest of the hill, has been delivering a constant and well-directed fire of grapeshot, shell,

6

musketry, glass, railroad iron, and even hickory nuts. To add to the embarrass-ment, a well intended but poorly directed fire from an Ohio battery in our rear works, is committing havoc in our ranks; the gallant Robb thus fell a victim to the excitement of the cannoniers. Imagine the surprise of the men who had crossed the plateau safely, to find a deep and wide ditch encompassing the enemy's works. For a moment, and but a moment, does the line waver, when with a jump the men are in the ditch, and force the enemy to keep under cover; a dead space is found under the salient of the fort, which partly screens the fire. They endeavor to scale the works and force an entrance into the bastion. Thirteen men succeeded in planting the colors on the parapet, and enter to contest for the possession of an angle of the work between one of the curtains and a bomb-proof magazine. The enemy was forced to surrender, and before night a lieutenant and twelve men were safely turned over to General McClernand.

All day did the flag remain on the works; no reinforcements came; our sharpshooters had dug their rat-holes on the outside of the parapet, and fired incessantly. The enemy, elated at the wholesale butchery of the morning, took courage and occupy all the main parts of the work. It was evident to the remain-ing few of the 22d Iowa, that it was necessary to leave the ditch at the first opportunity, or all would be captured. All hopes are given up of taking Vicks-burg. Favored by darkness, some return to the ground left in the morning; but Lieut.-Col. Graham, Capt. Gearky, and fifteen men are taken prisoners.

Imagine the picture presented to the eye that night. Vicksburg still in the hands of the enemy; the ground literally strewn with dead bodies; the groans of the wounded and dying so appalling; the assault a failure, merely from the want of more support. Within and on the banquette of the salient lie the cold corpses of Marvin, Hale, Kirk, Griffin, Robb, the two Drummond boys Jordan and Fry, who so fearlessly sacrificed their young lives in a hand-to-hand contest with the foe, and who in their ardor thought only of opening a passage into the Gibraltar of the South. Shades of those brave men who fell within the fort, and far from any succor! Ye fell not as victims but as martyrs in the cause of freedom, and in support of the Constitution! Alone, and seen only by Him who rules all things, ye fought the rebels with cold steel; and in giving up your lives forced him to sur-render. Your dead bodies formed a barrier to the enemy from touching yonder flag, which defiantly waves, though shattered and torn.

Not quite as far to the front, and in the ditch, fell Lieut. Robb (afterwards carried to the rear), Hamlin, and many others—an awful spectacle of slaughter. On the plateau, and fallen early in the fray, with upturned faces are Robertson, Lamb, and others. Col. Stone has been borne off the field, Lieut.-Col. Graham is a prisoner; few officers who were with the regiment in the morning escaped un-scathed; the fragments of the gallant band who received their "eighty rounds" the night before, were left on the night of 22d May. Scarcely a handful rallied

7

around that jolly old soul, Jim Sterling, the Quartermaster, whose forethought had provided a supper. A stern, silent, and sober array formed around the campfires behind the 1st U. S. Infantry that night. A shovel-full of dirt over each dead body, and a handful of cotton under the boys over the hill yonder in Carr's Division Hospital, is all the care necessary to-night.

The next morning, as if nothing had happened, those left formed in the trenches, and from that time until the Fourth of July, patiently and stoically they labor with the spade and musket; and on the anniversary day of American Independence, those hated flags of secession are lowered before the glorious old flag "which bears the stripes and stars."

Harvey Graham: Second Colonel of the 22nd Iowa Infantry.

Colonel Stone returned home to Iowa to recuperate from his wound. He never rejoined his regiment, for while home he became involved in the gubernatorial race. He secured the Republican nomination for Governor over Brigadier General Fitz Henry Warren, the first Colonel of the 1st Iowa Cavalry. Stone then went on to become Iowa's second "War Governor" by defeating Brigadier General James M. Tuttle, the second colonel of the 2nd Iowa Infantry who ran as a Democrat. Command of the 22nd Iowa then was given to Lieutenant Colonel Harvey Graham.

Following the surrender of Vicksburg on July 4, 1863, and the subsequent military action against Jackson, Mississippi, in the weeks following Vicksburg's fall, the 22nd Iowa entered a rather uneventful period of its Civil War service. During this time from August of 1863 to July of 1864 the 22nd Iowa was assigned to the Department of the Gulf where the regiment saw service in Louisiana and Texas. Part of this time period was spent in the ill-fated Red River Campaign led by Major General Nathaniel Banks.

In July of 1864 news reached the 22nd Iowa that they were to be transferred to one of the hotbeds of the war–the Shenandoah Valley in Virginia. Together with the 24th and 28th Iowa Infantry Regiments, the 22nd traveled by steamer from New Orleans to City Point, Virginia, and then to Washington DC, where they joined the forces of Major General Philip Sheridan's Shenandoah Valley Campaign. Originally more Iowa troops were to have been sent, but the situation in the western and southern theaters of the war dictated they remain where they were. Once the Iowa troops had arrived in Washington DC, they were greeted by crowds of curious onlookers who wished to see how these western troops compared to soldiers of the Army of the Potomac.

The Shenandoah Valley was a major source of food supplies for the Confederacy. If Confederates could be driven from this area, the Confederacy could be broken. Previous attempts had failed, but Sheridan's campaign finally succeeded. Costs, however, were high. Three battles were fought in Sheridan's Shenandoah Valley Campaign: the Third Battle of Winchester (Opequon) on September 19, 1864, Fisher's Hill on September 22, and Cedar Creek on October 19. In the Shenandoah Valley, once again the 22nd Iowa proved its fighting merit, as also did the 24th and the 28th Iowa. Nearly one half of the men who were with these three regiments in the Shenandoah Valley were casualties.

The 22nd Iowa remained in the Shenandoah Valley until January, 1865. The regiment was then moved to Savannah, Georgia, where they remained until March, when the regiment was sent to Morehead City, North Carolina. In May the 22nd Iowa was sent to Augusta, Georgia, where it performed duty for a brief time before returning to Savannah in July for its final muster and discharge.

A total of 1084 men (including replacements) had enrolled and fought with the 22nd Iowa during its tenure of service. Over one half of these men were casualties: 60 were killed in action, 267 were wounded (55 died of wounds they received), 128 died of disease, 187 were discharged for wounds or disease, and 79 were captured.

Four hundred and thirty-seven men were on the rolls of the 22nd Iowa at muster-out. These men set foot on Iowa soil, some for the first time in three years, on July 27th at Davenport. The regiment was paid and discharged on August 3, and on the 11th it was honored at a gala celebration at the fairgrounds in Iowa City. Here, Governor Stone gave the following address:

Soldiers of Iowa:—The conspicuous and honorable part you have borne in the arduous struggle for the preservation of our national government, has excited the admiration of your countrymen and secured for yourselves an imperishable name. Your constancy and patience so often tried, your patriotism and valor universally acknowledged, have culminated in the triumph of national authority and the perpetuity of the Union which our fathers established. With your bayonets the name of Iowa has been carved upon the brightest pages of American history. From the banks of the Des Moines you fought your way to the Gulf of Mexico and the Atlantic seaboard, stacking your arms at the close of the war on the banks of the Potomac in the shadow of the Nation's Capitol.

Such marches, sieges and battles the world has never witnessed before, within, ancient or modern times, surpassing in boldness of execution the world renowned, campaigns of Cyrus or Alexander, Caesar or Napoleon, they will give historic, grandeur to the age and render universal the glory of our arms.

In the name of the people of Iowa, whose country you have saved and whose State you have honored, I bid you the assurance of their pride, your fame, and their lasting gratitude for your heroic achievements.

Nobly have you maintained the honor of our State in every campaign and battle, and faithfully redeemed the confidence reposed in your valor. Looking upon your now thinned ranks, we are mournfully reminded of your comrades slumbering in their lonely graves in the fields of glory where they died. Your banners torn by the storm and dimmed by the smoke of battle we shall receive from your hands and safely deposit among the other valued memorials of your fame. The remembrance of your honorable scars and many victories will be reverently cherished and transmitted as a part of the common heritage. Soldiers in war, you return as citizens to mingle with your friends and engage in the pursuit of peace.

Committing to the care of a generous people the widows and orphans of those who are fallen, we invoke for the surviving heroes the continued guidance of Him who sheltered them amid the trials and dangers of war.

CHAPTER I.

A t the hour of 2 o'clock in the afternoon of April 11th, 1861, General
Beauregard, commanding the Provisional Army of the Confederate
States of America, at Charleston, S.C., sent a courier to Major Robert Anderson, of the 1st U.S. Artillery, commanding Fort Sumpter, demanding,
in the name of the Confederate States of America, the surrender of the
Fort, its garrison and equipment, and specifying the hour of 6 o'clock
p.m., as the limit of time allowed for answer to his demand. Within the
time specified, Major Anderson returned the following answer:

"*I have the honor to acknowledge the receipt of your communication
demanding the evacuation of this Fort, and to say in reply thereto, that
it is a demand that which I regret my sense of honor and of my obligations to my Government, prevent my compliance.*"

Beauregard at once wired Major Anderson's answer to the Confederate Secretary of War at Richmond, to which that official replied as follows:

"*Do not desire needlessly to bombard Fort Sumpter. If Major Anderson will state the time at which, as indicated by himself he will
evacuate, and agree that in the meantime he will not use his guns
against us, unless ours should be employed against Fort Sumpter, you
are authorized thus to avoid the effusion of blood. If this, or its equivalent, be refused, reduce the fort as your judgment decides to be practica-
ble.*"

At the hour of 11 o'clock that night General Beauregard conveyed to
Major Anderson the substance of his instructions from the Confederate

Secretary of War. To this communication Major Anderson responded by courteously, but firmly, refusing to surrender or evacuate Fort Sumpter unless compelled to do so by the success of the assaulting forces, or by order of the United States Government. There upon Beauregard telegraphed the Confederate Secretary at Richmond:

"He will not consent."

At 3 o'clock a.m., Major Anderson received Beauregard's ultimatum in the following message conveyed to him by Col. Chestnut and Captain Lee:

"By authority of Brigadier General Beauregard, commanding the Provisional Forces of the Confederate States, we have the honor to notify you that he will open the fire of his batteries on Fort Sumpter in one hour from this time."

Already Stevens' mortar battery at Sullivan Island was shorted, ready to open fire on Fort Sumpter. At precisely 4:30 o'clock in the morning of the 12th of April, 1861, Beauregard gave the fatal order. At once an old man, lean and long-haired, with eyes fairly blazing in their sockets, tottered forward and eagerly grasping in his long, bony hands a lanyard, pulled the string. A flash, a roar, and away across the waters of Charleston Bay speeds the shrieking shell on its mission of death and destruction. The old man worked his fingers in an ecstasy of fiendish delight, while he chuckled and raved to those about him:

"Aye, I told them at Columbia that night, that the defense of the South is to be secured only through the lead of South Carolina; and, old as I am, I had come here to join them in that lead–and I have done it!"

The first shot was followed by a most withering and continuous bombardment from the network of batteries with which the rebels had invested Fort Sumpter. Reinforcements failing to reach him, the fort in ruins, his guns dismounted, his powder magazines exploded–leaving him only four barrels and three cartridges of powder, his provisions all gone, fire spreading on every hand until there was not a portion of the fort left where a breath of air could be got, except through a wet cloth; the brave Anderson was compelled to capitulate and surrender the fort on the terms offered by Beauregard on the 11th. On Sunday forenoon, April 14th, with colors flying and drums beating, he marched his gallant command out of the wreck of Form Sumpter, bringing away company and private property, and saluting his flag with fifty guns.

The first blow struck at the flag almost paralyzed the North. The first reports of the conflict were discredited, many deeming such a thing impossible. But the announcement of the surrender of Fort Sumpter, the defiant editorials of the leading southern papers and the proclamation of President Lincoln calling for 75,000 volunteers which appeared in the northern papers on Monday morning, April 15th, arousing the North to a sense of the situation, and the terrible fact that the threats of the Southern fire eaters were at last put into execution, and the great civil war—the conflict and crime of the ages—was inaugurated.

The work of enlisting soldiers in response to the call of the President was carried forward with the greatest enthusiasm. Crowds of excited men marched and countermarched through the cities and towns of the North. Drums were beating, banners flying, while the air was rent with the wildest cheering for the Union. Not only was the call for 75,000 men at once filled, but over half a million men were clamoring for the privilege of being enrolled for the defense of the Union and the honor of the flag. It soon became apparent to President Lincoln that 75,000 troops were not enough to meet the demands of the war which was now on in full force, so in May he issued another proclamation calling for 42,000 additional troops whose term of enlistment would be for three years or during the war.

After some preliminary skirmishing, resulting in some loss on both sides, the first great battle of the war, known as the Battle or Bull Run, was fought on the 21st of July, 1861. The Union forces were repulsed and retreated in a somewhat demoralized condition on the City of Washington; but it is also true that the enemy was even more seriously defeated. General Stonewall Jackson, in his report of the battle, confesses that, although he had, at the last moment, broken the center of the Union line, both flanks of his own army were turned and placed in great danger of being totally defeated. The most that can be said for this first serious battle of the terrible civil war is that it was a drawn battle. The war was now fully inaugurated, and the loyal people of the North awoke to the fact that the forces already in the field were not sufficient to conquer the South and preserve the Union.

The battles which were fought in the early part of the war convinced President Lincoln and his Cabinet that the war was going to be one of vast proportions and in order to strengthen the army and put troops enough in the field to conquer the rebellious South, he issued his call for 300,000 additional volunteers. As soon as the old war Governor of Iowa, Hon. Samuel J. Kirkwood, received notice of Iowa's quota, he at once issued his proclamation calling on the loyal people of the State to meet it. Recruiting officers were at work in the towns and cities of the State and the work of enlistment went on rapidly and with great enthusiasm. Regiment after regiment was mustered into the service and was sent to the front, and in a very short time Iowa's quota was full and thousands were still offering their services to their country.

The author of this book was one of the many thousands who responded to this last call, enlisting in Company I, 22nd Iowa Infantry, at Iowa City, in the month of July, 1862, and was mustered into service August 9, 1862, by General Henderson, U.S. Mustering Officer. The regiment remained in Iowa City at what was known as "Camp Pope," until September 25th, when it was armed, equipped and sent to the front to become a part of the great army which had already preceded it. When the regiment left, most of the recruits had bidden good-bye to wives, children, fathers, mothers, brothers, and sisters. We left the comforts and safety of home for the privations and dangers of a soldier's life to engage in the great conflict for God and human rights with high hopes that the war would end long before the term of our enlistment which was for three years or during the war. Alas, how little we knew what those years would bring forth, or through what scenes and experiences of trial and suffering we would pass before the time of our service was ended.

The regiment arrived at Benton Barracks, St. Louis, Missouri, early in October, where we spent a short time, the greater part of which was devoted to the task of drilling. About the middle of October we were ordered to Rolla, Missouri, where we were assigned to garrison duty at that important post. Here we spent the greater part of the winter of 1862 and 1863, guarding commissary stores, protecting railroad trains, providing escorts to the wagon trains carrying stores and ammunition to the different detachments and army posts in western and southern Missouri. At that period, there were no large forces of rebels in Missouri. Price had been driven out of the State and his command broken up into detach-

Prior to the Civil War, four distinct parties of conflicting sentiment existed in Missouri. There were militant secessionists, equally militant Unionists, moderates of Southern sympathy and also Union moderates. In 1861 the state's newly appointed Governor, Claiborne Jackson, attempted to side the state with the Confederacy. That effort was stymied, Jackson was deposed, and the state remained in the Union. However, it was a divided state in which combat occurred throughout the duration of the Civil War with 1,162 battles engagements, skirmishes and other incidents of combat being fought within the borders of Missouri, a total exceeded only by Virginia and Tennessee. As a state Missouri mustered 109,000 men into the Union Army and 40,000 officially into the Confederate Army. Numerous other Missourians, however, fought as vigilantes or guerrilla warriors on behalf of the Confederate cause.

ments and guerrilla bands, whose business it was to attack scouting parties from the Union posts, harass

STERLING PRICE

Major General Sterling Price launched his Civil War career fighting to hold Missouri for the Confederacy, and he never stopped pursuing that elusive goal throughout the conflict. He had migrated to the Missouri frontier at age 21 with his father and soon became a prominent slave-owning tobacco planter and political leader. During the Mexican War he was military governor of New Mexico and earned a brigadier general's star. He was the embodiment of Missouri's rural aristocracy. He served as a Missouri legislator from 1836-38 and 1840-44; congressman, 1844-46; governor, 1852-56; and commander of state troops. Price at first opposed Missouri's secession but in May 1861 became outraged at the takeover of Camp Jackson, St. Louis, and offered his sword to the South as commander of state troops. In uneasy concert with Brig. Gen. Ben McCulloch, he defeated Lyon at Wilson's Creek, Mo., and soon captured the large Union garrison at Lexington. But he was to win no more major victories. He feuded with McCulloch, with whom he was teamed in the Confederate defeat at Pea Ridge, Ark., then commanded the ill-fated Army of the West at Iuka, Corinth, and Helena, Ark., in 1862-63. Early in 1864 he helped repulse Union Maj. Gen. Frederick Steele's Camden Expedition. Price's final bid for fame came late in 1864 when he was chosen by Gen. E. Kirby Smith to lead the Army of Missouri in the expedition known as Price's Missouri Raid. After driving spectacularly from southeast to northwest Missouri Price's depleted force was driven back into Arkansas. After the Confederacy fell, Price went to Mexico, returned to St. Louis in Jan., 1867, impoverished and broken in health. He died there eight months later.

and hinder the movement of supplies by rail and wagon trains. The men composing these roving, plundering, marauding bands were thoroughly acquainted with the country in which they operated, therefore it required the presence of staunch escorts to save the supply trains from being captured and destroyed, or turned over to the service of their friends. This kind of service, performed as it was, in all kinds of weather and over roads that were often almost impassable, crossing streams for the most part bridgeless, making it necessary for the soldiers to wade them neck deep in mud and water, impressed the men of the 22nd Iowa that real soldiering was not child's play.

On the 9th of February, 1863, we were ordered to break camp and be ready to march at the hour of noon of the same day. Our destination was West Plains, Missouri, thence over the Ozark Mountains to Iron Mountain, from there to St. Genevieve, on the Mississippi River, where we were to embark on a steamboat for Milliken's Bend, near Vicksburg. One morning a courier was carrying an order from Brigadier General Davidson, who was in command of the expedition, to Colonel Stone, who commanded the 22nd Iowa, when he was fired upon by a bushwhacker who was hidden in the dense undergrowth which lined the road on either side. Before the bushwhacker could make good his escape, he was captured, brought into our camp and placed under guard. Continuing our march over the mountains, we passed

John Wynn Davidson was a Virginia native who entered West Point in 1841, where he graduated 27th in his class. His military service began with the 1st Dragoons. At the outbreak of the Civil War he was a captain with the 1st U.S. Cavalry, and then the 2nd U.S. Cavalry. He recieved commission as Brig. Gen. of Volunteers in February of 1862 and Maj. Gen. of Volunteers in March of 1865.

through a desolate, uninhabited region, not a human being or habitation being visible in the heavy timber. Suddenly we came upon a small log cabin which our prisoner said was his residence. Having asked and gained permission to see his wife, with the injunction to make the interview very brief, he called her to the door where they engaged in conversation for a few moments. He was then ordered to close the sad interview and move forward, but being stubborn and rather slow to comply, he was brought to his senses, and to compliance with the order, by the sharp prick of a bayonet. He moved on with dogged steps about one hundred yards, and then, without uttering a word he made one desperate leap from the side of his guard, gained the timber and with the fleetness of a deer, ran down a steep hill. Instantly a dozen or more guns were leveled upon him. Three times he was ordered to halt, which he disregarded, when a volley was sent after the fleeing man, and he fell dead. His wife seeing the desperate leap he had made for his life, and seeing him fall at the report of the guns, came running to his aid, but she was too late to render him any assistance, his spirit had already ascended to God who gave it. The desperate man had paid the penalty of his attempt to commit murder. Leaving him in the care of his weeping wife, the command pushed forward to encounter other scenes of horror and bloodshed, but none more weird and tragic than the death of the unknown bushwhacker of the Ozark Mountains.

CHAPTER II.

At St. Genevieve we boarded a steamboat and were taken down the Mississippi River to Milliken's Bend, where we were assigned to the 13th Army Corps. General Grant was then engaged in making preparations for the speedy reduction and capture of Vicksburg and the opening up of the Mississippi River to the Union gunboats and transports. Almost insurmountable difficulties seemed to stand in the way of accomplishing that great work as speedily as it was at first intended. The river itself was at flood-tide, filling the innumerable bayous, creeks, and lagoons, which ran in almost every direction about the city. But at last the waters subsided sufficiently to make it possible for Grant's army, which had been wading and swimming the swollen streams, to find sufficient dry land to begin operations, and instead of wasting their time and strength fighting alligators and other reptiles, to begin the more useful, though dangerous work of fighting "Johnnies."

The plan of the Vicksburg campaign is now so well known that it is needless to dwell upon it at any length. General Grant's army was to be marched down the west bank of the river to a point below Vicksburg, and from thence, under cover of the gunboats, was to cross the river and attack that great rebel stronghold from the rear. This was one of the most desperate moments of the war. General Grant said it was a sight magnificent, but terrible.

At about 10 o'clock on the night of the 16th of April, 1864, eight gunboats and three transports started on the perilous undertaking of running the batteries which defended Vicksburg on the river front. All the skill and strength of the rebel government had been employed in making these defenses as complete as they could be made. The best engineering

DAVID DIXON PORTER

Admiral David Porter was destined for a Naval career. His father, David, was a distinguished naval officer and diplomat, his brother was Commodore William D. Porter, and his adopted brother was Adm. David G. Farragut, and his cousin was Gen. Fitz John Porter. He first went to sea with his father at age 10. Porter joined the U.S. Navy in 1829 after junior service in the Mexican Navy. His assignments were varied, but advancement was slow in peacetime service. On Apr. 1, 1861, Cmdr. Porter accepted command of the *Powhatan* and the naval portion of an expedition to relieve Florida's Fort Pickens. In Oct., 1862, he took command of the Mississippi Squadron and assumed responsibility for the Mississippi and its tributaries north of Vicksburg. In cooperation with the Federal army he was involved in the capture of Arkansas Post in Jan., 1863, and then Vicksburg in July. For the latter action he was promoted to rear admiral. After a courageous performance in the abortive Red River Campaign of spring 1864, Porter went east to command the North Atlantic Blockading Squadron. Immediately after the war Porter became superintendent of the Naval Academy and was made admiral in 1870.

talent had been employed in their construction and the heaviest and most powerful guns were mounted on their ramparts, or looked out from their embrasures. General Grant, from a tugboat stationed in the river, watched the brave men start on their perilous journey, while at a point further down the river, immediately opposite the rebel batteries, General Sherman, with a small detachment of soldiers awaited their coming, intending to render all the assistance he could to the crews of the boats if the rebel batteries succeeded in sinking them. Admiral Porter, who commanded the expedition, gave orders to his officers to get under way, his own flag-ship, the "Benton," taking the lead. The rebels kept a sharp lookout and the advancing ironclads, though only drifting with the current, moving as noiselessly as the

gentle flow of the river itself, were speedily discovered. In an instant, a huge solid shot shrieked through the darkness above the vessels and buried itself in the river beyond. The next moment was one of profound silence, and then, as if all the furies of Pandemonium were let loose at once, the calm was broken by the roar of Vicksburg's heaviest and most terrible batteries. Shot, shell and straight bolts of iron were hurled with the most terrific fury and precision through the trembling atmosphere. Immense piles of wood and rosin had been gathered at the various headlands, to which the match was now applied, and these, like monstrous torches, suddenly thrust up out of the earth, blazed forth, flinging their fierce light far out into the river, so that not only was the fleet brought into clear view, but the entire river for miles was illuminated as with the light of day. Two of Porter's ironclads were sunk, consorts and transports crushed into each other in their mad efforts to escape the awful effects of the tremendous, withering fire from rebel artillery. Some of the transports turned back, hoping to escape destruction by steaming up the river, but Porter had prepared for this and the retreaters were driven back by a gunboat which brought up the rear of the advancing line. Signal after signal went up from the deck of the "Benton," as though the noble vessel was lying quietly at her anchorage, while from the staff the Admiral's pennant floated out proudly, defiantly on the hot, night air. It took the boats two hours to pass through the awful storm of shot and shell hurled against them from the rebel guns, some of them at almost point-blank range. Strange to say, only two boats were sunk, the rest ran the gauntlet in safety. The fleet came to anchor below the danger point, and Grant's invincible army was in a position to cross in almost complete safety.

The point where the greater part of his army crossed the river was known as Bruinsburg, and from thence the march to Vicksburg was commenced. McClernand's corps led the advance of the army, having the 2nd Brigade of Carr's division, commanded by Col. Wm. M.

EUGENE ASA CARR

Eugene Carr entered the U.S. Military Academy in 1846, graduated 19th in his class in 1850, and was commissioned in a regiment of Mounted Riflemen, beginning a military service that lasted 43 years. For the next decade Carr's service was in the Western frontier, where he was involved in a number of skirmishes with hostile Indians. In 1854 he was severely wounded by an arrow. When the Civil War began, Carr was a cavalry captain at Fort Washita, Indian Territory. He joined Brig. Gen. Nathaniel Lyon's forces in Missouri and participated in the Battle of Wilson's Creek on Aug. 10, 1861; six days later he was commissioned colonel of the 3d Illinois Cavalry. Over the next months Carr was in the maneuvers that forced the Confederates out of Missouri. In the Battle of Pea Ridge he was wounded 3 times but refused to leave the field; later he received the Medal of Honor for gallantry in this engagement. On Mar. 7, 1862, he was made Brigadier General of volunteers. He commanded a division during the Second Vicksburg Campaign. Carr's military reputation rests mostly on his exploits as an Indian fighter after the war. He retired from the military as a Brigadier General in 1893.

JOHN ALEXANDER McCLERNAND

John Alexander McClernand, who was the Democratic U.S. representative from Abraham Lincoln's home district, was appointed a Brigadier General in May 1861. His only military experience was 30 years previous as a private in the Black Hawk War. Ambitious, selfish, and pompous, McClernand irritated professional soldiers, but was intelligent and bold enough to compile a decent war record. He was placed under Gen. U. S. Grant, who detested him, but promoted him to Major General in Mar., 1862. It was McClernand on the May 22, 1863, assault on Vicksburg, who reported exaggeration of his troops' success, therefore leading Grant to commit more men to the bloody effort. In June Grant removed him from command for issuing a bombastic congratulatory order to his men without sending it through headquarters. McClernand protested, but when Vicksburg fell 3 weeks later, so did McClernand. He was briefly restored to command of the XIII Corps in Feb. 1864, during the Red River Campaign, but only long enough to damage his reputation and become so ill that he resigned his commission. He returned to Springfield, IL., and his career as a Democratic politician.

Stone, of the 22nd Iowa, at the head of the column. Nothing of unusual interest transpired until about the hour of midnight, when the advance encountered the enemy about eight miles from Port Gibson. Here was fought the first battle in the new campaign against Vicksburg. That evening Grant's army marched into Port Gibson, and the first great victory was gained. On May 12th at 4 o'clock in the morning, McPherson's Corps struck the enemy's videttes in front of Raymond, and at 5 o'clock p.m. his troops marched into Raymond, the enemy falling back on Jackson, the capital of Mississippi. Then it was that the splendid generalship of Grant began to be manifest. Instead of pushing on to the immediate investiture of Vicksburg, he suddenly threw his entire army on Jackson and drove Pemberton into his works on Black River. This was one of the hardest battles fought in the vicinity of Vicksburg. The enemy had the advantage of numbers, position and defenses. But he was terribly beaten, suffering a loss of 24 pieces of artillery, 3,000 killed and wounded, and 3,000 prisoners. The Union loss was 2,441.

Before 9 o'clock on the morning of the 17th, another battle had been fought. While the battle was raging in its hottest fury, a dashing young officer rode up to General Grant, with an order from General Halleck, who was then at the head of the United States Army, commanding him to abandon his campaign against Vicksburg and take his army to Port Hudson and reinforce General Banks. Of course Halleck was entirely ignorant of Grant's movements and victories, because when the fighting General turned his back upon the Mississippi River, he cut off all communication between himself and the authorities at Washington. They knew nothing of him, he did not care to know much about them. General Grant's reply to the order was:

"I think it is now too late."

The words were scarcely spoken when, on glancing to the right, he saw a General officer in his shirt sleeves leading his brigade to the assault. That officer was General Lawler, and the brigade he was leading was composed of the 21st, 22nd and 23rd Iowa Infantry, and the 11th Wisconsin Infantry. The object of the movement was an as-

JAMES BIRDSEYE McPHERSON

James Birdseye McPherson graduated from West Point in 1853, 1st in his class. Posted to the Corps of Engineers, he was reputed to be one of the most promising young officers in the army. Following the outbreak of the Civil War he served as an aide to Maj. Gen. Henry W. Halleck, then chief engineer to Maj. Gen. U. S. Grant. He was promoted to Brigadier General in Aug., 1862 and to major-general 2 months later. In Jan., 1863, he became commander of the XVII Corps in Grant's army. In that capacity he performed excellently during the Vicksburg Campaign. Later he was transferred to Maj. Gen. William T. Sherman's command, where he continued his distinguished military service. Tragically, he was killed in the Battle of Atlanta on July 22, 1864.

sault on their works. At a given signal the brigade, with a mighty cheer, left the cover of the woods, and, in spite of a terrific fire from the enemy, crossed the open bottom on a run, waded the bayou, and in five minutes from the time the order to charge was given, the brigade was inside the rebel breastworks. General Grant said:

"It was a daring and splendid movement, in every way honorable to the skill of the brave officer who led it and the brave men who executed it."

Here let me say, there was something grand and terrible in the assaults which formed such a prominent feature in General Grant's tactics. Holding a part of his army in reserve for any emergencies that might arise, he managed to hurl the other part of it with full force upon the point which he saw to be the least protected and the most favorable for an assault. It was not a question of doing an astounding piece of "fancy work" that would surprise the nation, but with the straight forward, powerful push of the man of common sense, who is determined to crush his opponent at a single blow. He did not shelter nor spare himself from danger, and when his order was to "charge," he meant "CHARGE!" and he expected his men to understand that he wanted their bayonets kept well down at the point.

The same troops who had sailed and waded two hundred miles in a little over two weeks, fought and won six battles in as many days, were now asked to take Vicksburg by siege or storm. The attempts to take the city and free the waters of the Mississippi had already lost the Union army 10,000 men, killed and wounded. Other loyal lives were ready for the sacrifice and Grant's soldiers urged him to assault the works at once.

The morning of May 19th saw the Union army forming a semicircular line outside of Vicksburg's fortifications eight miles long. Ten o'clock of the morning of May the 22nd was the time set for storming the works.

Michael Kelly Lawler commanded the 3d Illinois in the Mexican War and in the 1850s farmed and ran a mercantile business near Shawneetown, IL. In 1861 he entered volunteer service as Colonel of the 18th Illinois Infantry. After serving in Missouri under Brig. Gen. U. S. Grant he was court martialed and acquitted of charges that he had used brutality in the discipline of his troops. He was promoted to Brigadier General in Nov., 1862. In the Vicksburg Campaign, Lawler, in brigade command, fought at Port Gibson, Champion's Hill and Big Black River Bridge. On May 22 he took part in the assault on Confederate Maj. Gen. Stephen C. Lee's troops along the Vicksburg lines and participated in the siege until its conclusion. Brevetted a Major General in March, 1865, he was mustered out in. Jan., 1866. Postwar, Lawler returned to his farm near Equality, IL.

Lawler's brigade of Carr's division, including the 21st, 22nd and 23rd Iowa, charged just south of the Jackson railroad. The principal fort in front of Lawler occupied a prominent hill close to the railroad. Up this hill the 21st and 22nd Iowa went with a cheer, defying the hail storm of bullets that met them on the way, and the awful enfilading fire from other angles in the entrenchments. Just as they reached the ditch of the fort, it was a hot and a dangerous time, when thirteen men, led by Sergeant N. C. Messenger, climbed out of the ditch over the shoulders of each other, right into Fort Beauregard, killing or dispersing the enemy within. Such valor is seldom witnessed in battle.

Brave as the action was, it accomplished but little, as the enemy's guns so covered the captured city that it was untenable. Our troops were forced to evacuate it, and it fell again into the hands of the enemy.

~ ~ ~ ~ ~

24

It may be of interest to the readers of this book for me to describe the part taken by my own regiment in the terrific assault on Fort Beauregard. It was one of the most desperate charges made during the war. It was one of those necessary experiments which, in offensive warfare, a commander is compelled by a sense of duty to make, even though the result may be in doubt.

The 22nd Iowa Infantry was commanded by Col. Wm. M. Stone, and it led the Division commanded by General Carr in its assault on Fort Beauregard. Steadily, and in splendid order, the Division moved forward. Not encountering any opposition from the enemy, we began to think the victory was going to be gained without any fighting. Just as we reached a point close to the rebel works, an obstacle in the line of march made it necessary to change the line to an oblique, which brought us very close to the fort, when, without any warning, and to our utter dismay, a host of riflemen sprang to the ramparts and poured such a continuous and deadly fire into our lines, that the division staggered and at some points fell back. In a moment the line was reformed and pushed forward to grapple with the rebels. Once more such a withering fire came from the rebel works, that, with the exception of the 22nd Iowa, and a few of the 11th Wisconsin, who steadily pushed forward to the ramparts of the fort, the division was driven back and finally retreated. Here Captain Robertson was killed, and the final assault was led by Sergeant N. C. Messenger, of Company, I, 22nd Iowa, who led eleven men into the fort, capturing the garrison consisting of a Lieutenant and twelve men. Sergeant Messenger and his little band of brave soldiers—Iowa soldiers—held the fort until the army fell back on either side, when the rebels again rallied, and having con-

> James Robertson was one of the unfortunate brave men who did not survive the heroic charge of the 22nd Iowa Infantry on the 22nd of May. He was twenty-six-years-old and had served as Captian of Company I since the unit's muster-in on August 18, 1862.

centrated their force, rushed to the attack and drove the captors out of the fort, inflicting heavy loss upon them. This charge of the 22nd Iowa on Fort Beauregard, on the 22nd of May, 1863, led by Col. Wm. M. Stone, and the final capture of the fort by a mere handful of the regiment under the heroic leadership of Sergeant N. C. Messenger, of Co. I, was one of the greatest exhibitions of northern bravery to be found in the annals of the rebellion.

CHAPTER III.

FALL OF VICKSBURG - ITS IRREPARABLE LOSS TO THE
SOUTHERN CONFEDERACY - WE EMBARK FOR NEW ORLEANS
GUARDING THE GOVERNOR OF LOUISIANA - HIS
IGNORANCE OF IOWA - THE CONDITION OF AFFAIRS IN 1864
WE ARE ASSIGNED TO THE 19TH CORPS
FIGHTING EARLY IN THE SHENANDOAH VALLEY
A REBEL CAPTAIN'S SUCCESSFUL SCHEME

The forty-two days of fighting, burrowing and besieging around Vicksburg were drawing to a close. Then came that memorable day, when every loyal man felt it to be a high privilege to be called a citizen of the United States. It was indeed the fete-day of the Nation, made memorable by the splendid victories which crowned the Union army's at Vicksburg, Gettysburg and Helena. All over the North the ringing of thousands of loyal bells sounded the death-knell of the bogus Confederacy. From that 4th day of July, 1863, the fate of the Confederacy was sealed. On that day 47,500 rebel prisoners, headed by Lieutenant General Pemberton, one of the bravest and best of the Confederate commanders, marched out of their defenses at Vicksburg, stacked their arms, and were paroled as prisoners of war. The glorious Stars and Stripes were already floating from the City Hall in Vicksburg. The Mississippi River was opened, the rebel armies were divided, their western supplies cut off, and their cause from that hour was hopeless. This was the most disastrous defeat suffered by the Southern Confederacy. The flower of their western army was destroyed and one of their best generals rendered powerless by be-

> John Clifford Pemberton, "The Defender of Vicksburg," graduated from West Point in 1837. He resigned from the U.S. Army in 1861 and accepted a Brigadier General's commission with the Confederacy while two of his brothers remained in the Union army. He was promoted to Major General in Jan., 1862, and Lieutenant General in Oct., 1862. He then took charge of the Department of Mississippi and East Louisiana where the focus of military affairs was upon the besieged river fortress of Vicksburg. Trying to follow the conflicting military plans of his two superiors, President Jefferson Davis and Gen. Joseph E. Johnston, he found he was unable to follow either and surrendered the fortress and 29,000 troops on July 4, 1863.

**NATHANIEL BANKS
AND THE RED RIVER CAMPAIGN**

The Red River Campaign began in March of 1864. Its objective was the Capture of Shreveport, Louisiana–the military, economic and political center of the Confederacy's Trans Mississippi Department. The Campaign was commanded by Maj. Gen. Nathaniel Prentiss Banks, who was appointed a General of Volunteers not because of any military expertise, but because of political muscle. A Republican, he was serving in his third year as Governor of Massachusetts at the outbreak of the Civil War, and thus found favor in the eyes of the Lincoln administration. His record as a command officer up to the Red River Campaign was one of failure, and this campaign would be no different. Banks moved up the Red River with a force of 25,000 Union soldiers and a large flotilla of gunboats and transports commanded by Rear Admiral David Porter. The campaign began with the Capture of Fort De Russy on March 14, but things worsened as Banks progressed up the river. On April 8 his forces were soundly defeated and retreated in disarray from the Battle of Sabine Crossroads. Confederates pursued Banks's defeated troops, but on the next day at the Engagement of Pleasant Hill, Banks's Union troops scored a victory. In spite of the victory, he continued to withdraw. Admiral Porter's fleet had difficulty making its way back down the river due to lowering water levels, and some of his boats were lost. In May, Banks's army arrived back at the mouth of the Red River (on the Mississippi), having accomplished nothing. This failure, in combination with his earlier displays of ineptitude for command, was cause enough for Banks to be permanently removed from military command. Returning to Massachusetts he served six terms in the U.S. House of Representatives.

ing a paroled prisoner of war. The Mississippi River was cleared of all obstructions, making it possible for Federal gunboats to patrol it from Cairo to New Orleans, so that the products of the North could be shipped to all the river cities and towns. The opening of the river also facilitated the shipment of army stores and communication of the eastern and western armies. The helplessness of their cause must have been apparent to the leaders of the rebellion from the moment Vicksburg surrendered to General Grant. The common instincts of humanity ought to have induced them to lay down their arms, disband their armies, acknowledge the supremacy of the Union, and thus avoid the farther effusion of blood and the ravages of war. But as will be seen, the bitter hatred and unrelenting malice of the rebel leaders, civil and military, prevented them from accepting the situation and following the dictates of reason.

After the fall of Vicksburg the 22nd Iowa embarked for New Orleans, and from thence was moved up the river to form a part of the well-known Red River Expedition, under command of General Banks. At the close of that expedition the regiment was again taken to New Orleans and from thence to

Opelousas, Louisiana, where we spent some time in hunting down and finally dispersing the desperate guerrilla bands led by John Morgan and Dick Taylor. While at Opelousas it fell to our lot to guard, at his own plantation, the rebel governor of Louisiana. Previous to this time he had been in the custody of the Provost Marshal of New Orleans, but one of his daughters having died at his home near Opelousas, the Governor had been granted permission to return to his home to attend the funeral of his child. Sorrow makes all humanity a great brotherhood, which even the stern necessities and exactions of war can not annul. Traitor to his government though he was, yet the magnanimity of the Union commander overcame all the obstacles, and thus it was that this man was permitted to return to his home for the purpose of kissing the silent lips of his beloved dead and consigning her remains to the grave. How many of our brave Union soldiers would have been glad to have enjoyed the same magnanimous action of the Confederate authorities in Southern prisons. But alas, still greater privation and suffering, if not death, would have been visited upon the man who would dare to make such a request. Judge ye angels and men, between the righteousness of the two causes, as manifested in the acts and dealing of their leaders!

Having been appointed on the detail made to guard the residence of the aforesaid Governor, and thus prevent him from violating the terms of his permit, it was my privilege to come into personal association with his fallen Excellency, and have frequent conversations with him. During one of these conversations, I was impressed with the fact that leadership, whether civil or military, in the Southern Confederacy, was simply a question of who had the most money and the largest political influence; not who had the most brains, the best character and the largest ability to discharge the duties of the position. It came about in this way: One day the Governor seemed to be unusually communicative and an interesting conversation took place between him, a comrade of the regiment and myself relative to the war and the difference between the value of the Greenbacks of the North and the Confederate Scrip (or "graybacks," as we called them for short) of the South. After our conversation on these topics had ceased, he asked us what regiment we belonged to. My comrade answered, "The 22nd Iowa Infantry." The Governor dropped his head and, as if speaking to himself, murmured: "The 22nd Iowa–the

22nd Iowa." Then, looking up, and raising his voice to a higher pitch, he asked this question: "Let me see; what State is Iowa in?"

How would such an ignoramus as that do for Governor of Iowa? Yet this man had been elected to govern the great state of Louisiana! He, one of the "Chivalry" of the great South, almost as ignorant as one of his own slaves, upon whom he was trying to rivet the chains of a criminal a per-petual bondage, was using all the resources of his State, and the power of his office, to prolong a bloody and wicked war. Had he kept his mouth shut his extreme ignorance and disgrace might have been concealed, but both were brought to view by his question.

Our campaigning in the vicinity of Opelousas was so severe—the regiment being engaged in almost continuous fighting and skirmishing during the summer and fall months—that our numbers became so de-pleted we were ordered back to New Orleans and from thence to Matagorda Island, Texas, to recruit our wasted ranks and get ready for active campaigning in the coming spring.

The year of 1863 saw the closing up of the third year of the war, of which, when the first guns were fired, and the first troops were ordered out, wise men, both North and South, predicted would last only a few weeks, or months at most! The men of the North had faith in the ability of the Government at Washington to crush the rebellion before it got a foothold; while the men of the South based their conclusions on the uni-versally cherished belief that one son of the Southern chivalry could eas-ily whip all the way from five to ten Northern "mud-sills"—but both were doomed to disappointment. And now, with the dawning of 1864, while the victories and advantages were undoubtedly on the side of the Union, yet the war was not ended, and no man was found bold enough to pre-dict when it would end.

However, important changes had taken place in the leadership and disposition of the Federal force. General Grant had been made Com-mander-in-Chief of the Union armies. Assuming the duties at once, he selected his subordinate commanders and placed them in charge of their respective Corps and Divisions. He believed the time had come to make a clean sweep of the Confederacy, and he resolved to do it. Richmond was his objective point, and the same plan of campaign which had re-duced and compelled the surrender of Vicksburg was selected for the capture of Richmond, and the final crushing out of the Southern Confederacy. General Sheridan was assigned to the command of the 6th, 8th, and 19th Corps. He was ordered to thoroughly reorganize these Corps and be ready to co-operate with the army against Richmond. The 13th army corps had become so greatly depleted that it was not strong enough to maintain a distinct organization, hence it was ordered to Washington, to be consolidated with the 19th corps. This was completed during the summer of 1864, and in August, Sheridan was ordered to move down the Shenandoah Valley, to co-operate with Grant and his final blow against rebeldom.

When we reached Harper's Ferry we found the rebel General Early's forces engaged in threshing grain, which the rich soil of the Shenandoah Valley produced abundantly. Sheridan at once gave battle to Early, and succeeded in driving him into Winchester, where a decisive battle was fought, which resulted in a glorious victory for Sheridan's army. A number of field batteries and many thousands of prisoners were taken. Early then retreated to Fisher's Hill, where Sheridan again attacked him and again routed him driving him down the Valley towards Staunton, the terminus of the railroad leading into Richmond. Sheridan then fell back to Cedar Creek, completely destroying everything in the Valley, leaving it so bare that he remarked, "If a crow should fly across the Valley he would have to carry his rations with him."

JUBAL ANDERSON EARLY

Jubal Early emerged from the Civil War as one of its great characters. Hard-drinking and sharp-tongued, he projected anything but the clean, noble image of a military commander, but he was one of the more popular Confederate generals. He graduated from West Point in 1837, 18th in his class. Although Early voted against secession in the 1861 Virginia state convention, he quickly stepped forward to defend his native soil, accepted a commission as colonel of state forces assigned to train volunteers at Lynchburg, and soon commanded the 24th Virginia Infantry. His superiors were so impressed with his performance that they appointed him Brigadier General. Continued impressive service won him promotion to Major General in Jan., 1863, and Lieutenant General in May, 1864. He ended the war fighting against Maj. Gen. Philip H. Sheridan in the Shenandoah Valley. After Lee surrendered, Early, disguised, traveled west to Texas, then to Havana, Cuba, and Toronto, Ontario. In Canada he wrote *A Memoir of the Last Year of the War* (1867), a lively, and colorful, account of his activities during the closing battles.

Lee at once sent strong reinforcements to Early, and in the early morning of October 19th, 1864, under cover of a dense fog, he attacked Sheridan. Our army lay diagonally across the Valley, the 6th corps on the right, the 8th corps on the left and the 19th corps occupying the center. At 3 o'clock in the morning the enemy succeeded in surprising and capturing our pickets, and thus succeeded in getting on the flank of our army, where it lay until daylight before making the general attack. A Confederate Captain conceived and executed the scheme for the capture of our pickets and the surprise of our army, which would have done credit to a genuine born Yankee. The Confederate army had been but in the lightest marching condition possible, everything that would in any way impede its movement, even to canteens, being dispensed with—and in perfect silence it was thrown across Cedar Creek, marched around the mountain to the east of our line, and as far north as the center of the 8th corps, coming into the Valley by a pass between two mountains. Here the main army rested, while strong detachments were sent forward to capture our picket line as if to relieve the posts. When challenged by the picket, "Who goes there," he would answer promptly in the usual manner, "A friend with the countersign," which he would give on further demand. Then he informed each guard that the army was preparing to move; that he had orders as officer of the guard to bring in all the pickets. Utterly ignorant of the scheme that was being played upon them, our men did not suspect the officer until they found themselves within the enemy's lines and received the surprising information that they were prisoners. In this treacherous manner all our picket posts along the east side of the Valley were captured, after which the Confederate army was formed into line of battle ready to move silently and swiftly up on Sheridan's unsuspecting troops. Early's plan was first to attack our right wing, expecting that Sheridan would move the left wing across the Valley, to the support of the 6th corps, which would make it an easy matter for Early to swing his army across the Valley and thus completely surround Sheridan, which would make the capture of his army an easy and certain victory.

The close proximity of the enemy led Sheridan to observe the greatest caution in all his movements, and in order to guard against surprise he had issued orders that one corps of his army should be under arms and in line of battle every morning from 3 o'clock until daylight. On this memorable morning the 19th corps were routed out at 3 o'clock, drawing from the men much grumbling and many remonstrances against the outrage which was thus perpetrated upon them by depriving them of the sleep they so much needed, because, so far as they could see, there was no enemy near, and they considered the whole arrangement a piece of foolishness. Poor fellows! They little knew how near the death-dealing guns of the enemy were to them at that moment, and that ere long many of them would take their places in that line of battle for the last time.

PHILIP H. SHERIDAN AND THE SHENANDOAH VALLEY CAMPAIGN

In 1848, Philip H. Sheridan falsified his birth date so that he could gain entry to West Point, from which he graduated in 1853, 34th in a class of 49. In 1861 he was called to war duty as a captain in the 13th Infantry in southwest Missouri. By March, 1863, he had risen to the rank of Major General of volunteers. His rise continued, and when Grant was promoted to Lieutenant General, he gave Sheridan command of all cavalry in the Army of the Potomac. In Aug., 1864, Grant made Sheridan commander of the Army of the Shenandoah with specific instructions to drive the Confederates south and to destroy all supplies that would aid the enemy. The fertile Shenandoah Valley had been the bosom of supplies and food for the Confederates throughout the war. In the Shenandoah he met and defeated Jubal Early's Confederate Forces in the Third Battle of Winchester and Fisher's Hill. Early's forces regrouped and assaulted Sheridan at Cedar Creek on Oct. 19, 1864. This surprise action caught the Federal troops unprepared and almost resulted in their defeat. Sheridan made his famous ride to the front and rallied his troops, turning near defeat into victory. He was rewarded with the thanks of congress, and promoted to Major General in the Regular Army. Also in the Shenandoah Valley, Sheridan developed his "scorched earth" policy, a tactic for which Southerners hated him because it laid waste to the land and reduced the populace to starvation. He continued fighting with fervor until war's end. "Little Phil's" meteoric rise is attributed to two traits he himself recognized: a willingness to take the offensive wherever possible and as aggressively as possible, and a willingness to exploit every edge over an opponent. These two principles, carried out against the weakened and diminished Confederates of 1864-65, yielded him a string of victories. In 1869 he was promoted to Lieutenant General when William T. Sherman was advanced to commander-in-chief of the army following Grant's election to President.

33

PART 2

CAPTURED & LIBBY PRISON

D estiny shapes men's lives, and war is a place of destiny for many men. So it was for Benjamin F. Booth on October 19, 1864, that the destiny that would forever after pattern his thoughts and attitudes was provided by war. On that day, as he was in a detail of sharp-shooters in the Battle of Cedar Creek, Booth was captured. The incident of his capture and the particulars of the 22nd Iowa Infantry's involvement in the Battle of Cedar Creek are detailed in Colonel Graham's official report:

Lieut. B. F. Copeland
Actg. Asst. Adjt. Gen., 2d Brig., 2d Div., 19th Army Corps.

HEADQUARTERS TWENTY-SECOND IOWA INFANTRY
Cedar Creek, Va., October 22, 1864.

SIR: I have the honor to report in brief the part taken by the Twenty-second Iowa Volunteers in the late action of Cedar Creek, Va., on the 19th instant:

On the evening of the 18th orders were received from the brigade commander to be in readiness to move at 5.15 o'clock in light marching order. In obedience to this order my regiment was in line at the stated time, momentarily expecting to move on a reconnaissance in the direction of Strasburg. While thus in line a heavy fire of musketry broke out on the left of the line, in front of the Eighth Corps, which proved to be an assault upon our works by the enemy. In a short time we were ordered to move forward in support of a battery; but had no sooner arrived upon the ground before the enemy had possession of our works and were advancing in heavy force, pouring a deadly fire of musketry and artillery in our ranks. There being but two regiments in this perilous situation (Twenty-second Iowa and Third Massachusetts), and the troops in front having fled in confusion through our ranks, it was impossible to hold the enemy in check with this small force, and our lines were broken and the men retreated in disorder. About three-fourths of the regiment having reached the crest of the hill, rallied and held the enemy in check for a short time, but could not stand against such an overwhelming force of the enemy, and again fell back. In this stand the enemy were so close to our ranks that their fire burnt the clothes of our men, and while falling back many were captured. Having fallen back to the rear a considerable distance our lines were again ordered to advance with the brigade, and after an obstinate fight drove the enemy from our front, and in a short time unfurled our flag in the camp occupied by us in the morning. In this part of the engagement the enemy were completely routed and fled in every direction. We found our camp totally destroyed by the enemy, losing all of our tents, knapsacks, blankets and haversacks, and rations, leaving the regiment almost entirely destitute of clothing and subsistence, in consequence of which the men have suffered from the effects of the cold weather. In view of this fact, that we were ordered out in light marching order, with not sufficient time to break camp, before the enemy had attacked our position on the left and had broken our line, rendering it necessary for us to lose no time in getting to the scene of action, I deemed it proper that the men should be remunerated for the losses which they have sustained by the casualties of war in thus being deprived of everything through no neglect of their own.

The casualties in my regiment were 72 in number, a nominal list having been forwarded to your headquarters.

I cannot close this brief report without mentioning with pride the gallant conduct of both officers and men in this severe engagement, ending in the most brilliant victory of the war.

Hoping that this report will meet your approbation, I have the honor to be, sir, your obedient servant,

HARVEY GRAHAM,
Colonel Commanding.

Total casualties officially reported for Cedar Creek to the 22nd Iowa Infantry were 1 officer killed, 6 officers and 43 enlisted men wounded, and 2 officers and 21 enlisted men captured or missing. Further particulars of the day's events are found in the journal of Confederate Captain Jed. Hotchkiss, a Topographical Engineer with the Second Corps, Army of Northern Virginia:

Wednesday, October 19.—We went through Strasburg and took Kershaw to his position on the top of the hill above Bowman's Mill. He was there by 5 a.m. Wharton was also in position on Hupp's Hill. The hour fixed for Rosser, then Gordon, and then Kershaw to attack. Page and myself examined the route ahead, and I urged the moving of Kershaw nearer. A light mist hung over the creek and river. Soon we heard Rosser driving the pickets on the left, then Gordon on the right, then Kershaw advanced across Cedar Creek in gallant style, and in almost a moment he was going up the hill and over the breastworks. A few flashes of musketry, a few shots of artillery, and he had the works, guns and all, surprising the enemy, though they had sounded the reveille in many parts of their camps before we attacked. Then, in conjunction with Gordon, Kershaw swept over the Eighth and Nineteenth Corps, and drove them in wild confusion across Meadow Run, upon the Sixth Corps and through Middletown, Colonel Payne at the same time charging their train, &c. Wharton and the artillery came up and helped across Cedar Creek. Our troops then formed and drove them from their camps northwest of Meadow Run to the ridge in front of Middletown, where the Sixth Corps made a stand and drove Wharton and Pegram back. Then we had the artillery brought up to near Middletown and massed it on them and drove them from the ridge. The fog concealed the enemy some time. The vigorous use of their artillery and advance of the infantry drove the enemy beyond Middletown, and by 10 a. m. we had formed a new line, extending through Middletown at right angles to the pike and along the Cedarville road on the right and the Furnace road on the left. Gordon was on the left, near Stickley's; then Kershaw came across the ridge; then Ramseur down the slope to Meadow Run; Pegram from that up to the turnpike; Wharton to right with Wofford's brigade, of Kershaw's division, on his right at the angle of the Cedarville and Buckton roads; then Payne's cavalry extending to the woods. Rosser had driven the enemy by the Grove road and was to the left and in advance. We lay there some time, using some artillery on the right and left and advancing our skirmishers a little, but making no decided move. We skirmished with the cavalry on the right and they charged our line several times, but were repulsed. Thus we lay until 4 p. m., making a few efforts to get off the immense captures we had made of artillery and everything else. We had some twenty-three guns. The enemy having had time to rally, had collected in rear of the large body of woods in our front and formed a line of battle and advanced at 4:30 p. m., obliquely to the left, and struck our left, or rather between the two brigades on the left, where the line was weak, and it gave way with little resistance, and was followed by all the rest of the line toward the left, and soon everything was in full retreat toward Cedar Creek. The artillery nobly fell back fighting and kept the enemy in check, and everything was getting off well, when Rosser, having fallen back, the Yankee cavalry crossed by Hite's old mill and came up to Stickley's and fell on our train and artillery just after dark, on Hupp's Hill, and dashed along, killing horses and turning over ambulances, caissons, &c., stampeding the drivers, thus getting 43 pieces of artillery, many wagons, & c., as there was nothing to defend them and we had no

organized force to go after them. Only a few Yankee cavalry did it all. They
came as far as Spangler's Mill, and there tore up a bridge which had broken and
impeded our train, but had been repaired and we were passing over it. The gen-
eral and staff got to Fisher's Hill and tried to rally the men. We succeeded in
getting many of them into camp, but could get none to go back and recapture the
wagons, & c., at Strasburg. Colonel Brown got eight or ten to go on guard at the
Stone Bridge. We got 1,300 prisoners off safely. The general was very much
prostrated when we learned the extent of our disaster and started the wagons for
the rear, and sent Rosser to stop the stragglers. Thus was one of the most bril-
liant victories of the war turned into one of the most disgraceful defeats, and all
owing to the delay in pressing the enemy after we got to Middletown; as General
Early said "The Yankees got whipped and we got scared." I got to Edenburg
and put the engineer troops on guard at the bridge to stop fugitives. A very fine
day. Cool at night. I spent the day with the general; carried orders, & c. We had
many narrow escapes. We were frequently fired at and much exposed. Colonel
Godwin was wounded in the neck. General Ramseur was killed. Payne had 326
men and took 399 prisoners.

The following men from the 22nd Iowa are listed as captured with Booth at
Cedar Creek:

Calvin Bray, Company D
George W. Bell, Company F
Charlie Bowen, Company K
Andrew Crain, Company G
David Connelly, Company I
Oliver Crocker, Company I
Robert Davis, First Lieutenant of Company C
Francis C. Flint, Drummer of Company H
Lewis Goben, Company F
Isaac Halderman, Third Corporal of Company F
Joseph W. Jennings, Company E
Elias Lively, Company E
Jehiel McDonald, Company E
Westel W. Morsman, Captain of Company I

Abraham Myers, Company E

William Oldacee, Fourth Sergeant of Company K

George S. Post, Second Corporal of Company C

Francis M. Payn, Company F

Edward Shoemaker, Company E

Benjamin West, First Corporal of Company C

Joel Webb, Company D

James F. Wiley, Company E

Eighteen-year-old Francis Flint, the Drummer of Company H from Shueyville, IA, would be spared the hazards his comrades captured at Cedar Creek faced. Flint died in Harrisonburg, VA, from disease a mere six days following his capture. To die so quickly, he was no doubt already in some state of ill health before his capture. George S. Post and Benjamin West were both paroled for some reason, perhaps because they were officers or perhaps due to illness. When they were paroled is lost to time. Nonetheless, there were no fewer than twenty troops from the 22nd Iowa Infantry who began their prison experience together, and that experience began at Libby Prison in Richmond, VA.

The Commandant of Libby Prison was Major Thomas P. Turner. Libby Prison was a three-story tobacco warehouse that had been secured in 1862 for use as a prison. It bore the sign of its previous use, LIBBY & SON SHIP CHANDLERS & GROCERS, throughout much of its term of use as a prison. It's use was to be for housing Union officers in its eight rooms, which explains why Booth's stay at Libby was brief. Though troops held at Libby had the advantage of being inside and out of the elements, and they did have running water and primitive toilets, there were problems. Tobacco warehouses are designed to retain heat, which added to the misery of its occupants. Sanitation practices conducted in the prison were neglected by rebel authorities and cramped quarters with sometimes as many as 1,000 men packed into a single room definitely did not add to the comfort of the men held within it. And prisoners had no place to get any exercise or to move about.

CHAPTER IV.

A DREAM AND A RUDE AWAKENING - THE BATTLE OF CEDAR
CREEK - OUT ON THE SKIRMISH LINE - CAPTURED BY THE
REBELS - OUR ARMY DRIVEN BACK - SHERIDAN ARRIVES AND
WHIPS EARLY - OUR SUSPENSE - START SOUTHWARD
SUFFERING BEGINS - ROBBED BY REBEL GUARDS
YANKEE SHARPERS

Just as the drums were beating the "long roll" that morning I was in dreamland. I dreamed that I was in a large three-story brick building in which I was wandering around in a dazed condition, but could find no way out of it. I tried to open the doors but they would not yield to my frantic efforts. One after another I tried the windows, but with no better success. I thought I could see across the valley, and on the opposite side were great heaps of bread, but I was powerless to free myself from the awful depths of that building to go to it. Finally, after a long time, during which I became wild with fear and faint with hunger, I found a door which was standing ajar. I pushed it open, walked out, and started towards the break, but before I reached it I became very thirsty. Then I began to search for water. I socn found a stream and lying flat on the ground began to drink. I thought I drank the stream dry. Just at this moment I was awakened by the roll of the drums, the orders of the officers, and the confusion of the men as they once more fell into line. I then laughed at the remembrance of my dream, but the time was not far distant when all the minutiae of that dream became vastly too real in my experience–too terrible for laughter. It is said that "dreams go by contraries," but my dream is one instance which had an almost literal fulfillment, so literal and real that the memory of what followed, even as I write these words, almost chills the blood in my veins.

Daylight having come and no enemy being in sight, we had just stacked arms preparatory to getting breakfast, when, to our surprise, firing commenced on our left wing where the 19th corps was in position.

The approach of the enemy was so stealthy and the attack so unexpected, that but few of the men in that corps were out of their beds. The 19th corps sprang for their arms and awaited orders. General confusion prevailed all through the army. It soon became apparent that, for the present at least, the 8th corps was the center of attack. Major General Wright, who was in command of the Union forces, came riding along the line of the 19th corps and at once ordered a detail of sharpshooters to deploy across the Valley to the east and if they found no enemy to go south until they were fired on, or until they uncovered the enemy's position. I was one of that detail of sharpshooters who started that morning on our perilous reconnaissance. We marched in silence eastward to the base of the mountain, when, to our dismay, we were in the very presence of the rebel army and heard the ominous order, "SURRENDER!" Knowing the great responsibility which rested upon us for the safety of the army, and knowing that to surrender then would be equivalent to surrendering our forces to the enemy, and with almost certain death staring us in the face if we did not surrender, we chose the alternative of death by firing into the ranks of the enemy, almost at point blank range. The rebels returned our fire with deadly effect, and those who were not killed were speedily captured. But the single volley we fired told General Wright that the enemy was near at hand.

> Horatio Gouverneur Wright graduated from West Point in 1841, 2nd in his class. In Apr., 1861, he acted as chief engineer of the Federal expedition to destroy the Norfolk Navy Yard before it fell into Confederate hands. In Aug. he was promoted to major and Sept. was jumped to Brigadier General. In May, 1864, he was promoted to Major General and given command of the VI Corps. He directed the VI Corps at Cold Harbor, and during the early phases of the Petersburg Campaign. In July the VI Corps moved to the Shenandoah Valley, where it opposed Lt. Gen. Jubal A. Early's Confederates. Wright conducted the pursuit after the Southerners abandoned their raid against Washington, DC, and acted with deliberate caution. His corps then fought in Maj. Gen. Philip H. Sheridan's campaign against Early in the valley. On 19 Oct. 1864, at Cedar Creek, when Early surprised the Federals, Wright commanded Union troops in Sheridan's absence. Slightly wounded, Wright regrouped the broken troops, but it was Sheridan, when he returned, who rallied them to victory. Wright and the corps subsequently went back to Petersburg and fought well until the war's end. After the war he returned to engineer duty in the Regular Army. He was promoted to colonel in 1879 and that year was commissioned Brigadier General and named chief engineer. He directed many projects, including the completion of the Washington Monument.

The battle now began in dead earnest. Our left wing was driven back and the main attack was then made against the center of the 19th corps, which succeeded in holding the enemy in check until the 8th corps fell back and took position in the line. In this first attack we lost 1300 prisoners and 28 pieces of artillery. Our army was driven back about a mile. General Wright was severely wounded but remained on the field and directed the movements of his army during the terrific assaults of the enemy. No men ever fought more bravely, but for the time being they were fighting against odds which they could not overcome. General Wright had succeeded in reforming his line of battle, when General Sheridan, hatless and covered with dust, dashed up on his famous black charger, now covered with white foam. The presence of Sheridan inspired the army with new hope and courage and turned what seemed to be a crushing disaster to the Union army, into a glorious victory. This great achievement of wringing victory out of the very jaws of defeat, in that eventful battle with Early, added new laurels to the fame of General Sheridan, and will live in history long after the great commander, and his famous black horse, ceased to live.

Two newspapers, one published in the South, the other in the North, improved the peculiar circumstances of that battle, especially the fact of the early hour in which it began, to make it the occasion of some sharp and witty sparring. The Atlanta Constitution took occasion to say in its report of the battle: "It is still a true saying, the Early bird gets the worm." To which the St. Louis Globe-Democrat responded: "The Early bird gets the worm, and he also gets his Phil."

It fell to my sad lot to be one of the sharpshooters captured, as already stated. We were at once turned to the south side of Cedar Creek where we were corralled with many others, and from which point we could see all the movements of the contending armies, until our forces had been driven out of sight. *Imagine the anguish we felt in seeing our brave boys driven before the fierce assault of the desperate enemy.* And as the cannonading grew fainter and fainter, we knew that our army was being beaten, if not entirely destroyed. This was a dark hour for the prisoners, but an hour of triumph for the rebels, who took great delight in tantalizing us—boasting that in a short time they would capture the entire Yankee army. However, we retorted by telling them it was *"a long lane that had no turn,"* and they would find lots of fighting Yankees there in the woods that were not yet, and would not be whipped. I remember one little upstart of an officer who was blowing around what they had done, and what they would do with us, "barn-burners" and "thieves," as they were pleased to call us. Comrade D. W. Connely, of my company, told him he had better be up with his army, as they would need him before the battle was over. This enraged the little dandy and he threatened to shoot Connelly for insulting an officer, but his threats had no effect upon the brave man, who told him he had better reserve his ammunition for the Yankee army, for without a doubt they would be coming back that way about noon, as they had left their cooking utensils in the morning and would be back to get them to cook dinner.

At this time fully twenty per cent of the rebel army were engaged in the work of pillaging our camps. Our men were compelled to leave everything when the battle began. The 6th and 8th corps were routed out of bed and a large number of the men succeeded in getting only their guns and cartridge boxes. Hence, the rebel foragers and stragglers had a rich field from which to gather spoil. After they had looted the camps they came to the prisoners and began a wholesale robbery of those helpless men, taking from us our best clothes, money, valuables and every metallic article we had about us, "as memorials of the Yankees." While this was going on, Captain W. W. Morseman, of my company, together with others, were brought in as prisoners. He had on a very good pair of boots, which soon attracted the attention of a rebel Major, who walked up to him, and ordered him in the most insulting language, using the foulest and most villainous epithets, to *"get out of them boots."* Captain Morseman began to remonstrate with him, telling him that he had been captured while on duty with a detail guarding private property, and thought that such treatment should not be visited on him. The Major pulled out a revolver and told him to dry up and get out of them boots, or he would make a pepper-box out of him, adding, he supposed he was there for the purpose of burning property. Captain Morseman reached him the boots and informed the rebel Major that if he had it to do over again he would burn the property and also the old hypocrite who lived in the house.

About 3 o'clock in the afternoon the firing began to grow more distinct. The tide of battle was evidently drawing nearer and nearer to us. The cannonading was plainly heard, and it became more distinct to our wide-open ears, and fast-beating hearts. Messengers began riding hither and thither, and we could read in the very countenances of the rebel soldiers, the glad tidings that the rebel army was in full retreat before the Union forces. This fact inspired within us a joyous hope that an opportunity might be given us to stampede, seize and throttle our guards, break through the lines and fight our way back to freedom. But this we found to be impossible. The firing became more distinct, and in a short time we could hear the rattle of musketry. All was confusion and excitement among the rebels who were about us. Connely asked some of them what was up over there in their army, adding, *"It is about time our boys were coming back to dinner."* Soon we could see the rebels coming from every direction at a breakneck speed. Orders were given to move the prisoners toward Staunton.

We were at once formed in line with guards all around us, and were soon on our way south. Despondent and discouraged as we were on account of our own deplorable condition, we were rejoiced to see the rebels in full retreat before our victorious troops. We could hear our guards inquiring of those who had left the front, how the battle was going. They were told, and we heard it with unspeakable joy, that it was such a stampede as is rarely witnessed. The fighting was kept up all the day, Early making his escape under cover of the night. The loss of my regiment in this battle was fifty-two killed and wounded and twenty taken prisoners.

The terrible truth began to dawn upon us that we were destined for one of those awful prison pens of the South, of which we had heard so much. Visions of Andersonville, with all its horrifying terrors, haunted us by day and troubled us during the night. We continued to march until about midnight when we were halted, and weary, hungry and heart-sick we threw ourselves on the ground for a few hours rest and sleep. Several of the prisoners were wounded, but able to travel. After lying on the cold, damp bed of earth, they became so sore that when they arose they could scarcely move. Next morning, October 20th, we were ordered to fall into ranks. I remember one poor fellow whose wound pained him so severely that he moaned piteously and begged them to shoot him and thus put an end to his sufferings. Another man who was unable to move because of his wounds, was left lying on the ground. I do not know what became of him, but as he was lying near the road, I suppose he was picked up by our troops, if he was not dispatched by the rebels.

The rout of the rebel army being complete, we were in ranks very early and resumed the retreat southward. An attempt was made by the prisoners for the purpose of making an attack on our guards hoping thereby to throw them into confusion, during which we could disarm them and make our escape. We had reason to believe that our army was still in pursuit of Early and if once at liberty it would be an easy matter to rejoin our own troops, but before our plans were perfected, the guards, in some way, became apprised of our purpose. Immediately the guards were reinforced and orders were given strictly forbidding any prisoner, under any pretense whatever, to leave the road. This order was accompanied with the cheerful information that any man violating it would be shot down in his tracks. The guards marched in parallel lines with the prisoners, about twelve feet away, and so close to each other that it was impossible, without courting immediate death, to make any attempt to escape. About noon, while still marching, one of the prisoners fell asleep and stumbled. In catching himself, to keep from falling, he staggered outside the road-line and realizing the danger he was in, started to get back into ranks, but before he could do so, a guard thrust a bayonet into his arm, making an ugly and very painful wound. This cruel act convinced us that the villainous rebels meant to do all they had threatened, and were only too anxious to find an excuse to execute their murderous designs.

Many hours having passed since we tasted food of any kind, we were becoming faint and weak from hunger. The marching was exceedingly difficult and painful. We were required to march two and two, in closed ranks, and as we went on, the road seemed to get narrower, making it exceedingly difficult for men who were tottering from physical weakness and weariness, to keep within it's limits as we were required to do under penalty of death. As we approached Staunton the thievish propensities of our rebel guards began to develop more shamefully. Not satisfied with the robbery they had already practiced upon us of what little we had left. Blankets, shoes, hats, and everything else they coveted, were taken from us at their own pleasure.

APPEARANCE WHEN CAPTURED, WEIGHT 181 POUNDS.

Connely and myself had each a blanket and a piece of tent cloth, and during one of our halts we rolled the two pieces of shelter-tents together as closely as possible, then wrapped one of the blankets about them. The second blanket we mutilated as much as possible, without entirely destroying it, to make it appear worthless in the eyes of our covetous friends. This we wrapped around the good blanket and pieces of tents, in such a way as to make it appear as worthless as possible—in fact, a veritable specimen of "hard-scabble," which even a rebel-thieving guard would scorn to pick up. By this sharp bit of Yankee ingenuity we succeeded in deceiving the Johnnies, and saved our tents and one good blanket which I have always felt was the means of saving our lives during the long months of exposure and hardship which followed. But this was not all. We saw that the rebels took an especial fancy to the hats and shoes worn by the prisoners. Whenever an opportunity offered they did not hesitate to appropriate them to their own use. My witty comrade, Connely, did not relish the idea of entering Staunton in such an undress condition as he would be if he was hatless and shoeless, so he improved the first opportunity he had to cut holes in his hat and in the uppers of his shoes, thus mutilating them so badly that the rebels would not want them. When one of the guards discovered what he had done, he asked him why he had cut his shoes in such a manner. He replied:

"So they will not hurt my feet in walking."

He then asked him why he had cut such large holes in his hat. He again replied:

"To give a free circulation of air so my head will be cool."

However, his answers, while very ingenious, did not deceive the rebel. He knew why he had mutilated them and emphasized that knowledge by furiously cursing him and threatening to put a hole in his head that would be more effective in keeping it cooler than the holes he had cut in his hat. After the guard got tired of cursing him and left, I said to Connely, *"Your Yankee genius has saved your hat and shoes but it has brought curses down upon your head."*

"Yes," said he, laughing, *"but to be bare foot and bareheaded would be worse than his curses."*

CHAPTER V.

Our second night in captivity - Encouraging(?) announcement from a drunken rebel - Connely in danger - Hungry and no food - A generous comrade More robbery by the guards - Richmond - Southern deviltry - The brutality of rebel soldiers Libby prison

About sundown we were halted for the night, more faint with hunger and weary from marching then ever. Not a bite of anything have we had since about 4 o'clock of the morning of the 19th, and even that meal was scanty, having been cut short by the opening of the battle. Our march has been over a dry and dusty road. The rebels appropriated all our canteens, so we have been unable to get a drink of water, only as their good pleasure saw fit to grant us the boon, which was very seldom. Before Connely and I had retired for the night an officer came through the corral where we were herded, and began a tirade of abuse against the prisoners, ending it with declaring the awful punishment the Confederate authorities intended to inflict upon us for burning the Valley. He said we would be put in Libby prison, and if Jeff Davis did not order it burned down, he would set fire to it himself. That was the punishment we deserved and he would personally see to it that it was meted out to us in all the length and breadth, height and depth of its just proportions. Great is Southern chivalry!–especially when full of whisky and in the presence of helpless prisoners. After this encouraging announcement of the awful doom which awaited us, he commenced talking about the war in general, and expressed his opinion that, instead of disaster they were now winning an overwhelming victory. Connely made bold to ask him how long he thought they could hold out? His answer was:

"Until hell freezes over."

Connely then asked him why they stripped our dead on the field of battle, and the prisoners they captured? His explanation was, because the

MY CHUM, D. W. CONNELY.

Federal army could get clothing from foreign countries, *"but,"* said he, *"our government is shut off and can't negotiate with foreign powers; consequently we are compelled to rob the dead and prisoners to clothe our armies."* Connely repeatedly emphasized the words, *"Our Government, Our Government!"* *"Why,"* said he, *"you have no Government, nor will you ever have one."*

This so enraged the drunken officer that he pulled out a revolver and snapped it at Connely, but it failed to go off, and while he was making ready to try it again, I shoved Connely in among the crowd of prisoners, where he was soon lost from his would-be murderer. Had it not been for the failure of the Rebel's pepper-box to fire, I fear my brave but somewhat rash chum would have been killed. I ventured to suggest to Dave that he had better keep a padlock on his mouth when he was talking to a drunken rebel officer, but he only laughed and said, *"I am like a woman, bound to have my say, let the consequences by what they may."*

We lay down for the night, and rather than run the risk of exposing our good blanket and pieces of tents we did without them, although the night was very cold and we suffered a great deal. Forty-eight hours, have now passed since we had anything to eat, and from all appearances we are likely to go forty-eight more in the same condition. Our sufferings are indescribable.

October 21st. Another dreary, dismal, toilsome day has dawned. Nature is robed in all her matchless beauty; the air is sweet and balmy; the woods are musical with the songs of birds and fragrant with the perfume of myriads of beautiful flowers. But even the beauty of Nature fails to minister hope, comfort and strength to weary, hungry men who are on their way to weeks and months of still greater privation and suffering. The early morning saw us again in our accustomed places in the line, ready to take up our march. We received the usual instruction to keep to the middle of the road. Here we received the first encouraging information we have had since we were captured, namely that when we reached Staunton we would receive rations. This was indeed joyful news and had a tendency to raise our spirits and inspire us with new hope. But even that humane announcement was accompanied with the inhumane one, *"You ought not to have any; you justly deserve to starve to death."* Well, that might be their opinion, for which we did not care a fig, because we knew they were too cowardly to put it into execution. We reached Staunton between 9 and 10 o'clock in the morning. I was so nearly exhausted I at once sat down to rest. According to the promise made us, they undertook to issue rations to the prisoners, but such confusion prevailed that they failed to do it decently and in order. It was a time when might prevailed, and men–hungry famished men–forgot the sacred rights of those who were equally hungry and worthy. The cracker barrels were rolled among the crows and the strongest got the lion's share. I saw the awful struggle which was going on among the hungry men to reach the food, goaded on to desperate efforts to get all they could, not knowing when they would get any more. Weak as I was, I concluded it was useless for me to struggle with that crowd, and choose to starve rather than run the risk of being trampled to death. While viewing the scene of confusion with disgust, and yet with pity, Connely, noble fellow that he was, approached me with a handful of crackers, which he promptly divided with me, saying, *"It is equal to a cyclone to get into such a conflict as that."* We ate the crackers, which were of a very poor quality. But, no meal that I had ever eaten in the past was eaten with such relish and enjoyment as those spoiled crackers, which composed our dinner in the city of Staunton, Virginia, about the hour of noon of October 21st, 1864, after a fast lasting from the early morning of the 19th, during which interval we had been marching hard all day and lying on the bare ground at night. We were not so particular about the quality as we were anxious about the quantity of the food, for the quantity was just about sufficient to aggravate our appetite and tantalize us with the memory that up yonder in "God's country," "hard tack and sow bosom" were plenty and to spare.

After we had finished our first meal as guests of the Southern Confederacy, and while we were waiting for coffee and cigars to come (in which expectation circumstances beyond the control of our generous hosts, doomed us to disappointment), we were loaded into stock cars and were soon speeding on our way to visit the Honorable Jefferson Davis, President of the Southern Confederacy, in the celebrated city of Richmond. Old Jeff, presumable not knowing that so many of us were on our way to visit him, failed to send palace hog cars enough for our comfortable transportation, hence, we were crowded until there was scarcely room to stand with comfort. After being loaded into the cars, new guards took charge of us. This change made the occasion for a new onset of pillage and robbery of the already twice-robbed prisoners. These new guards seemed to be of a higher-toned order than the other fellows. While they would not hesitate to take anything they could find loose, or could succeed in unloosing, yet money–Greenbacks, Gold, Silver– seemed to be their principal game. Not finding much of that article among the prisoners, they soon fell back on what few hats, coats, shoes, etc., were left–taking even the photographs of our loved ones at home, which, of course, were of no use whatever to them, only as it helped to make their torture of helpless men the more bitter and unbearable. Those of the prisoners who chanced to have money resorted to every means they could invent to save it. Some hid it in different parts of their clothing; some under the soles of their shoes; others would take a bill, chew it up so that it would pack closely, then lifting the top off a brass button would deposit it there, replace the cover, fastening it down carefully so as not to attract attention, hoping in this way to save it. But alas; as will be seen farther on, even this Yankee trick failed to escape the sharp eyes and greedy paws of the rebel thieves.

About 2 or 3 o'clock in the afternoon, we reached Richmond, where we were unloaded and formed into ranks preparatory to being reviewed by the citizens who had been apprised of our coming, and were anxious to inspect the Yankees. While undergoing the critical scrutiny of these excellent(?) citizens of the Confederacy, and every moment expecting cards of invitation to dine with his royal nibs, President Davis, we were ordered to march–and march we did. We continued our march through the city until we reached a large three-story brick building on one corner of which was a sign which read:

"LIBBY AND SONS, SHIP CHANDLERS AND GROCERS."

We then awoke to the realization that we were about to enter that infamous place of torture known as "Libby Prison."

On our march from the depot to the prison we were escorted by two lines of Richmond citizens, embracing all sexes, ages and classes, each and every one of whom were doing their very best to entertain us with such choice and encouraging words as these: *"Say, you Yankee sons of b's, what you'uns want to run off our niggers for?" "Oh, is these the kind of brutes that has come down here to kill our noble sons?" "Say, Yank, where is your* arms?" "Ho, you bluebellies, where is the rest of you'uns?"

The women would hiss at and spit upon us, and ask us if we would burn down Richmond as we did the Valley? While on this eventful march, we found one woman whom we took to be a friend–she was either that or a vicious foe, whose scheme to poison us, if she had such a scheme, failed. This woman reached out a loaf of bread to Connely, who was nearest to her, which he readily took. Oliver Crocker, of Company I, remarked to him, *"Connely, that bread may be poisoned."* Connely replied, *"All right, Crocker, to die by poison is preferable to starve to death, and a good deal shorter and pleasanter route to go out on."* He broke the loaf of bread in three pieces, giving one piece to Crocker, one to me, keeping the third piece himself. He said, *"Let us eat it; if it kills us it is poisoned; if it does not kill us, we will give the woman credit for being a friend to the Union soldiers."* We ate it and still lived, so the woman was undoubtedly a friend to the men who had fought bravely, were captured and now suffered all manner of torture and insult from these devils in human shape.

When we arrived at Libby Prison, we were ordered to march in, at the same time receiving the encouraging and helpful information that we would "catch hell" before we got out of there; that we were to be roasted for burning the homes over defenseless women's heads in the Valley. Our devastation of the Valley seemed to be the uppermost thought in the minds of both soldiers and civilians, and furnished the excuse for all manner of insults and threats of vengeance from men, women and children. As the last of our column was marching in through the wide doorway, Charley Bowen, a member of Company K of my regiment, being the last one, was seized by the shoulders by a great, big, burly specimen of humanity, jerked back and ordered to pull off his jacket and trousers, or he would shoot him on the spot. At this moment, another guard stepped in the doorway ahead of him, thrust his bayonet at him, and ordered him to obey. There being no relief for him, he was forced to comply with this fiendish order. He was then pushed inside the door of the infernal prison with not a vestige of clothing on him but his shirt, drawers and socks–his shoes having been taken from him before he reached the prison. To make his condition the more pitiable, winter was approaching and no covering of any kind to protect him from the cold days and nights which were sure to come. With all these facts before us, who will dare say that the Union soldiers were engaged in fighting chivalrous and brave men? No, no! We were fighting fiends in human form—things having the semblance of men, but who were guilty of deeds so atrocious and inhuman that devils would blush for shame.

LIBBY PRISON IN 1864

Photo Courtesy U.S. Military History Institute

CHAPTER VI.

ROBBED AGAIN - UNSUCCESSFUL ATTEMPT TO HIDE OUR MONEY - PRISON RULES - CORN DODGER AT LAST THOUGHTS OF HOME - A SLEEPLESS NIGHT - GRAYBACKS GALORE, AND DIRT SUPREME - THE PRISON DOCTOR PLANS FOR ESCAPE A SHOT FIRED, BUT NO HARM DONE

After we were safely inside the prison walls, about a dozen rebel officers came in and divided up our battalion, ordering one half to take the second floor, and the other half to occupy the third floor, at the same time placing guards at the stairway leading to the third floor. When this arrangement was completed, a rebel officer stepped in front of our division, with a revolver in his hand, and ordered us to fall into two lines across the building at the same time announcing that any man who would attempt to secrete any money or other valuables he might possess, or who would refuse to obey any orders that should be given him, would be shot down like a dog. After our lines were formed as he had directed, we were next informed that we must turn over all the money and valuables we had; that he would take down our names, the name and number of our regiment and company, and when we were exchanged, all valuables would be returned to us. After the money had been turned over, they then began to search our clothing. Every button was subjected to the closest scrutiny and every one that had the least appearance of having been opened was cut off, the owner being asked if he had a twenty or a fifty dollar bill inside of it. Those whose shoes were left to them had those articles so closely inspected that only one man in all our number succeeded in saving his money–a five dollar bill which he had in some way hid in his shirt collar. While this plundering was going on, one of our boys told the officers if they would set up their headquarters nearer the front they would stand a better chance of obtaining more plunder, although it would be a little more dangerous over there; that "to

59

the victor belonged the spoils," or at least, they seemed to be working on that system, as robbers number one and two had had the lion's share from us, leaving but little for them to take. After they had finished going through our division, they went upstairs and repeated the same mode of plundering on the boys up there, until every dollar of the money which they had thus far succeeded in keeping, had passed into the possession of our enemies. One man on the third floor had a $20 Confederate bill. He told the plundering officer that was all the money he had. The officer looked at him in a pleasant way and said:

"If that is all the money you have, you may keep it, poor fellow."

We well knew his kindness was not inspired by any love he had for the "poor fellow" but because he knew the miserable bill was not worth taking.

~ ~ ~ ~ ~

But, do not judge these Confederate robbers too harshly! Let us all be charitable in our judgment of even such light-fingered gentry as these were. Perhaps, after all, they were doing us a kindness by compelling us to practice lessons of economy. They did not want us to spend our money foolishly, or squander it in riotous living. But, unfortunately for us, they took the entire matter of guardianship into their own hands—we did not have a single voice in the selection of who should be the custodians of our wealth—we did not have even the right of veto. We were all tumbled into "innocuous desuetude." Mind you, they sought to quiet our fears, and alleviate our pain, as we saw seam after seam ripped open, patch after patch torn off, shoe after shoe dissected, button after button uncovered and the previous "greenbacks" which they contained, and upon which we had built such high hopes of comparative comfort, transferred to the pockets of these the meanest of all robbers, by telling us, on the honor of gentlemen(?) that, the very moment we started towards home again, all our money (they did not promise to pay us loan brokers' interest), would be returned to us again. But, alas!, few, if any, of those noble, brave, heroic sons of the Confederacy who had thus, unsolicited, and out of pure benevolence, become our guardians for the purpose of taking care of our money were present when, what few of us who lived to return, started homeward. And we who did survive the terrible ordeal, were magnanimous enough toward our southern guardians not to demand a

*return of our money, because their banks, at that time, were in sore financial
straits—in fact they were badly and irretrievably busted. We love our southern
guardians—indeed we do. May their breed never again rise up to curse the earth
and pollute the land.*

~ ~ ~ ~ ~

After they had completed their work of robbery, they then kindly informed us concerning the rules and regulations of the Hotel de Libby.
One was, that to indulge in the simple and innocent privilege of putting
an arm outside a window, or to stand with our face near a window, was
an invitation for a minnie ball, which would be sure to come from the
rifle of a guard. With these, and some other friendly(?) suggestions, they
left us, stating we would probably get a bite to eat before night, but, as
they were short just now on account of our burning the Valley, we must
put up with what we got, and be thankful for it. To all of which we responded *"Amen!"* and bade our dear guardians *"good night."*

Our first night in Libby Prison was gloomy and discouraging
enough. Nearly famished with hunger—our only food since the 19th being the few damaged crackers we got at Staunton; our money all appropriated by the rebel officers; our clothing all gone—some being left with
nothing but their underclothes—over half of our number hatless, shoeless
and blanketless, and all this robbery having been carried on upon helpless prisoners, by men who professed to be waging a war for human
rights, the love of liberty and the glory of God—well, it is enough to make
one cry out, as did the spirit in Jean Paul Richter's dread, "Is there no
God?" We soon learned that among the authorities of the Confederacy
there are no men—only fiends.

About sundown the long-looked for rations came, conspicuous only
for their scantiness. This evening's repast, as issued to us by the prison
authorities, consisted of a piece of cornbread about three inches square,
and not to exceed one and a half inches thick. On this we feasted thankfully—and rapidly. It did not take us long to finish supper that night. Brutus asked concerning the corpulency of Caesar:

"Upon what meat doth this our Caesar feed that he hath grown so fat?"

Confident we are that unless our rebel hosts become more generous in our quality, no latterday Brutus will ever be troubled with such a question.

Being very weary, Connely, Crocker and myself laid down for the night with the hope of getting some sleep, which our poor jaded bodies, weary minds and sickened hearts needed so much but my own mind was too much engrossed with perplexing things to admit of sleep. My thoughts went homeward to beloved ones who were there. No doubt by this time the news of the great battle and my capture by the rebels had reached the ears of my dear wife, who was even then mourning for me as dead. To have let her know the true situation in which I was then placed would be to her worse than death. I tried to console myself with the hope that she would remain ignorant of my sufferings, and would continue to pray for my release and return. But relief did not come from those musings. Memories of my aged father, my brothers and my only sister, came thick and fast. They, too, would soon learn that I was listed among the "missing," and in their sorrow and despair would look upon the darkest side and consider me dead. But would honorable death on the battle-field present a "darker side" than the insults, the wholesale robbery, the cruel and unnecessary sufferings to which I, with my noble comrades, had already been subjected, and were yet to come? No—a thousand times, NO! Death would have been as a bright summer morning radiant with the glory of the sunshine, beautiful as a garden of roses, in comparison to the conditions under which I was then placed. The darkest picture that the human mind could possibly paint, might have taken from that first, sad night in Libby Prison, as we lay on its rough, hard floor, weary, and famished with hunger, trying to drown our sorrows in blessed sleep which would not come.

~ ~ ~ ~ ~

That was one of the longest nights I ever lived. I could hear the guards walking their beats, and commenting on "the catch of fresh fish" which they had succeeded in bringing in. But gloating as they were over our capture and misfortunes, they were not happy over their own position by any means. The battle in which we had been captured brought no joyful tidings to them. They could not understand how it happened that Early allowed his army to be so badly whipped after he had routed the Yankees in the morning and driven them so many miles towards Washington. One of the guards confided his opinion of the affair to another guard in the following expressive language:

"I don't see how Early could get himself whipped so damned bad after such a glorious victory in the morning!"

One of our boys who was standing at the window and overheard this choice bit of conversation, yelled out:

"Say, Johnnie, I can tell you; Sheridan just came from Winchester and he turned the battle against Early! No flies on Phil, I tell you!"

This retort dried up the conversation between the rebel guards about the "fresh fish" and Early's defeat in the Valley.

~ ~ ~ ~ ~

With the close of a long, weary, sleepless night, came the dawning of the 22nd of October, 1864, and the fourth day of my captivity in rebellion. Life is still sweet, but the hunger which is gnawing like the grinding of two mill stones, with no wheat in the hopper is exceedingly bitter. There is one favor, however, for which we are truly thankful, we have plenty of good water. A daylight survey of the building in which we have taken up our residence for an indefinite period of time, reveals some conditions which are not so easily discovered after night. For instance, I find that it is in an exceedingly dirty condition. Evidently the chamber-maid forgot to bring her brooms, or, perhaps, chamber-maids and brooms have ceased to be a part of the retinue of Libby Prison. Then, that peculiar species of "song birds," or, more scientifically speaking, "scratching birds," known to the ornithology of southern prisons as "Graybacks," are very numerous and seem to be as voracious as the human "graybacks" who robbed and insulted us without let or hindrance. As between the two, the original "Grayback" is very much more of a gentleman than his human counterfeit.

About 10 o'clock this morning breakfast was served consisting of the regulation corn bread, the pieces being a little

> "Grayback" was a term used by Civil War soldiers to describe body lice, a principal agitator of the soldiers that was particularly prevalent in prisons. Aside from the irritation they caused, they also spread disease. A prisoners general health was often directly related to his ability to rid himself of "graybacks," which often became a time consuming effort.

larger in length and breadth, but somewhat skimped in thickness, they being about four inches square and one inch thick, so taking the actual number of square inches in each piece, there was a slight advance over the rations of yesterday evening. Still the increase was scarcely sufficient to make any appreciable improvement in their ability to satisfy the demand. I am now determined to make as much of a royal feast out of this piece of "dodger" as I can. Therefore, I select my position. I sit down by an upright post in the middle of the building, first of all spreading out my blanket which I imagine to be the easy cushion of a sumptuous dining hall chair. Then I regulate the size of my bites, not according to the craving of my stomach, but according to the size of my piece of "dodger" in ratio to the vacuum it is destined to fill. I chew very slowly—not wishing to impair my digestion—in fact I try to keep each bite in my mouth as long as I can but the law of gravitation inside of me seems to be so strong that it is all I can do to keep the bread in my mouth long enough to get the taste of it. However, dear reader, I must say that this ration of corn bread tastes sweeter to me than any I ever ate in all my life before. I wish there had been more of it to relish.

About noon the prison doctor came in to make his daily round of the different rooms. The man who was stabbed in the arm with the rebel guard's bayonet, before we reached Staunton, is suffering a great deal from his cruel wound. He belongs to an Ohio regiment. The arm is terribly swollen and it is very painful. The doctor gave him some liniment to put on it. He seems to be a kind-hearted man, and freely condemned the guard for his brutality in stabbing the man under the circumstances. There are quite a number of sick men in the prison but the doctor is doing all in his power for their relief. It is comforting to find one man belonging to the Confederacy who has not, as yet, become dehumanized. It is to be hoped this man will escape the contagion of brutality which seems to be so universal among the civilians as well as soldiers of rebeldom.

A drowning man is said to catch at straws. The more desperate and hopeless one's situation, the more vivid and active are one's mental anticipations of relief from distressing conditions. So it is with the prisoners in Libby. We know that we are confined within the strong walls of an immense building from which escape seems to be impossible. We know that we are in the clutches of a cruel and relentless foe who will not only guard every avenue of escape, and visit the most bitter and condign punishment upon any who dare attempt such a hazardous feat. A foe who will close his ears against all appeals for such treatment as honorable prisoners of war are entitled to, as well as against all proposals of the United States Government for a just and speedy exchange of prisoners, his purpose being to torture the prisoners of the Federal army, whom he has failed to kill in battle. Yet, notwithstanding the hopelessness of our situation, the all-absorbing topic of our conversation by day, and of our dreams at night, is either exchange or escape. But our pleasant dreams were brought to a sudden awakening by one of the guards shooting at a man whose arm was protruding through the bars of the window. He was holding in his hand a handkerchief which he had washed and was trying to dry by holding it outside the window. Fortunately the guard's aim was not good and the ball sped wide of its mark. This act told us that all hopes of parole or exchange from such a foe, was not to be entertained.

When we were marched into the prison, all commissioned officers were taken from the ranks and put in a part of the prison by themselves, but we were ignorant of their whereabouts. This evening two Confederate officers came into our room and ordered all commissioned officers, if any were present, to step to the front, but as none obeyed the order, the officers were satisfied there were none present.

I have already stated that we had breakfast about 10 o'clock a. m. We waited patiently and hopefully for dinner, but none came. We then looked forward with eager expectation to the supper hour, being satisfied to accept two meals a day, if we could not get three. But the supper hour came and passed and still no waiters bearing platters of food appeared. The truth then began to dawn upon us that the Hotel de Libby was a kind of sanitarium, in which they served only one meal a day, and that very scanty in quantity, and not much to brag of in quality.

Night is again coming on and I shudder at its approach. Not many weeks, or even days, ago I welcomed it with gladness because it brought rest to the body, peace to the mind—a blessed recuperation of all the mental and physical powers. But now, instead of sweet, restful sleep, the long and dreary hours of the night are spent in thinking of home and the loved ones there whose hearts are bleeding because of the uncertainty which surrounds my fate. And I am not alone. As I look into the sad and haggard faces of the comrades about me, I know that but few men in Libby Prison are free from the harassing thought which drives "sleep from our eyes and slumber from our eyelids."

CHAPTER VII.

OUR RATIONS OF DODGER DECREASING - FAULKNER MUST
LOSE HIS ARM - JEFF DAVIS AND LEE VISIT THE PRISON
RUMORS OF EXCHANGE - OUR SUFFERINGS ON THE
INCREASE - "WHY DOES OUR GOVERNMENT LET US STAY
HERE?" - CHANGE OF DOCTORS - AN IRISHMAN'S RETORT
A GREAT CALAMITY: OUR TOBACCO ALL GONE
THE PHILOSOPHY OF GRAYBACKS
POOR FOOD AND NOT MUCH OF IT

The morning of October 23rd was ushered in with a cold drizzling rain. The most absorbing feature of our prison are the multitudes of graybacks, whose principal business is to draw all the vitality from our poor bodies. This is their principal and continual occupation during the hours of the night but when daylight appears they skedaddle, like their human prototypes (the rebels), for their hiding places, from which they watch our movements and prepare for a more vigorous assault when night again throws her mantle of darkness over the earth and thus hides their movements.

About 11 o'clock the squad of men to whom is entrusted the distribution of our daily rations was ordered to the door to receive our corn-dodger which, in quantity but not in quality is about the same as yesterday. While the rations were being distributed, one of our men made bold to ask a rebel guard if he could tell him anything about our chances for being exchanged or paroled, or about how long he thought we would remain guests of this hotel. He received the polite and characteristic answer:

"You'uns will have to stay here until hell is froze over, and you might as well keep quiet about it."

Our rations were divided as usual, and, as usual, are just enough to aggravate, but not appease our appetites. The quality this morning is not as good as it has been, the cook having allowed the bread to bake heavy and soggy–scarcely more than half baked–but it is licked up with a voracity which cares little for such trifling accidents.

This morning we were compelled to admit there was one man in Libby Prison, wearing the Union Blue, who is mean enough to disgrace it, and render himself despicable in the eyes of all the prisoners, by his thievish conduct. While the rations were being distributed, one man came down from the division up stairs, stood in our line, and got a ration of bread which did not belong to him, thus leaving one man of our own number without any. The fellow had gone back before we found it out, so the rest of us divided our share with the poor fellow who was cheated out of his scanty ration. We vowed among ourselves that we would guard against such rascality in the future.

The doctor did not make his rounds to-day until after 12 o'clock. One of our boys was taken very sick and the doctor had him removed to the hospital, which is across the street but a little south of this building. Faulkner, the man with the wounded arm, is very bad to-day. The doctor expressed his fears that the arm would have to be amputated to save his life, gangrene having set in. The more we get acquainted with the doctor the better we like him. He is kind and gentlemanly in all his bearing toward us. He freely and candidly answers our eager questionings concerning the probability of our exchange or parole, but is unable to give us any reliable information on the subject. Although disappointed in our expectations of receiving some encouragement and hope from him, yet we feel grateful for his kindness and appreciate the generosity of his treatment.

This afternoon we were treated to a rare privilege, nothing less than a sight of the high dignitaries of the Confederacy. His royal "nibs," President Davis, accompanied by his staff and the famous General Robert E. Lee, commander of the rebel army rode by our prison, looking up at the windows and seemed to take great delight in seeing the fine catch they had already made. From all appearances they were well satisfied and rode away.

This evening a ray of hope beamed in upon us by a rumor circulated through the prison that we were to be exchanged, but the longer we tried to hunt up the authority for the rumor, the fainter became the trail, until it was lost entirely and we were compelled to fall back upon the cheerless task of trying to hope against hope.

October 24th. This is a beautiful morning. The sun is shining brightly and doing its best to dispel the gloom from our hearts by flooding our prison with glorious sunlight. How bright and beautiful the world which lies outside our barred windows looks to our weary, longing eyes! But what a chill comes over us as we turn our eyes from the world outside to the smaller, but none the less conscious and sensitive world inside the prison walls. What mysterious changes have taken place during the past few days. Only six days ago we were reveling in plenty to eat, and the joy of association under honorable and fraternal (even if they were dangerous) conditions. Now, this is all changed. Separated from companions, weak and famished with hunger, in the clutches of a foe so cruel and inhuman that they seem to take supreme delight in torturing and insulting us. They meant very much more than they expressed, when they told us they were going to starve us to death here. How long can mortal flesh endure this agony?

Our rations were served to us again as usual, quantity and quality being about the same as yesterday. When the doctor came this morning he was besieged on every side by men eager to gain any information he was able to give them on the all-absorbing subject of exchange. He received our importunities with great patience and kindness, but the only response we could elicit from him was:

"Cheer up, boys! Cheer up, boys!"

This was all he would say, but the way in which he said it led us to believe he knew more on the subject than he dared tell us. After visiting the sick he ordered Faulkner to go with him to the hospital, his arm having become very much worse. This visit of the good doctor, and the peculiar manner in which he expressed himself, has sent new blood coursing through our veins and brought new hope into our lives. Some of us feel that there must be some meaning in the look of his face, the flash of his eye and the tone of his voice, while others say they are only trying to awaken within us false hopes for fear that we will become mutinous from desperation and hunger. Of course, every man has his own views of the situation, and does not hesitate to speak freely what is in his mind.

The question often arises as to why our government allows us to remain here, subject to such torture as we are enduring? Is it possible that we are to be thus rewarded for all that we sacrificed when we responded to the Nation's call for help in the hour of her peril? It must be that President Lincoln is entirely ignorant of the treatment we are receiving as prisoners of the rebel Government, because if he was apprised of the real facts he would either order the Union armies concentrated and Richmond crushed at a single blow, or else he would see that we were exchanged at once. No, no! That great-hearted man in the White House at Washington would not allow his boys to perish from starvation at the hands of a relentless foe. Oh, this torture from hunger and vermin makes life a burden which cannot be endured much longer! We cannot rest by day nor sleep by night. The walls and floors are literally packed with vermin. They cover our clothing, they fill our hair. They, too, are prisoners; hungry as we are and like us in every respect, except this, that while they can and do feed upon us, we cannot feed upon them.

October 25th. Another night, long and lonesome, has passed, and another day (to be) long and dreary has dawned. I had a dream last night, full of pleasure, but its awakening was full of pain. I dreamed that I was at home. I could see it in all its comforts and beauty just as I had left it the day I started to the "front." My wife was getting supper, I could see every movement she made and everything she did, as plainly and vividly as sight itself could make it. I thought to myself; "Now I will have one good meal–farewell hunger and pain!" But, alas! just as my wife said, "Supper is ready!" and I went to my old place at the table, I awoke to find myself in a veritable rebel hell, hungry, weary, and with every bone in my body aching, while the graybacks were fighting for what little blood is yet left in me. While I lay on my back meditating on the future, a ray of consolation came to me in this way: If our rations do not increase our flesh will soon be gone, and then our enemies; the graybacks, will have to starve as well as we. O revenge, how sweet thou art!

A great calamity has befallen the prisoners, both sick and well. Our kind-hearted, humane doctor has been taken away from us, and in his place has come a young, dapper, dandyish fellow, evidently endowed with about as much brains as third grade army mules. He puts on lots of professional airs; tries hard to look wise, but fails to make us believe that his wisdom is equal to his vanity. One of the boys so far forgot himself in the presence of this medical prodigy as to run the risk of asking him if he could tell us how long we would have to stay in this prison? He drew himself up to the full height of his stature and replied:

"That sire, will depend on how long your constitution will stand it."

A little Irishman, belonging to a New York regiment, replied:

"Say, doctor, if you will furnish us with a kettle to boil these graybacks in, and some salt to season them with, we will be here to scatter flowers on your grave—bedad we will, sir."

This raised quite a commotion, which was followed by such a loud burst of laughter, that the little dandy "pill-bags" went flying out of our room—no doubt swearing vengeance on us all.

October 26th. Another day has dawned, and the same routine of prison life has to be gone over. About midnight we were aroused from sleep by a fire in the west part of the city. How extensive it was we could not tell. That it was not very far from the prison we were sure, because the light from the fire illumined the interior as well as the exterior of the building. We were cautioned by our guards not to get too close to the windows. The prison authorities evidently feared if the fire should spread we would make a break for liberty. To prevent this the guards were reinforced, and stringent orders for our safe-keeping were issued. We were hoping that the fire might prove to be extensive enough to involve this part of the city, and seriously threaten, if not actually destroy this old prison house, and thus give us a chance to escape, but to our chagrin the fire was stopped before it got under much headway. Our organization for escape, if an opportunity offers, is now very complete, and we were all on the watch for some movement on the outside, to favor our making a dash upon the guards, hoping, if once outside the prison, to reach our lines, which we knew to be east of Richmond. At 2 o'clock all was quiet and we went back to our hard beds.

A great calamity befell me this morning—I took the last chew of my tobacco. It is all gone and no means of getting another supply. None but those who have undergone the experience can tell what a solace and comfort tobacco is to those who are enduring the tortures of prison life. It really allayed the pangs of hunger, so that when we were deprived of our tobacco we suffered far more than we would have done if our rations had been cut short. The rations we received to-day were short enough to satisfy the most rigid advocate of abstemiousness. However, an addition to the quantity was made in the way of giving us a pint of what they call "bean soup." It consisted of one black-eyed pea and two spoonfuls of worms in about a pint of water. This is the "standard" bean soup of Libby Prison. But we are losing much of the fastidiousness which was such a marked characteristic of our soldier-nature before we began boarding at this "hotel." We are now perfectly content to adopt the doctrine that "what won't poison will fatten." Hence our anxiety is not about quality but quantity. Whatever will help to "fill up" is received with thankfulness and no questions asked. When the life is being slowly but surely starved out of a man, anything, even worms, that will cheat the destroyer and sustain life, is appreciated and vigorously devoured.

An old subject, in somewhat altered form, has appeared and is furnishing great opportunities for the naturalist, "bugologists," philosophers, and other professionalists among the prisoners viz: the history, including the habits, origin, customs, propensities, capabilities and general character of the "Grayback." These discussions, and the organization of regular campaigns for the extermination, afford much amusement and serve to pass away many of the dreary hours of prison life in comparative forgetfulness.

Our French cooks were rather slow in preparing our breakfast this morning, as it was 12 o'clock noon, before rations were distributed to us. The only striking thing about this late meal is that it was composed of a small quantity of sour, soggy, half-baked cornbread. We shall be compelled to petition our hotel-keeper to dismiss these cooks and employ better ones if our food is not more expeditiously and palatably prepared. The rights of guests, as well as of cooks, must be regarded with proper regularity, or the Hotel de Libby will loose its reputation as a first-class hostelry, and travelers through this part of the Confederacy will shun it– indeed, its present corps of guests would like to have a chance to shun away from it.

Our new doctor made his rounds again. The dear man was late in coming. The whole Confederacy seems to be getting into the bad habit of "slow movement," except when Sheridan is after them, when they move with increased celerity. The doctor left a very little medicine for some of the sick, while a great many who needed medicine were left wholly unsupplied. His excuse was that his supply of medicine was so short he could give it only to those who needed it the most. What a stain on American civilization that even sick and helpless men are left to die without proper medical aid! Did the world ever witness such inhuman treatment as that bestowed by the rebel Government on honorable Union prisoners? But the day of vengeance is not far distant!

October 28th. Our prison is all excitement this morning. Men who were despondent and ready to give up and die have taken new courage and feel that life is still worth fighting for. I have determined not to "swear off" using tobacco yet. The reason for all this commotion and "backsliding" is that news has reached us that we are to be exchanged. This time the rumor seems to be well authenticated, our informant being no less a personage than Major Turner, Commander of Libby Prison. He told us that negotiations for an exchange of prisoners were actually in progress, and there were strong probabilities that in a few days we would be sent within our lines. My soul is already aglow with bright visions of plenty to eat and plenty of tobacco. To-day our rations of corn dodger were devoured rapidly and thankfully. Men could scarcely stop talking about the prospective exchange long enough to eat. But there are many who refuse to be carried away by the rumor. They fear it is only a ruse of the enemy to add to our torture by starvation and suffering, the keener and deeper anguish of disappointment. Another new doctor has made his appearance among us to-day. This one is an elderly man and, I am glad to say, a different man to the upstart whose place he has taken. This one seems to be a gentleman and treats us with the consideration becoming his profession.

CHAPTER VIII.

REBEL CRUELTY - FOOD ONLY ONCE A DAY, AND
DECREASING IN QUANTITY - "NO EXCHANGE OF PRISONERS"
GUARDS KEEP A CLOSE WATCH OF THE WINDOWS
INTENSE SUFFERING FOR TOBACCO - THE FIRST DEATH - THE
AWFUL FILTH OF LIBBY PRISON - STILL TRYING TO BE
CHEERFUL - GRAYBACKS STILL ON TOP
STARTLING NEWS: WE ARE TO LEAVE LIBBY

October 29th. The longer we remain in prison the more we are learning the lesson that our enemies take special delight in deceiving us by creating in our hearts hopes of exchange and speedy release, which have no foundation at all. This is one of the bitter lessons we have to learn. It is so easy to get such rumors afloat among men who dream of release by night and pray for it by day. It is hard to believe that human beings could be so cruel. Would-be philosophers might say that, situated as we were, it was foolish to put so much confidence in these rumors. We ought to have known better than to allow ourselves to be carried away by them. But it is the very circumstances under which we were placed which made it so hard to control our judgment. Intense desire for release is the ruling power in the case. Anything which gives us the faintest hope of being released from this worse than living death–this unceasing succession of days and nights of indescribable horror and suffering–is grasped at and cherished with a spontaneity of feeling and belief that is irresistible. But thus far our confidence has been misplaced. Our expectations of being exchanged have come to naught, forcing upon us greater depression of spirits and hopelessness of the future. These hopes and disappointments are beginning to tell seriously on the health of a great many of the prisoners. One of these days the brittle thread of life will snap with some of them. Who will be the first?

Our rations of dodger come regularly once a day. The ration is constantly decreasing in size, but it has a corresponding increase in weight.

However, the increase in weight does not indicate an increase in the nourishing quality of the dodger–it simply indicates cupidity and downright cussedness in the cooks. How any one can make so small a piece of corn dodger weigh so heavy is a problem that all the scientific culture of the inhabitants of this "School of Economy" have not been able to determine. But that which the mind cannot grasp the stomach can feel to its fullest satisfaction–of misery.

The doctor banished the last hope of exchange from our minds this morning, by informing us that the negotiations for an exchange of prisoners between the two governments have failed. The latest rumor is that our government has positively refused to exchange any prisoners under any circumstances. This is sad and distressing news, not only to us who are enduring all the horrors of prison life, but to the loved ones in our homes, who are enduring agony almost as great, because of their anxiety concerning our fate. I am afraid this shock, which is the severest of any we have yet had, will be more than many of the poor boys can survive. Is it possible that our government is going to desert us and leave us to the malignant cruelty of our enemies? It looks that way to us. I have already mentioned the fact that one of the positive orders of the prison was that no prisoner should stand in close proximity to any of the windows. This rule the guards seemed to take great delight in enforcing, because they were always on the alert for an opportunity to shoot one of the hated "Yanks." At almost any hour of the day they could be seen in attitudes of expectancy, with rifles cocked and ready, watching the windows to find a man close enough to give them a reasonable excuse to fire. They were many times seen to go into the street, many feet away from their regular beats, for the sake of getting a shot at a prisoner whose shadow, even, might fall on the window, although the man himself may have been many feet inside the deadline. A prisoner, to-day, received a bullet in his arm, while he was in the act of throwing water out a window. Another was saved from death by a nail turning the course of the bullet. When the matter was reported to Major Turner, the prison commander, he flippantly replied:

"The boys need practice."

Such outrages as these are of daily occurrence from which we have no protection nor redress. Will not God send both to such cruelly wronged men?

October 30th. Exchange stock is way below par this morning, and the spirits of the prisoners have fallen in proportion. The quantity and quality of our rations range from bad to horrible bad. Our ration of corn bread is contracting in size so rapidly, that a few days more and all that will be left to us will be the memory of the dodger that once came, but comes no more. I wish I could give a faint description of the stuff they are pleased to call "food," and which they give us to eat. It is composed entirely of corn bread, distributed among us once a day. This is every thing we have to eat. It is made out of the poorest and roughest grade of corn meal, large pieces of cob and husk being often found in the bread. Sometimes it is not more than half cooked; at other times, as to-day, the crust is baked so thick and hard that it would make a good substitute for grape-shot. Such is the food upon which the chivalric(?) Confederacy is feeding the prisoners it has captured in open and honorable battle.

While exchange stock, vitality of spirits, hope for the future, and our rations of corn dodger are all going down, there is one commodity that is constantly going up in price, but slowly vanishing from the market, viz: tobacco. Every tobacco chewer—and they are legion—is out of tobacco; not a chew to be had at any price. We are a great company of "reformers," the advance guard of the forces of anti-tobacconists. But it is not because we "want to," but because we "have to." I suppose we could buy tobacco from the guards, if we had anything to buy with, but our guardians—the men who took our money into safe keeping—are so anxious to break us of this nasty habit, and perfect our purification, that they will not replenish our exchequers, which are as empty as our tobacco-bags. When I was a boy I used to hear the old adage, "There is honor among thieves," but we have found there are exceptions to this rule as well as to all others; at least we have found a lamentable absence of honor among the class of thieves into whose hands we had the misfortune to fall on the morning of October 19th. And the more we see of them, and the more we have to do with them, the more we learn of their thievish and disreputable characters.

To-day occurred the first death on our floor. A young man belonging to a Pennsylvania regiment. He was not sick, but died from sheer despondency. No words of encouragement and cheer that we could utter served to revive his poor broken heart. No man ever more surely suffered martyrdom for his country than did this young man. It is a great cost to pay. Might not that life have been spared to do better service for the country? How many men will have to follow this first one, God only knows.

One thing which adds to the severity of our sufferings is the absolute impossibility of maintaining personal cleanliness. No effort whatever is made by the prison authorities to keep the rooms in anything like decent sanitary conditions. The inside of the awful hell is so foul and filthy that no pen can describe its true condition. As I have already stated, it is overrun with the vilest of vermin, and the floors are encrusted with filth of every description. The naked and starved men lie down at night on the slimy floor, not to sleep, but to kill time, and arise in the morning with hair and beard matted with the expectorations and filth of the day previous. One old blanket, full of dirt and vermin, has to serve for the only covering of half a dozen poor, naked sufferers, whose only moments of quietude come with the semi-oblivion enjoyed in snatches of half-delirious sleep, on a bed whose mattress and pillows were all of one substance—a hard, board floor, reeking with filth.

~ ~ ~ ~ ~

Unpleasant though the subject may be, a better understanding of the conditions under which we were compelled to live by day and sleep by night, can be appreciated if I briefly describe the sanitary conditions of the prison. Here, more than anywhere else, the barbarous and devilish characters of the men who had us in their power was manifested. Circumstances which they could not control, may have made it necessary for the prison authorities to keep us on short rations, but no reason under the sun could exist why we should be compelled to live in the midst of such reeking filth as existed in Libby Prison. There was an abundance of fresh, pure water. The prisoners would have been glad of the opportunity to scrub and clean the floors as well as our persons, but all this was wickedly denied us, for which there was not the shadow of an excuse. It was done to add still farther to the misery we were compelled to suffer by day and by night.

The sanitary(?) arrangements were conspicuous only for their great simplicity. Of waterclosets, there were none. A sink, made something like a large trough, is furnished for each floor, and is free to all. The convenience of this simple arrangement is admirable, and reflects credit on the great men who conceived and executed the plan, but the effect upon the sense of common decency is simply abominable. Every day an old darkey comes around and removes any accumulations of filth. Following him comes another parading through the building, carrying an old coal hod filled with pine knots, which he would set on fire, and the smoke from which was supposed to fumigate the rooms and kill the awful stench which filled the atmosphere of the prison. Comment on this is unnecessary.

Notwithstanding these terrible conditions under which we were compelled to live, not all the prisoners were of a morbid, inconsolable turn of mind, who did nothing but mope around, gradually waste away and die for the want of something better to do. Far from it. These cases were the exception, not the rule. Never did men try harder to devise ways and means for "killing time" and making dreary hours pass as pleasantly as possible. We had lots of fun as well as lots of sorrow. There was much loud, ringing laughter, as well as much groaning and weeping. Songs—love songs, patriotic songs, humorous songs, plantation songs—often made old Libby ring until the rebel guards would wonder "What on earth them there renegade, fool Yanks were a-doin." Some men of lymphatic temperament were blessed with the ability to sleep from ten to eighteen hours a day, and they were envied by those who were differently constituted, because sleep was considered to be the most priceless blessing God could bestow on men situated as we were. Those whose temperaments were of a different character, and who could not render themselves oblivious to their surroundings by sleep, devised many ways to make life bearable. Some would improvise checkerboards on the floor, and many a hard-fought game of checkers was carried on in this primitive manner to the delight of the spectators as well as of the participants. Others would engage in the old game of "Fox and geese," while other's played and romped like a lot of happy school boys on a stormy day. Many employed their time and skill in cutting their names on the wood-work and brickwork, while many exhibited the Yankee proclivity of whittling from morning until night. Thus the days were passed, and life in Libby Prison was lived.

~ ~ ~ ~ ~

October 30th (continued). Owing to a lack of proper food, the foul condition of the prison, and the want of medical attention, the sick are rapidly increasing. The types of disease are becoming so malignant, and the danger of infection so great, that quite a number were taken to the hospital to-day. One of the men taken out was a peculiarly sad case his malady being insanity caused by the want of tobacco. It is strange, but true. This privation is felt more keenly than even the lack of food, and causes greater despondency among the prisoners–that is, among those who have been accustomed to the use of it. Blessed is the man (in Libby Prison) who has never used, required, or "hankered" after the weed.

November 1st. No change as yet in the value of exchange stock. It is as low in Libby Prison market as Confederate scrip is on the New York stock exchange. An order was read to us to-day which recited that the Federal Government had rejected all proposals made by the Confederate Government for an exchange of prisoners; that there would be no exchange whatever, and we could now make up our minds to remain in the Confederacy until the war closed. Here after we might consider ourselves to be permanent and distinguished guests of President Jefferson Davis. When this announcement was closed, some one remarked that we would soon be the "extinguished guests of the Confederacy" which will certainly be the case if a radical change in our treatment is not made by our hosts. The question is on many lips, and throbbing in many hearts, "Can it be possible that our Government; the Government under whose flag we enlisted, for whose defense we went into the fire of battle, and for whose sake we are now enduring prison torture, will leave us here to rot and die?" Surely the authorities at Washington are not ignorant of the awful agony we are enduring–the living death by which we are being slowly tortured? Many are utterly broken down with despair, while others take a more hopeful view of the situation, refusing to believe the statements made to us this morning. They continue to talk cheerfully and hopefully, and are free in expressing their opinion that Turner lied for the purpose of increasing our despondency, thus making our lot more bitter and our lives more uncertain. Thank God for the healthful effects of one cheerful, hopeful soul.

Our scanty rations did not reach us to-day until 2 o'clock P.M. They were smaller in quantity, and no improvement in quality. We suppose the alarm clock in the quarters of our rebel cook failed to awaken that worthy dignitary, and hence the lateness of our breakfast. But we are at a loss to account for the continued and gradual decrease in quantity. The nights are becoming colder, and having little, if any covering of clothing, we suffer a great deal from the cold. Our condition is becoming more deplorable every day.

November 2nd. Another long and sleepless night has been passed and, so far as we know, or can see, at the opening of the day, there was nothing to break the monotony of our prison life, or make the day more bearable than the former days. We supposed our principal business would be a call to make another concerted attack on the great army of graybacks which are constantly gaining reinforcements from every quarter, and with the decrease of the vital fluids in our bodies, are becoming more voracious and desperate. They are becoming as cruel towards us as their human prototypes who are standing guard over us. However, a great and unexpected surprise came to us in the shape of an announcement, which created quite a commotion in our ranks. It was, that as there is no hope of an exchange of prisoners being effected, and as the winter is drawing near, the rebel authorities have decided to send us to a more southerly location, as we suppose, for the benefit of our health.

Tomorrow at noon we are to be marched out and transported to some destination, at present unknown to us. The most earnest pleading failed to induce the rebels to tell us where they were going to send us. The only answer we could get out of them was, to be ready to move promptly at the hour of noon tomorrow. After giving us these orders the officers left us to wonder what it all meant, and whither we were going.

Excitement runs high; many theories and explanations are advanced, discussed and decided. But one thing is certain to all of us, the last hope of exchange has died out. The prisoners are discussing the probabilities of our destination, but not even the most hopeful and sanguine have courage enough to suggest even the possibility of exchange. The effects of this loss of hope are indeed painful in the extreme. Those who have already given up hope have become almost wild with despair, while those who continued to keep the spark of hope alive, are giving way to the awful strain under which they have been living. Still there are some who are even rejoicing that we are going to leave this terrible place, hoping that we will receive better treatment and be in the midst of more decent and healthful surroundings, while others whose natures are such that nothing can dismay them, are encouraging us to cheer up, be brave and bold, because under the very worst circumstances we can imagine, conditions cannot be much worse than they are here. Therefore, instead of complaining, we ought to be thankful that we are going away from this living hell. But who can tell what a day may bring forth, or a change of location mean?

There is not an uncomfortably large number of prisoners confined in Libby Prison, owing to the fact that its capacity is limited. Large numbers are brought in here, but they are allowed to remain only temporarily, they being transferred to other prisons farther south. One of the remarkable facts of our prison life is the remarkably low rate of mortality which prevails. Notwithstanding the wretchedness of our surroundings, the lack of food and of medicine, the death rate of Libby Prison is smaller than that of many other southern prisons. Of course I am speaking of the relative death rate. The deaths in Libby are numerous enough to satisfy even the hellish desires of our enemies, many hundreds of our brave and noble men having died in the midst of wretchedness which this feeble pen cannot attempt to describe. The few who survived and still live, are able to bear testimony to the martyrdom of our brave comrades, imposed by rebel brutality, which so wrecked their poor bodies that they were unable to endure the strain, and so laid them down and died.

This day has passed and not a morsel of food of any kind has been given us to eat. Why this is so is more than we can tell, but rebel inhumanity can devise more hellish means of torture than Satan himself.

PART 3

SALISBURY PRISON

After a stay of less than a month in "Hotel de Libby," Booth and his comrades were destined for a new home in the Confederacy: Salisbury Prison in Salisbury, North Carolina. Little has been done to perpetuate knowledge of this particular prison, yet those held within its confines certainly endured as much if not more privation and hardship than those in the infamous Andersonville.

Salisbury Prison was established in 1861, and was the Confederacy's first prison camp and the only prison in North Carolina. The town of Salisbury was established in 1755 and had a population of 2400 when the prison was opened. This was a rich farming and industrial area, and a typical southern community with the characteristic antebellum homes. Good railroads served the community. It had a distillery during the Civil War, and some arms manufacturing was done there along with the manufacture of shoes, an item of great need by the southern army. Rowan County, in which Salisbury was located, had a population of 14,500 in 1860, twenty-six percent of which were slaves.

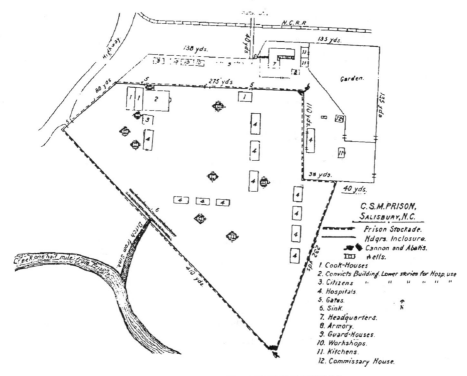

PLAT OF SALISBURY PRISON

(Taken from *The War of the Rebellion: A Compilation of the Official Records of the Union and Confederate Armies*. Series 2, Volume VIII, p. 252.)

Salisbury Prison was itself originally a cotton mill. The Confederacy was unprepared to hold prisoners (as also was the Union) and depended upon the states to supply prisons. Hence it was that large unused structures such as the tobacco warehouse of Libby Prison and the cotton mill at Salisbury were quickly pressed into service for holding prisoners. Sixteen acres comprised the grounds of Salisbury Prison. On it was a four-story building measuring 120' x 45'. This building housed all prisoners until 1864, when it was put to use as a hospital. Six brick tenement buildings of four rooms each, a frame building which was used for the superintendent's house, and two or three other miscellaneous small buildings also occupied the grounds of Salisbury Prison. The stockade was constructed around these buildings to encompass a yard enclosing five or six acres. Inside the stockade was a dead line beyond which no prisoner was to pass under the threat of being shot. The dead line consisted of a trench three feet wide and two feet deep that was six feet inside of the stockade walls. Along the outside of the stockade walls, and three feet below the top, was a platform upon which sentries walked. Near the entrance gate to the prison was a blacksmith shop. This building became the "dead house." Inside the yard, in the northeast and northwest corners, howitzers loaded with canister were positioned, their purpose being to force back riotous crowds should such an occasion arise.

The first prisoners arriving at Salisbury Prison were forty-six captives of the first big battle of the war–Bull Run at Manassas, VA, on July 21, 1861. These prisoners had been held in Raleigh, NC, and arrived at Salisbury Prison on December 9, 1861. Along with them were seventy-three Union sailors captured when their ship, the *Union*, ran aground along the North Carolina coast in November. Early prisoners were treated with little or no hostility. Many were paroled and allowed to roam the town at will–even to have visitors. Up to August of 1864 the capacity of the prison was 2500. Then with the encroachment of combat action upon areas of the deep south, coupled with suspension of prisoner exchanges by the Union, the prison population of Salisbury took a big jump to 8,000-10,000 men. The flood of prisoners which swelled Salisbury Prison's population began in October of 1864. Under Lieutenant General U. S. Grant's authority, the last official exchanges of prisoners had occurred on April 17, 1864, with the exception of some special and battlefield exchanges which still continued. Grant explained his rational for suspension of prisoner exchanges to Major General Benjamin Butler as thus:

It is hard on our men held in Southern prisons not to exchange them, but it is humanity to those left in the ranks to fight our battles. Every man we hold, when released on parole or otherwise, becomes an active soldier against us at once either directly or indirectly. If we commence a system of exchange which liberates all prisoners taken, we will have to fight on until the whole South is exterminated. If we hold those caught they amount to no more than a dead man. At this particular time to release all rebel prisoners North would insure Sherman's defeat and would compromise our safety here.

Dr. Braxton Craven, the president of Trinity College (predecessor of Duke University) served as Salisbury Prison's first Commandant. By the time Benjamin F. Booth arrived at Salisbury in November of 1864, seven Commandants had came and gone, and the prison was now under command of Major John H. Gee. In December of 1864, Brigadier General Bradley Johnson was appointed commander of Salisbury Post and Prison. Gee remained as prison Commandant and medical officer.

In addition to Union soldiers, Salisbury Prison was also used to house Confederate convicts and deserters, conscientious objectors, civilians who were disloyal to the Confederacy, ex-slaves, and some Union soldiers who had fled to the south. Perhaps the most famous prisoner to reside at Salisbury was Robert Livingstone, son of the famous Dr. David Livingstone. He was serving in Company H, 3rd New Hampshire Volunteers, and was captured in the Battle of New Market Road on October 7, 1864.

Until the fall of 1864, conditions at Salisbury Prison could probably be considered good in comparison to what was to come. At that time the overcrowding which occurred created immense problems for the prisoners. Most of the prisoners kept in the main building were pushed out when the building became a hospital. Consequently, like Andersonville and Florence Prisons, the 8,000-10,000 men held at Salisbury, were forced to live in confinement out in the elements, resulting in a density of well over 1,000 men per acre.

But overcrowding was just one problem. The logistics of supplying such a large population of inmates was something the Confederacy had not anticipated and was not prepared to handle. Hence came the problem of supplying the prisoners with food, shelter, clothing, medical supplies and wood for heat and cooking. At this time the Confederacy was having extreme difficulties providing the same supplies for its own soldiers. Food was by far the biggest want of the prisoners. It was a constant problem from the very beginning, but in 1864 the beleaguered status of the Confederacy added to the problem. Other contributing factors were the 77-day drought of 1864 which had taken its toll upon local crops, and the fact that most of the men who had been raising the crops were off fighting the war and the slaves they would normally have relied on to help them with their crops had by this time fled or abandoned them. Uncooked food was served at Salisbury Prison until November 13, 1864, when a bakery oven became operational.

Under such conditions of crowding and deprivation as existed at Salisbury Prison, morale of the prisoners naturally took its toll. At this time the morale of the town of Salisbury residents was itself low, they having tired of the privations of the war. There were, however, some bright spots. At one time in 1862 a hand-written newsletter was published and distributed among the prisoners. Baseball was played in the compound, and prisoners actively engaged in making trinkets which they exchanged among themselves for needed commodities such as food or tobacco, or when they could, with guards and town of Salisbury residents who were generally sympathetic toward the Salisbury prisoners. Salisbury residents were eager for the trinkets the prisoners made as souvenirs.

One thing frequently mentioned by prisoners of Salisbury, and any other southern prison, was the supposed willingness of guards to shoot prisoners. The description given by prisoners lends itself to the impression that guards were a bloodthirsty lot bent on shooting a Union prisoner for the purpose of obtaining a promotion or a furlough. Such was not the case, as a guard would receive neither if he did indeed shoot a prisoner for crossing the dead line. It must be remembered that prisoners would probably naturally develop a bad attitude about those responsible for holding them within their confines, as it was those men who stood between them and freedom.

With so much depravity, and conditions so contrary to human survival no matter how anyone might have tried to relieve them, it was inevitable that death should occur wholesale within the confines of Salisbury Prison. The tragically high death rate at Andersonville Prison is well known, but an equally high death rate also occurred at Salisbury. During the months from October, 1864, through February, 1865, 10,321 Union prisoners were sent to Salisbury Prison and 2,918 of them, or roughly one in four died. These figures are based upon Confederate reports; other reports claim the number of deaths was higher. Another contributing factor to such a high death rate in 1864 was that men imprisoned at Salisbury were outside in the weather during this time period, and the cold and harsh conditions of winter naturally requires more energy from the body and a larger input of calories. This is exactly what they did not receive; no doubt wearing the men down even faster.

Total number of deaths in Salisbury Prison has been the subject of some distortion, with some having made estimates (with questionable substantiation) of from 11,000 to 15,000 as having died there. For that many to have died, the death rate would have been 100%. The exact number will never be known because of incomplete records and conflicting reports, coupled with the fact that when the death rate did become wholesale, as it did in those months when the prison population was at its peak, the situation necessitated burial in mass graves (trenches) with no means of identification affixed to an individual soldier's body location. The exact number to die at Salisbury Prison, from all reliable sources, can at best be placed at somewhere around 4,000. As for the claims that Salisbury deaths were greater than those at Andersonville, this is a distortion, as over 12,000 identifiable graves exist at Andersonville, which at times had more than 30,000 confined within its 26-acre compound. However, it remains unarguable that anyplace where 4,000 men die within five acres is definitely a bad place, in fact one of the worst places of the war. Though such death is an atrocity, sight must never be lost of the fact that the Confederacy was not alone in the toll its prison system had taken on its occupants. Elmira Prison, a Union prison, had a death rate higher than either Andersonville or Salisbury.

BIRDS EYE VIEW OF SALISBURY PRISON IN 1864

Photo Courtesy Louis A. Brown

CHAPTER IX.

RAW SALT CODFISH FOR OUR RATIONS - TERRIBLE
SUFFERING ON ACCOUNT OF THIRST - "GOOD-BY LIBBY
PRISON" - ORDERS TO SHOOT - THE START SOUTHWARD
PERMISSION TO DRINK FROM JAMES RIVER - SEQUEL TO MY
DREAM OF OCTOBER 19TH - A NIGHT OF UNPARALLELED
SUFFERING - DEAD MEN IN THE CARS - ARRIVAL AT
SALISBURY PRISON - THE STOCKADE - TERRIBLE SIGHTS
RAW, UNCOOKED CORN MEAL FOR FOOD

November 3rd. About 10 o'clock this morning notice was served on the sergeants having charge of the ration squads, that rations were awaiting them. They promptly reported, and soon returned with our day's rations, consisting of about one pound of uncooked hard, dry, salted codfish–this and nothing more. To eat this terrible stuff we knew would create the most intense suffering, but having gone nearly forty-eight hours without a mouthful of any kind of food, our hunger was so great that we devoured it with the same relish, and in much the same manner, that a ravenous wolf would devour its prey.

About 1 o'clock orders came to us to leave Libby Prison. We were marched out with a heavy guard completely surrounding us. To show the spirit of the rebel authorities toward the Federal prisoners in their power, the following is a verbatim copy of the order received by the guards who were to escort us from Libby Prison:

"C. S. Military Prison,
Richmond, Va.,
Nov. 3rd, 1864.

Special Orders, No. 3.

Sentinels are instructed to shoot down any prisoners upon first attempt to escape.

Major Turner, Commanding."

And well we knew that our inhuman guards would be only too glad to find the least excuse for obeying that brutal order.

As we were marched out of the prison, we were formed into four columns, close marching order, and then ordered to stand at "parade rest." In that exposed condition we stood for over an hour. During this time we were reviewed and interviewed by the hospitable(?) citizens of Richmond, of both sexes, and, I might add, of all colors. Some of these men and women were just as venomous in their speeches and actions toward us as they were upon our first arrival among them; but others, seeing our ghastly appearance, almost naked, and so emaciated, became more softened in their speech and humane in their actions. But we paid little attention to either their venom or their pity.

At last the order, "Forward march!" was given. Marching west, we crossed the James River, and then turned south until we reached the railroad depot. Here we were crowded into cattle cars, and started southward, whither no one knows except those who have us in charge.

We now began to suffer most intensely from thirst. The salt codfish which we had eaten for our breakfast created a thirst which was terrible. We had no canteens in which to carry water, and no facilities had been provided by the rebel authorities whereby water might be conveyed to us in the cars. The prospect ahead of us made the prisoners almost desperate. As we crossed the James River I was so thirsty that I ventured to ask the guard to permit me to go down the bank and get a drink. Strange to say, he granted me the coveted favor. As I laid down at the edge of the river to drink, as I seldom, if ever, drank before, my dream on that memorable morning of October 19th, already related, came into my mind. Involuntarily, I turned my face up stream and wondered if it were possible that I was going to drink the James River dry. I almost felt that my raging thirst would make me equal to the task, and that I must do it before it could be satisfied. The only hindrance to my desire was the lack of capacity to hold it all. If my capacity had been equal to my craving desire I should have swallowed all the water and thus wreaked my vengeance on the city of Richmond by leaving it to die on the banks of a dry river, and depriving it of the protection of its great ironclads. What a fine scheme that would have been! But, alas! I could not accomplish it. I drank of the water until I was in actual misery, and still my thirst seemed to be as fierce as if I had not tasted a drop. The torture of the hours following, no pen nor tongue can describe.

About 5 o'clock P.M., our train started southward, destination still unknown, and about which we were not very greatly concerned. Every train coming north to Richmond, and there were many, had the right of way over our train, which subjected us to not only many tedious delays, but to a great deal of switching and bumping. About 4 o'clock in the morning we reached Greensborough, North Carolina. No words can express the sufferings of that night. Every car was packed as full of prisoners as it could hold. There was scarcely room to stand, none whatever to lie down. One door in each car was closed, barred and bolted, while at the other door two guards were stationed, with guns loaded and bayonets fixed, each man carrying in addition thereto two large revolvers, having full power and authority to shoot down any prisoner who made even a movement toward the door. In addition to these guards, there were two cars loaded with rebel troops, to be used against us in case we made any attempt to escape during the journey.

~ ~ ~ ~ ~

That long and weary night can never be forgotten by any of the unfortunate men. The appeals for water would beggar description. Men fairly frothed at the mouth. Some of the prisoners begged the guards to let them get off at the water tanks, many of which they stopped at, pledging their most sacred honor to return immediately after getting water, but to all such piteous appeals the answer was:

"It is against orders."

We had hoped that when we halted at Greensborough we would be supplied with water, but we were doomed to disappointment. No one was allowed to leave the train until after daylight, although a large water tank was not more than one hundred yards away from us, with plenty of good water in it. I want to here record my profound belief that this terrible night of torture was deliberately planned by the rebel authorities at Richmond. Why did they give us the dry, uncooked, salt codfish instead of the usual ration of corn bread which, up to that date we had invariably received? Why did they allow us to go for forty-eight hours without a bit of food of any kind before giving us the salt codfish? Knowing that we had no canteens, why did they not make some provision for furnishing us with water, or at least allow us to procure it from the water-tanks at which the engine pulling our train took water? Could all this have happened by mere chance? By no means! They knew what they were doing, and it was a deliberate plan to torture their prisoners, hoping that many of them would go insane from the terrific thirst, and would thus furnish an excuse for speedily dispatching them.

~ ~ ~ ~ ~

November 4th. About half past 6 o'clock we were permitted to leave the cars and go to the railroad water-tank and get water. Many of the prisoners could not control their terrible, devouring thirst, and drank to such excess that they were injured for life. One man dropped dead while in the act of drinking. Others seemed to lose their reason and acted more like maniacs than like rational human beings.

After we had finished drinking, a detail was made to go through the train and carry out the unfortunates who had died during the night. Connely and myself were among the number detailed for this sad duty, and from the car in which we rode we took out four dead men. The sad, pleading eyes of the dead, together with the cries of despair from the living, were scenes that can never be effaced from memory. I did not help bury the dead; in fact, I felt more like being buried myself than assisting to bury others. Thirteen dead men told how successful were the cruel and devilish plans of our barbarous captors during that first night ride from Libby Prison towards our unknown destination. Thirteen noble, honorable, brave soldiers foully and premeditatedly murdered! God will hold the wicked murderers responsible, and there will yet come a day of accounting.

We were corralled here until about 10 o'clock, when we were ordered to get into the cars again. We are no longer in the dark as to our destination, as it has been made known to us that we are bound for the prison at Salisbury, North Carolina. We reached that famous place about 5 o'clock P.M. A cold drizzling rain was falling. We were welcomed with shouts of *"barnburners," "thieves," "robbers." "Now, we will fix you." "It will be a long time before you burn any more barns." "We will send you where there won't be any barns to burn!"* As we marched into the dismal place we became fully

94

convinced that suffering beyond the power of man to conceive was in store for us. We knew that so far as our enemies could carry out their threats they would do it. It has been said that a cat cannot travel so far away from home but the tail will follow him. So it seemed to us that "barn-burning" was our supreme crime. We thought it must be stamped on our faces, because wherever we went these words greeted our ears, "barn burners."

~ ~ ~ ~ ~

Salisbury prison was a brick structure about 40 feet wide and 100 feet long, four stories high. It was erected for a cotton factory. In addition to the main structure, there were four or five tenement houses adjoining. This prison was first used for deserters from the rebel army, violators of military orders, cut-throats and criminals of all kinds. During the early part of 1864 it was converted into a military prison by building a stockade around it and enlarging its area to about six acres. This stockade was formed by setting pine logs in the ground to a depth of about three feet and extending about twelve feet above the ground. They were boarded up and down, so as to make a solid wall. On the outside of this enclosure, and about three feet from the top, a platform, or walk, was erected on which sentinels were placed about ten paces apart, and who walked their beats by day and night. The guards had orders to be on the alert and shoot down every Yank who dared to cross the "dead-line," or in any way give the least provocation. This stockade enclosed the large brick building and two of the small tenement houses heretofore mentioned. At the northwest and northeast corners of this stockade howitzers were placed loaded and trained on the interior, so that in the event of an attempted outbreak every portion of the prison was covered, and the guns would scatter death and destruction among the prisoners. Along the east, west and north sides of the stockade, about six feet in the inside a ditch was dug about three feet wide and two feet deep, forming what was called "The Dead Line." Any prisoner crossing this line, whether accidentally or purposely, or even found leaning against it, was shot down without warning. As early as September, 1863, a few prisoners were kept in this prison. In the early part of 1864 another building was erected, about twenty feet wide and seventy or eighty feet long. It was a frame structure and was used for hospital service. This building was two stories high, poorly ventilated in summer and very uncomfort-

able in winter. The brick prison proper, the frame hospital building, and a small building used as an office in the early days of the prison, supplemented by about six Bell tents, and six or seven log huts, furnished all the shelter we would have. How scanty these accommodations are can easily be imagined when I state that, in addition to the large number of Union prisoners, there are also about 300 rebel convicts here, a large proportion of them being from the very lowest classes of humanity that ever disgraced the earth. These convicts made the night hideous by gathering together in squads, roaming over the prison grounds, and wherever they find a Union prisoner alone, overpowered him and robbed him of his clothing, blanket, or whatever else he might chance to have, or that their thievish propensities might covet. Their method of robbery was to pounce on their victim unawares, crush him to the earth, seize him by the throat so that he could not cry and make alarm, and then rob him at their own pleasure, after which they would hurry away to their own wretched quarters, which received the appropriate name, "The Devil's Den."

**THE MAIN BUILDING AT SALISBURY PRISON
WHICH EVENTUALLY BECAME THE HOSPITAL**

CHAPTER X.

FIRST IMPRESSIONS OF SALISBURY PRISON - HUNGRY, BUT
NO RATIONS - SLEEPING UNDER DIFFICULTIES - AN
ADVENTURE - DESTITUTE OF CLOTHING - OUR RATIONS
ARRIVE - WHAT CONNELY AND I SAW - RECRUITING FOR THE
REBEL ARMY - THE DEAD WAGON - COMRADES DISCOVERED
BETTER SHELTER - STOCK COMPANY FORMED - WE PREPARE
BETTER QUARTERS - HOW WE DUG OUR CAVE - DRAWING
RATIONS UNDER DIFFICULTIES - NEW STOCKHOLDERS
TAKEN IN - STARVING IN THE MIDST OF PLENTY

On the 4th day of November, 1864, in the midst of a cold, drizzling
rain, we were marched inside Salisbury Stockade to become a part
of its wretched inhabitants. Our condition was pitiable in the extreme.
Not a mouthful of any kind of food have we had to eat since we ate the
terrible ration of salt codfish in Libby Prison two days before. We were
wet to the skin, and so cold that I trembled like an aspen leaf. The only
way I could keep my teeth from chattering was by holding them shut
tightly together. In this condition I took a hasty survey of our new quarters, but the more I saw of it the more its unspeakable horrors were impressed on my mind. I saw no relief for the present, and could only anticipate increasing misery, want and suffering for the future. Darkness
coming on, the terrible conclusion is forced upon us that we are to lie
down again without any food being furnished us to satisfy our awful
hunger. Connely and myself had been successful in keeping our roll,
consisting of a blanket, and two pieces of shelter tents. These we divided
between ourselves, he taking the blanket and I the pieces of tent; these
we placed over our shoulders and sat down in the mud, leaning our
backs against a tree. In this position I soon fell asleep, being so wearied
and exhausted that I could not keep awake. I was soon roughly awakened from sleep by some one violently pulling at the pieces of tent with
which I covered my shoulders. I immediately took in the situation and

called to Connely for assistance. He awoke and came to my aid, and together we succeeded in beating off the thief, who, seeing that we had the better of him, fled in dismay.

November 5th. Our reinforcements filled the quota of Salisbury Prison to 10,321 men, besides the 300 cut-throats and convicts already mentioned. Thousands are exposed to all kinds of weather, day and night, winter and summer. A large majority of prisoners have neither blanket, overcoat, shoes or hat. Many were reduced to only a shirt and pair of drawers. In this forlorn condition the poor fellows burrowed in the ground, and as long as there was room crept under the buildings, while others went through the cold, bleak nights in the open air, lying on the muddy or frozen ground absolutely shelterless. I have seen unfortunate men lie down in the mud, fall asleep, and on awakening would find their clothes frozen to the ground, holding them fast as if pinioned to the earth. To see these brave men suffering such untold agonies, was a sight which, when once beheld, could never be forgotten.

The grinding mills throughout the south were not equipped with bolting cloth to separate the cob from the cornmeal used to make cornbread. Southern women used sifters to accomplish this task. Such equipment was not available to the commissary or cookhouse staff of Confederate prisons. Some prisoners were able to manufacture their own sifters, but this was rare. Ground cob that was in the cornmeal turned hard as the meal dried and took its toll on the delicate walls of men's intestines, irritating the diarrhea and dysentery which weakened so many of the prisoners.

About noon we were counted off in squads of about one hundred men to a squad. Each squad was commanded by a sergeant, whose duty it was to report the number of men under his command, draw and divide their rations. When our squad was organized and reported, rations were issued to us, consisting of one pint of corn meal, the cob being ground with the grain. Having no facilities for cooking it in any way, our only recourse was to eat it raw.

November 6th. This morning the sun is shining bright and beautiful. Connely and I took a survey of the prison, if such a desolate place could be deemed worthy of even such a name. It is indeed the most forlorn place the eye of man ever beheld. Prisoners were standing on the sunny side of the trees gathering all the heat possible with which to warm their poor, emaciated bodies. As we came to the frame building used for a hospital, we looked on a scene that beggars description. Here lie the dead bodies of our prisoners, eyes shrunken, faces emaciated, their ghastly countenances telling the awful tale of the terrible struggle they had fought with death, but, alas! in vain. Here they lay unnoticed and uncared for. Suffering reigns everywhere. The only smiling faces we saw were those of the rebel guards. Every eye was dull with despondency, and every lip denoted pain. From every hole in the ground and every place where men could crawl away there came forth what were once strong, able-bodied, happy men, but now changed into gaunt and ghastly forms, slowly perishing from hunger, exposure and ill-treatment. About noon our attention was drawn to a crowd of men congregated at the big gate. Our curiosity was excited and we went to see what it meant. We found a fair specimen of a rebel perched on a box, pleading for recruits to enlist in the rebel army to go to the extreme south and garrison forts. This was in order to relieve the able-bodied soldiers there who were greatly needed at the front. He was especially desirous to get wagon-makers and blacksmiths, and as an inducement to these mechanics to prove disloyal to their country, by enlisting in the rebel army, he offered an extra inducement of one hundred dollars in southern scrip, a suit of clothes, full rations and twenty dollars a month while they served. A few accepted the offer. They saw no hope of gaining their liberty alive; they had barely clothes enough to cover their nakedness; they thought, perhaps, they could save their lives and find a better opportunity to escape to the Union lines. But the majority of the prisoners looked upon these excuses with contempt, entirely unworthy of men who had worn the Union blue, and followed the old Flag. Personally, I felt then that I would starve to death a dozen times before I would be guilty of such a cowardly and traitorous act—and there were thousands of others of the same mind. After the recruiting officer was done exhorting for recruits, he informed us that they were scant of rations and would not be able to furnish us anything to eat that day; that we must be as patient as possible as they were expecting rations from the Shenandoah Valley, and they would probably be at hand the next morning. It seems as though we will never hear the last of the Shenandoah Valley. Most of the prisoners in this pen were captured in the Shenandoah Valley during the campaign of 1864, and hence were especially obnoxious to the rebels, and were treated accordingly.

~ ~ ~ ~ ~

About 2 o'clock the "dead-wagon" made its daily tour of the grounds, halt-ing at the "Dead House" to load in the bodies lying there, and then passing out at the south gate to the grave yard, or trenches, which are about 250 yards southwest of the prison. The "dead house" was a small brick building, situated near the center of the stockade. In the days when "Cotton was King," and raised in abundance, this building was used for an office in connection with the cotton factory. Here they kept their books and supped their Kentucky Bourbon. It is again used as an office. Here books are again kept. But the long line of figures do not represent dollars and cents–the business of a prosperous concern, sending its valuable commerce into many regions–they do indicate the numbers of brave and true soldiers who have been literally murdered by starvation and brutality, the work of an inhuman so-called, Government, whose barbarity is sending sorrow and dismay into thousands of northern homes. The dead are gathered up during the forenoon, brought to the "dead house," piled up against the end like sacks of grain, and counted by a sergeant who registers the number in a book kept for that purpose. An accurate account is thus kept of each day's mortality. When this is done, the dead wagon hauls them out in the same manner they are piled up in the dead-house.

~ ~ ~ ~ ~

November 6th (continued). The night is drawing near and we must be looking for a place to sleep, as it is certain we will get nothing to eat this day. We have found some of our regiment who were captured at Winchester, September 19th, one month earlier than we were. They have a piece of tarpaulin stretched over a pole, and we–Connely and myself, are invited to lodge with them over night. Our quarters are very much crowded, but it beats hanging up on the rainy side of a tree. We did not sleep much the first part of the night as we were too busy talking over the battles we had fought in together, but towards the latter part of the night, one by one, wearied and exhausted, hungry and heartsick, we fell asleep.

November 7th. This morning we have made a fortunate discovery– one which we hope will add a little to our comfort. Connely and I found two members of Company H of our regiment who are the fortunate pos-sessors of an old tent. These, when spliced with the two pieces we have, will make two whole tents. Then we started out to look up a location on which to pitch them, and succeeded in finding room just south of, and about five paces from the deadhouse. A large oak tree grew near by. The location seemed to be quite favorable, especially, as one of our number remarked, *"our friends would not have very far to carry us in order to reach the dead-house."* Here we began to dig a basement over which to erect our tents. With the aid of an old case-knife, and the half of a canteen, we commenced until about noon when our squad, known as "Squad No. 10" was called to get our rations, which consisted of the same as day before yesterday, viz.: one pint of corn meal, including the cob. Unfortunately, the quality was as poor as the quantity, the meal having been heaped together in such quantities that it had heated and become very musty. However, we waived all objections against the quality of the stuff, but we could not reconcile ourselves to the limited quantity. This, together with the absence of fuel and all facilities for cooking it, made it very hard to bear. It was eaten raw. This course of diet was of the same order as that of eating dried apples for breakfast, drinking a pint of water for dinner, and allowing the mass to swell for supper. This traditional plan we changed somewhat. We ate the corn meal for dinner, drank the water for supper, and let it swell for the next day's rations. Some of the poor fellows had neither cup nor can in which to get their ration of meal. Some resorted to their hat, while those who were not fortunate enough to possess a hat substituted a corner of their blouse, and if neither hat nor blouse were available–they would draw their hands together and receive their meal in that way. In any way possible, the precious meal, poor as it was, would be carried to some secluded spot, where it would be devoured as only famishing men could devour it.

After we had eaten our dry meal, all hands went to work digging with a will. We reinforced the case knife with a sharp stick, and the canteen was kept going by changing operators, so that by sundown we had a hole about one foot deep, five and one-half feet wide, and eight feet long. *Will some of my readers try to do the same amount of work in the same length of time, using only the same kind of implements?* But suffering men will nerve themselves to do almost superhuman deeds. One of our party climbed the tree and with the assistance of the case knife and mallet succeeded in cutting off limbs for a ridge-pole, end poles and stakes, which enabled us to put up our tent. And in this domicile, rude as it was, we were as happy and contented as Diogenes in his famous tub. Our family numbered six, all told. But we had only two blankets, and one we had, early in our capture, cut up so badly in order to deceive our rebel guards, by wrapping it around our good blanket and pieces of tent. Something had to be done in order to increase the supply of blankets because by no manner of stretching or "spooning" could one good blanket and one mutilated blanket be made to cover the bodies, poor and emaciated as they were, of six men. A meeting of the "stockholders" was called, the situation discussed, propositions made, and, by a unanimous vote we agreed to take in two more "stockholders" but upon the express condition that they would each furnish a blanket. This swelled our "family" to eight, and all to lie down in a space five and a half feet by eight. Six of the number were members of the 22nd Iowa Infantry; the other two belonged to a Maine regiment.

JOHN H. GEE

Major John H. Gee was perhaps the best known of all Salisbury Prison Commandants. Gee was a Florida physician, and was appointed to Command of Salisbury Prison and Post on August 24, 1864. His appointment was because of his "prudence and discretion," but it was short served, with his remaining in this position until December 17, 1864 when Brig. Gen. Bradley Johnson took command. During Gee's term the population of Salisbury Prison expanded from the 2,500 residents the facility was designed for to over 9,000 (perhaps over 10,000) prisoners. Problems of supply and provision for the prison population were incredible and Gee, aware of his inadequacy to deal with these problems, offered his resignation several times before it was finally accepted. He was also stymied by rank problems, as many of the Confederate officers at the prison outranked him, thereby making it difficult to issue orders and maintain discipline in the ranks. Though he had resigned his position, he remained at Salisbury Prison until the end of the war as Commandant and Physician. Following the Civil War he was arrested and tried for crimes against the Union prisoners but was found not guilty, basically because he had been dealing with circumstances beyond his control.

~ ~ ~ ~ ~

Some of the prisoners sold every article of clothing they could possibly spare—some retaining only their shirts—in order to obtain money enough with which to buy bread. It took from $5.00 to $10.00 in Confederate money to buy a single loaf of bread. It may seem impossible that at this very time, when we were receiving only one pint of dry, corn cob meal once a day for our rations; when men were selling the clothes off *their backs to buy bread to keep from starving, the commissary store-house in Salisbury was packed from floor to roof with corn and pork, but such is the fact. Are we not forced to the conclusion that the systematic starvation of the Federal prisoners was a willful and deliberate plan to kill them off! This purpose of the Confederate authorities was most faithfully carried out by John H. Gee, Post Commander. When a subordinate officer, knowing that plenty of food was packed away in the commissary store-house, asked Gee for permission to issue full rations to the prisoners, this fiend answered:*

"No sir; it is against the orders issued to me. Give them quarter rations."

CHAPTER XI.

FIRST NIGHT IN OUR NEW QUARTERS - THE RECRUITING
OFFICER AGAIN - SALISBURY BUILDINGS AND THEIR USES
DIRT, VERMIN AND DEATH REIGN SUPREME - GREAT
SUFFERING FOR WANT OF CLOTHING AND SHELTER
HEARTLESS PHYSICIANS - TRYING TO FORCE THE PRISONERS
TO ENLIST - HOW WE GET OUR FUEL AND WATER
A MURDEROUS ORDER - GOOD FORTUNE - A PETITION AND
ITS WICKED REFUSAL - "BARN-BURNERS" AGAIN - A
CONVICT WHIPPED - A TERRIBLE SCENE - AN AFFECTING
PARTING BETWEEN TWO COMRADES - A VALUABLE
PURCHASE

November 8th. The night was passed in comparative comfort in our new quarters. Although somewhat crowded, yet by sleeping in the same relation to one another as mother used to put away her silver spoons, and, when the squad wanted to turn over or change position, by observing the command "Spoon to the right!" or "Spoon to the left!" as the case might be, we slept very comfortably. Fortunately, we were so tired and slept so soundly, that we had to "spoon over" only once during the night.

I enjoyed a rare luxury to-day in the shape of a chew of tobacco–the first I have had for several days. Words cannot describe the joy I received in rolling that sweet morsel under my tongue. The nectar and ambrosia of the Grecian gods were as "green persimmons" to the sweetness and richness of the "chew"!

To-day the recruiting officer has again made his appearance and is working hard to get men to enlist in the rebel army. Every inducement is held out to Union prisoners to take the oath of allegiance to the Southern Confederacy. They take advantage of the awful despondency which prevails among the prisoners, telling us that they have not the wherewithal to feed us, and that our government at Washington will not consent to an exchange of prisoners. A few of the poor boys are won over by these ly-ing statements–but, only a few and these have to run the gauntlet of fly-ing clubs and other missiles. The great majority prefer death to disloy-alty.

The large brick building and one of the frame buildings are full to overflowing with sick men. To look in upon them is to witness a sight that is heart-rending beyond expression. The lower story of the brick building has only a dirt floor. On this the sick are placed in rows running the full length of the room. At one time a very little straw partially pro-tected the poor, sick bodies from contact with the dampness and filthi-ness of the dirt floor, but the straw has become so broken and scattered by long use and no replenishment that it no longer affords any protec-tion. The dust is so very thick and is so full of vermin that they are seen crawling around like ants on a ant-hill. The suffering of the helpless sick is fearful to contemplate, and the sight enough to make one's blood run cold. It is not an uncommon thing to see sick men who are so weak that they cannot brush the vermin away, completely covered with them, face, whiskers, hair, in fact the whole body, is devoured and tormented by the pests. No effort whatever is made by the prison authorities to cleanse the place or give any protection to the sick and tormented men. Their living hell is called a "Hospital," and the villains who are in charge of it are called "men." What a travesty on truth and justice!

The second story of this building is also used for the sick. It differs from the lower story only by having a floor, but so far as dirt and vermin are concerned, it shows no improvement whatever. On this floor also the sick are laid in rows and so closely packed together that there is no room to step between the bodies. The ventilation in this room being very poor, words cannot describe the terrible odor which filled its atmosphere, and which the poor fellows were compelled to breathe day and night. No man ever left the pen, however feeble he might be, who had a friend to attend his wants, or render him aid of any kind. The only advantage gained by going into one of these buildings is shelter from the storms, and even this is counterbalanced by being brought into immediate con-tact with such masses of filth and contaminating disease that the open stockade was a much more decent and comfortable place, even for sick men than their boasted "Hospital."

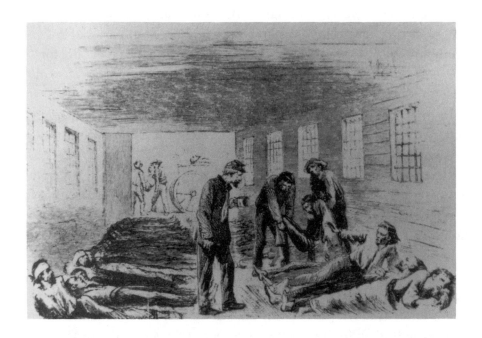

INTERIOR OF BRICK HOSPITAL, SALISBURY PRISON

Nearly all the prisoners are without covering or shelter of any kind. During the long, chilly nights, they suffer a great deal from cold, which, during the day, is followed by the other extreme of intense heat from the sun. The effect of these changes upon men who are comparatively well, is to impose intense suffering. What must it be to the poor fellows who are helpless from disease? The rebel surgeons seem to give little or no attention to the sick. They go the rounds in a cold, perfunctory manner. Very little medicine is given. Only those who were so far gone that there was no hope for a cure received the least attention from the hospital surgeons. Nearly as many die inside the stockade, without having received any medical attention whatever, as in the hospital. At the other hospital, that is, the frame building, the same conditions exist, and even worse. No brushes, no brooms, are furnished to clean the floor and walls. The nurses could not even procure water enough to wash the faces and hands of the sick and dying men. There they lay, right in their filth, and no means of removing either it or them. No pen can properly describe the conditions: God only can see and understand.

From what my own eyes have witnessed, I am compelled to believe that, with very few exceptions, the doctors of the South are a set of inhuman scoundrels, unworthy to bear the dignified title of "doctor." They are a burning disgrace to that honorable profession. Because of their utter neglect of duty, and their inhuman treatment of the sick, so loathsome has this place become that it is next to impossible for even a well man to endure it. It is not strange that the mortality of this prison is greater than that of Andersonville.

The policy of the prison authorities now seems to be to force us to join the rebel army by withholding our rations, as not a mouthful of food of any kind have they given us since yesterday. But the great majority of the Union prisoners are determined to endure torture and suffering, even unto death, if need be, rather than prove disloyal to the old flag.

Our wood for cooking and heating purposes is received in the following manner: A squad of men is detailed each morning to go into the woods and cut down green pitch-pine trees. This wood is then loaded on flat cars and taken to the northwest corner of the stockade, unloaded and carried within the stockade about 150 yards distant. Each one hundred men are allowed what three men can carry away on their shoulders. The men who go out to cut the wood are guarded like prison convicts. This break on the fearful routine of prison life is a great blessing to the men who are detailed to go out, as well as to their friends who remain inside, because on their return to the prison from work, they are permitted to take blackberry roots in with them, which we find to be an excellent remedy for diarrhea, the disease being very prevalent among the prisoners. The men who are detailed to cut wood receive double rations. This is the greatest inducement of all.

Our water supply is brought to us in barrels, the allowance being the amount that two men can carry in a barrel for every 100 men. A hole is cut through the staves of the barrel, into which a pole is put. This is carried by two men to a stream about 200 yards southeast of the stockade. About three pails of water is an average load for two men in our condition. These water carriers go out in squads of ten and twenty, under strong guard. Along the road to the stream are numbers of citizens who are eager to trade a sweet potato or corn dodger for a Yankee relic. Wells were dug in the stockade and water found at a depth of eighteen feet, but the wells became so contaminated with filth that, although suffering for water, as we often do, it is impossible for us to drink it. A few deeper wells were dug on higher ground, but even these became so contaminated and foul that they were rendered useless.

~ ~ ~ ~ ~

When the reader will bear in mind that there was no arrangement whatever made for sewerage, and the prison contained a population of from 1500 to 2000 men on each acre of ground, some idea may be had of the vast accumulation of filth of all kinds which covered the ground and saturated it during the wet season. These wells became the only and most natural catch-basins, and their condition after a heavy rain may be better imagined than described.

A trench, or sink, was dug along the east, and some ten feet from the inside of the stockade fence. It was about three feet deep and four feet wide, and it was no uncommon sight to see some poor fellow fall in there knee deep in filth. Some idea of the sanitary conditions of the grounds may be had after reading the following order issued to the guards, copies of which were posted up at conspicuous places along the line:

"C. S. Military Prison,
Salisbury, N.C.,
Nov. 1, 1864.

Sentinels are requested to shoot down all prisoners in the future who are seen moving about camp after taps.
Major J. H. Gee, Commanding."

~ ~ ~ ~ ~

November 8th (continued). Rations were issued to-day consisting of one pint of corn meal, musty as usual. The wood squad also came in with wood, and as the squad is divided up into so many messes, it makes it necessary to divide the wood, which has to be worked up with a railroad spike and a case knife, in this manner: The spike is driven under a sliver of wood, then one end of the sliver is cut off with the knife and a mallet, and holding on to the other end, it is pulled off. In this laborious manner green pitch-pine logs, eight and ten inches in diameter, are worked up and divided.

Guttapercha is a rubberlike substance made from the sap of trees that grow in Malaysia from which hair combs of the Civil War era were made. Booth was able to secure these combs from time to time and make his rings by cutting the combs up and heating the plastic so as to be able to form it around a stick. The sets he used in the rings were most likely buttons, as that is essentially all that the prisoners at Salisbury would have had for such use.

Good fortune befell me to-day. I was on the water-carrying detail, and met a kind citizen who gave me a plug of tobacco for a guttapercha ring, adorned with two sets. May blessings, many, fall upon his head.

A committee was appointed to-day to confer with the Commander of the prison, with instructions to do all in their power to move him to allow us to go into the woods and cut pine logs with which to build barracks and huts for shelter from the storms and the severity of the weather. The grounds around the stockade are covered with a heavy growth of pine timber, and with a little work we could soon build huts that would shelter all the poor fellows from the cold and bitter wintry winds. The committee reported to the west gate and sent word by a sentinel to the Commander that a committee wished to confer with his honor(?) on important business. The sentinel returned and ordered the committee to follow him. They were at once conducted in to the presence of his august majesty, to whom they made known their business, pledging their honor that no one would attempt to violate his parole if such permission was granted them. The doughty Major held his head, looked very wise, and at last broke the silence by saying:

"No, your request cannot be granted for two reasons. First, it will destroy our forests. Second, you fellows can live without houses as well as the inhabitants of the Shenandoah Valley."

This ended the interview, and the committee returned and reported the Commander's answer, which caused great grief among the prisoners. Here it is again. It seems that all our hardships and sufferings are due to the unfortunate fact that we were captured in the Shenandoah Valley. I wonder if any of us should be so fortunate as to be permitted to knock at the "Golden Gate," if Peter will put out his hand and say:

"Depart, ye damn barn burners! Ye who were captured in the Shenandoah Valley Begone!"

But if St. Peter should be tempted to say that to us, what will he not say to the miserable brute who rejected our reasonable request for permission to erect some kind of shelter to protect us from the snow and frost of winter? If the righteous (Union prisoners) can scarcely be saved, where shall the ungodly (Major Gee) and the sinners (the rest of the rebel gang) appear? We give it up, but the anticipation is comforting.

November 10th. Last night about dark an event took place which nearly caused bloodshed. One of the rebel convicts was arrested and taken to a place near the west gate, where he was lashed to a tree, his body stripped naked, and in this condition he was unmercifully whipped by two stout Confederate soldiers, the entire camp looking at the brutal work going on. The hot blood of the prisoners was up, and all resolved to die rather than stand by and see a prisoner whipped in such a brutal manner by miserable slave drivers. The guards ordered the crowd to disperse. Excitement ran high, when an officer stepped to the front and announced to the crowd that the man who was being whipped was a deserter from the Confederate army, and he was being punished for insulting an officer. Being satisfied that the officer told the truth, the crowd dispersed. I did not want to look at the terrible sight, so I went to my hut, but I could plainly hear his piteous appeals for mercy. I knew he was an enemy to my country, its righteous cause and beloved Flag, but for all that, I remembered he was a human being, and if they would rend it asunder. The terrible punishment lasted until the cries of the poor wretch were scarcely audible, when the surgeon who was watching his pulse told them to stop.

The recruiting officer is at his place again as usual. His earnest appeals and great inducements won Jerry Daniels, of Company "H," over to his cause. Jerry came to his hole in this ground, where he had a sick comrade by the name of Miller. Jerry said to him:

"Jacob, I can't do you any good if I stay, and I will desert and make for our lines at the first opportunity. If I live this way much longer, I shall die. I am already on the verge of insanity, and before I get too

> Jeremiah Daniels, from Jefferson, IA, was twenty-four when he enlisted with the 22nd Iowa on August 11, 1862. He was wounded severely at the Battle of Port Gibson on May 1, 1863, and wounded again in the famous charge of the 22nd Iowa at Vicksburg on the 22nd of May, 1863. On September 19, 1864, along with 31 other members of the 22nd Iowa, he was taken prisoner in the Third Battle of Winchester. The destination for some of the captives, but not all, was Salisbury Prison.

weak to travel I will try to escape. To stay here is certain death. I will lose nothing by leaving, and here, now, comrade, I leave you my piece of blanket. That is
all of the world's goods I have. It will do you more good than I can if I stay, and
with my blessing, I bid you farewell, hoping to meet you again on earth; if not, I
hope to meet you on the sunny banks of Eternal Deliverance, where there will be
no rebel prisons and bloodhounds."

They bade each other farewell, and it was the most touching and affectionate parting between two friends I ever witnessed. I marched up to
the gate with poor Jerry, and the tears came into my eyes when I saw
him march out under that infamous rebel rag. In that sad moment I renewed my allegiance to the dear Old Flag, for whose honor and defense
I, with thousands of others were suffering untold agonies. I vowed never
to aid its enemies to the value of anything, or to the extent of a moment
of time. When Jerry was well outside the stockade he turned and bade us
all farewell.

The work on the bakery is progressing, but not speedily enough for
us. The chief topic of conversation now is "Bread!" We have been in here
six days and nothing has been given us to eat but three pints of coarse
meal, cob and all ground together, and so musty that a decent hog would
not eat it. This having been the day for soliciting recruits for the rebel
army from among the prisoners, it is certain we are doomed to go without even our musty meal.

I made a valuable purchase to-day in the shape of a pair of small pin-
cers, or pliers. They will be of great service to me in making finger rings,
and these, in turn, will enable me to add to my scanty store of tobacco,
food, etc. How fortunate I am after all!

CHAPTER XII.

STARVING, BUT NO RATIONS - MANUFACTURING RUBBER
RINGS - WHO OUR GUARDS ARE - A RIVAL BUSINESS
CONVICTS AGAIN RAID THE CAMP - SKIRMISHING FOR
GAME(?) UNDER DIFFICULTIES - CONNELY MEETS WITH AN
ACCIDENT - TRADING - CRUELTY OF THE PRISON
AUTHORITIES - PLENTY, BUT STARVING - ANOTHER LOT OF
"FRESH FISH" ARRIVE - HIGH LIVING - "BREAD! BREAD!!
BREAD!!!" - MISERABLE PRISONERS - THE PRISON
AUTHORITIES DISCOVER A TUNNEL - A CHANGE IN OUR
RATIONS - A REBEL TOUR OF INSPECTION

November 11th. This morning finds us nearly famished, no rations being given to us since the day before yesterday! In this way the minions representing Jeff Davis and his so-called Government wreak vengeance on Union prisoners who will not consent to become traitors to their Flag by enlisting in the rebel army.

I commenced the manufacture of a rubber ring this morning. The process of manufacture is as follows: I commence by taking the center portion of a fine-tooth comb, cutting it in three strips about one-fourth of an inch wide. These strips are warmed sufficiently to make them pliable like leather, and are then wound around a stock until the ends meet. Each strip is kept on the stick until it is perfectly cold, so that it will retain its circular form. Then a set is put on the ends, a place having been cut out sufficiently large and deep to hold it. The set is made secure by rivets being put through it and clinched on the inside of the ring. Then the rubber is filed round and smooth, and the set polished and the article is ready for the first vain rebel who wants to possess it. These rings sell for from $5.00 to $10.00 in rebel scrip. A good and ready market is found for them in going for water, many citizens being eager to buy or trade them as relics of the Yankee prisoners. We very much prefer trading them for eatables as we can get more for them in that way.

Our rations of meal were distributed to us to-day, consisting of the same quantity and quality. We received the welcome news that hereafter our rations will consist of bread, baked, I suppose, in the new oven, and will be issued to us daily. If these promises are faithfully kept we shall be very thankful, but we cannot help doubting the sincerity of their promises and intentions.

We are guarded by two classes of rebel soldiers. One class is called the "senior reserves." To look at them, one would conclude the Confederate authorities had been robbing the graves of their dead, and had, by some magical process, infused life into the skeletons, put clothes on them, armed and equipped them, and then assigned them to the heavenly(?) task of guarding Yankee prisoners, and shooting them as opportunity offered. They are old men, and would show us some compassion if they dared to do it. To do so would be to place their own lives in jeopardy.

The other class is called the "junior reserves," and one could easily conclude that the cradles of Southern homes had been robbed to get them. This class is composed of boys ranging from 15 to 18 years of age. Of course they have never seen actual field service, and the great ambition of each youngster is to "shoot a Yankee." They watch the dead-line very closely, and woe be to the poor fellow who either willfully or accidentally steps on, or falls over, the prohibited line. A flash, a fall, a groan, and the youthful murderer receives his reward by being called a "Warrior"! By such inducements held out to these boys, our enemies give many a Union prisoner his eternal and speedy parole. Will not the blood of these cruelly murdered men curse the very soil on which their blood has fallen?

I have two rivals in the relic-making business—one, Lewis K. Auringer, of the 81st Pennsylvania Infantry, who works in bone, making bone Bibles, finger-rings, cuff-buttons, etc. The other, W. B. Hill, of Co. B, of my regiment, who is an expert in making wooden spoons. His wares are in good demand, but those who need his goods the most are the prisoners, and they have not the money with which to buy.

November 12th. The sick are increasing with alarming rapidity, and the dead likewise. The record of yesterday's mortality was thirty-two corpses taken to the dead-house. No doubt the terrible exposure and lack of food and proper medicine is the chief cause of the increased death rate. And it promises to grow worse instead of better.

Major Gee remarked to-day that he would have us all in hell or the Confederate army in thirty days.

The convict prisoners were out raiding the camp last night. They robbed two men of their clothing while the poor fellows were walking about to keep warm. The nights are getting very cold and those who had no huts to shelter them suffer beyond description. One problem will soon be solved, viz: how long can a man live on one pint of corn meal issued to him every other day, and compelled to tramp about all night to keep up body heat, or else lie down on the bare ground huddled together like so many swine? The solution is not far off.

During the middle of the day, while it is warm, the poor boys may be seen sitting and supporting their poor, emaciated bodies against a tree or building, shirts and pants off, trying to rid themselves of the awful vermin which are sucking the very lifeblood out of them. But even this, while it is an imperative necessity, is a very dangerous proceeding–in fact, no man dare attempt to take off a garment for any purpose unless he is surrounded by friends who will protect him; and even then, he must sit on one end of the garment while he is skirmishing for game at the other end. If this precaution is not observed, some one stronger than he will soon have the garment. Such occurrences are so frequent that we have to look upon them as scarcely deserving of condemnation.

The ubiquitous, and exceedingly annoying, recruiting officer is out and at work again. To us who refuse to accept his invitations and promised rewards, it means no rations, and a farther fast of twenty-four hours. But let it come. We are determined to die rather than prove disloyal.

Comrade Connely met with a very severe and painful accident to-day. He crushed his thumb while carrying wood. He applied for aid to the prison surgeon and got some salve to put on it. I hope it will not prove serious. I had the good fortune to go out with the water squad to-day and succeeded in trading a finger ring for three sweet potatoes, which I ate raw. I also cut off two brass buttons from my blouse for which I got the half of a sweet potato pie. From its appearance and consistency it must have been baked in the sun, on a board. It was nearly as tough as rubber; but it tasted delicious. While I was out to-day I had a conversation with one of the guards, and I am perfectly satisfied from the information I received from him, that there has been no time since this prison was opened, that the authorities could not have furnished the prisoners an abundance of corn meal and bacon were they so disposed. And from my own observation, I know they could have furnished us with abundance of lumber with which to build comfortable huts for the thousands of shelterless prisoners.

~ ~ ~ ~ ~

With such glaring facts before us, is it not reasonable to believe that their inhuman treatment was willful and premeditated cruelty? It was a part of their plans to wreak vengeance for their disappointed hopes.

~ ~ ~ ~ ~

November 13th. The dawning of this morning brought no ray of cheer or comfort to the thousands of poor fellows who are compelled to be shelterless and exposed to the cold, drizzling rain which fell during the night, and still continues this morning. This kind of weather greatly increases the mortality of the prison, where men have no shelter to pro-tect them from the weather. When they get sick they receive no medical treatment. The barbarity of our enemies is inexcusable and beyond ex-pression.

Another lot of what they lovingly call "fresh fish" (these are "black bass") arrived to-day. About 300 colored soldiers, or to use the favorite southern term, "niggers," and about 1200 or 1300 white soldiers were brought in to become the guests, or victims, of Major Gee and his butch-ers. Judging from their appearance, they must have come over the same route we traveled. They are only half-clad, barefooted, bareheaded, and but very few of them have even a blouse lift. They are a sorry, forsaken looking lot. But how will they look after they have been in here a few months? The young guards are making all the fun they can out of them at our expense, asking such questions as, *"do you'uns want an introduction to your brothers?"*

The number within this stockade at the present time is about 12,000. Our rations have come again consisting of corn meal after the regulation pattern, or Salisbury Prison standard. Nine days ago we came to this rebel hostelry and during that time only five pints of course corn meal have been given to us. This comprises the entire amount of food supplied to us by the representatives of Jeff Davis' government who are supreme in authority here. This system of slow, but sure, starvation is having its effect in rapidly diminishing out numbers. The prisoners are dying at the rate of twenty-five and thirty a day. It takes a man of exceedingly strong constitution, buoyant hope and cheerful, enthusiastic temperament to live under such conditions. The man who allows himself to become depressed and gloomy soon dies. Two poor fellows have gone totally insane, but are still left within the enclosure; no attempt whatever is made to protect, restrain or give them relief. They run around the ground crying:

"Bread! . . . Bread!! . . . Bread!!!"

This one word they scream at the top of their voice. Their eyes are glassy, their walk unsteady. They are indeed objects of pity, but of that virtue there is none to be found among the rebel officers and guards of Salisbury Prison. A more desperate, heartless set of fiends never walked the earth.

The most pitiful objects among the prisoners are those men who have no friends or particular associates in the prison. Where a few old acquaintances have been able to keep together, they could keep up at least a semblance of cheerfulness. The old saying, "Misery loves company," may or may not be true, but it is true that men who have been associated together under better and more favorable conditions, if misfortune chances to overtake them, are able to encourage each other, enliven the surroundings, and thus make their fate, however distressing it may be, more bearable. Not so with those who are so unfortunate as to be compelled to bear their grief and endure their sufferings alone. There is still another class of prisoners who are compelled to endure agonies unspeakable–those who have no huts, or tents, or holes to go into, but are forced to crawl under buildings, or tramp over the grounds all night to keep up sufficient warmth to save them from freezing. These poor fellows suffer the most because when morning comes, instead of being refreshed by rest and sleep, they are completely exhausted and worn out.

To-day the prison authorities made an important discovery–a tunnel which was being dug by some of the prisoners for the purpose of aiding them to escape. To avoid any such operations hereafter, the authorities have stationed a special guard of fifteen men in different parts of the stockade to watch the prisoners and their movements. While exchange stock is low, stock in tunnels is at a high premium, many a poor fellow imagining he can see Paradise in all its glory through a tunnel. Alas! how few live to see their hopes realized.

November 14th. Morning has again dawned, a little brighter so far as nature can make it, than yesterday morning, but presenting the same blank, cheerless, hopeless aspect. The rebel raiders were abroad again last night, and had a high time stripping the dead, robbing the poor colored prisoners of what few remnants of blankets were left to them by the other rebel raiders, their captors. Their opportunity for raiding these unfortunates was favorable to success, as the poor fellows, not expecting such raids from those whom they supposed to be fellow prisoners, had divided themselves into small groups and laid down wherever an opening could be found. Such small groups not being able to defend themselves against the onsets of the stronger force of raiders, they were easily robbed of whatever they had. It is wretched enough to be in here as a white prisoner, but to be a "nigger" prisoner is to be subjected to brutality and cruelty indescribable. It is a heart-breaking sight to see these poor fellows, the colored soldiers, this morning almost destitute of everything in the shape of blankets and coats. As the weather is fast increasing in severity their sufferings will be beyond endurance.

A change was made in the rations issued to-day. Instead of the usual ration of meal, baked bread was given to us, but it is made out of the same material heretofore given to us. The loaves are said to weigh one pound each, and one loaf is divided between two men. What this means may be understood when I declare on my honor as a soldier, that the entire loaf would not be sufficient to satisfy the hunger of one man: what must it be when it is divided between two? To make matters worse, the bread is only half baked, is sour and musty, and inside the loaf is corn as raw and hard as when first ground.

Some of the officers took a walk through the prison to-day on a tour of inspection. If they were men possessed of any souls or consciences they must have seen sights that would haunt them with remorse until their dying day. But there is no danger of any thoughts or feelings of pity entering their minds. How I do wish they were compelled to live as we have to live, and subsist on the rations we have to subsist on! Possibly they might then be induced to order better conditions and more food for the prisoners–if they were the prisoners.

CHAPTER XIII.

COLD, NAKED AND SHELTERLESS - LIME-RAISED BREAD TO EAT - A SUTLER - PATROLS IN SEARCH OF TUNNELS - NEWS OF LINCOLN'S RE-ELECTION - A JOYFUL NIGHT - BURYING THE DEAD - A SIDE DISH - BREAD - COFFEE - A VISIT TO THE DEAD HOUSE - RATIONS DIMINISHING IN QUANTITY BUT INCREASING IN STRENGTH - THE RECRUITING OFFICER CHANGES HIS TACTICS - THE LOCATION OF A TUNNEL BETRAYED - THE BETRAYER FOUND - REWARDED - DEATHS IN THE STOCKADE - A COLORED PRISONER SHOT BY THE GUARDS - ROBBED AGAIN

November 15th. Last night was very cold, and this morning a cold, blood-chilling wind is blowing from the north. Things have come to such a state with us that it is absolutely necessary to strip the dead to relieve the needs of the living. It looks inhuman to carry the poor dead bodies to the dead house naked, but it is only fulfilling the scripture which says, in substance, "we brought nothing into this world with us, and we shall carry nothing out of it." The Scripture has its literal fulfillment in the condition in which we find ourselves here–for sure we brought nothing in with us (the thieving rebels having robbed us of all we had) and from the appearance of the dead bodies brought to the dead house, it is certain they will take nothing out of here with them, because they are carried out and buried as naked as when they were born.

Rations of bread, the same as yesterday, were issued to-day. However, the bread had an additional ingredient in it which we were not expecting. We wondered where the yeast came from to raise the bread, but to-day's rations solved the mystery. Crocker and I drew our rations together–one loaf for both of us–and when we divided it, to our amazement, we found a piece of pure, genuine lime, about the size of a hickory nut in it. The bread is flavored so strong with the lime that we can

121

scarcely eat it. It is of a yellowish color, like a piece of pine soaked in lye, and it is nearly as strong. If the cook puts this lime in the bread to make it light and spongy, like pound-cake, or "angel-food," they made a miserable failure of it, because the bread is soggy, heavy and strong enough to make soap. What effect it will have on our poor, empty stomachs, time alone can tell. One thing is in our favor, there is nothing left inside us for the lime to work on–fortunate are we, after all!

Good news reached us to-day through one of the old prison guards; Abraham Lincoln has been re-elected as President. The news was hailed with lusty cheers inside the prison, and was responded to with jeers from the outside. They know that with President Lincoln in the White House at Washington and Grant in command of the armies in the field the doom of the traitorous South is sealed. Nothing but "unconditional surrender" will be accepted–and it must come very soon.

November 16th. A Sutler established his headquarters in a tent within the stockade to-day. His price-list is posted up at the door of his tent and is as follows:

> Potatoes, per bushel—$40.00,
> Onions, per bushel—$50.00,
> Rice, per lb.—$2.00,
> Salt, per lb.—$1.00,
> Corn bread, per lb. loaf—$5.00,
> Black pepper, per oz.—$5.00,
> Bacon, per lb.—$5.00,
> Sugar, per lb.—$1.00,
> Tobacco, per lb.—$5.00.

If we only had plenty of rebel scrip we might live like kings, but as we have not, I fear his majesty will do a slim trade.

Rations are coming in now with commendable regularity, but the stuff they call bread is so strong with lime that a dog would have to be on the verge of starvation before he would eat it and even then he would not, because he could not. A starving Union prisoner will feast on what a starving dog would refuse. What they mean by making it this way is more than we can tell. We would much prefer the raw meal as they for

122

merly issued it to us.

The guards now make special patrols of the camp in search of tunnels, but fortunately they do not stay inside the stockade during the night. The workman are busy in the tunnels during the hours of the night. The dirt is carried out in a shirt or coat, tied like a sack, and is scattered over the grounds. It is then covered with surface dirt so as to disguise it, because the dirt which is taken out of the interior of the tunnel is a red, hard clay, and is easily distinguished from the surface dirt. It is scattered by throwing a small quantity in a place, and when it becomes muddy, the tunnel dirt is mixed up with the surface dirt which hides it. In this way the opening of the tunnel is kept from the prying eyes of the guard.

November 17th. The Sergeants in command of the squads, and whose duty it is to draw rations, have their rendezvous in one of the small tenement houses. They were having a jubilee last night when the news of President Lincoln's re-election was confirmed. They were making speeches, singing "The Star Spangled Banner," and other national airs, and were having a good time generally, when their jollity was brought to a sudden close by one of the guards ordering them to stop. He then fired into the building, wounding one of the sergeants.

Jacob Miller, Daniel's comrade, died last night and was taken to the dead house this forenoon. The light has gone out in one more northern home, but if the loved ones in that home, when the sad news reaches them, could only know from what an awful living hell, death has released their loved one from, they would sing songs of praise to God instead of weeping tears of sorrow.

I went out with the water squad to-day and through the kindness of the gray-beard guards, we went to the creek by way of the grave yard. We were there while they were unloading the dead, and hardened as we were to sights of suffering and acts of inhuman treatment among the living, the scenes at the grave yard were such as made the blood almost run cold in our veins. There were twelve or fifteen corpses piled on the wagon, laid in like logs, and entirely destitute of any covering of any kind. Two men stood on the wagon and each taking hold of a foot and a hand of a corpse, would give it a swing or two and then heave it headlong into the trench, piling them up three or four deep, and hastily covering them over with a few shovels full of dirt. This was a sight I had never witnessed before, and I hope I will never be called on to witness again.

~ ~ ~ ~ ~

Mothers and fathers of the North, think of your beloved children; wives think of your darling husbands, who went forth to defend the Flag and the Nation that treason and rebellion might be beaten back, and while engaged in this righteous and honorable duty, taken prisoners, transported to a rebel prison, starved to death and then buried in this manner! What shall we say when asked to forgive and forget these people who so cruelly and needlessly committed these barbarous acts? What man or woman, whose sense of right, justice and honor is not entirely dead, could witness such a sight as this and then forget it or forgive it? It might be possible to forgive, but to ask me to forget it is to ask me to become dead to my own existence. No, forget it we never can! To do so would not be consistent with human nature. I expect to remember this terrible scene as long as I live, and not only will I carry it in my own memory, but I will teach it to the rising generation that they too may remember it. I want them to know what sufferings while living and what shame and indignities when dead were heaped upon the brave men who went into the nation's battles from 1861 to 1865, and were taken prisoners and incarcerated in southern prison pens. I want them to know why and how these numberless, nameless, graves were filled with noble, patriot soldiers. And as we hand the Old Flag down to coming generations without spot or blemish on it, honored and respected by all nations, may they imbibe the patriotism of their fathers and maintain the honor, integrity and safety of the Flag and Nation against all foes at home and abroad.

~ ~ ~ ~ ~

November 18th. The rations issued to us to-day had a "side-dish" attached to them, made out of the offals of the beeves butchered for the rebel troops at this garrison. We got the hearts, livers, lungs and heads, etc. My friend Connely got one eye of a beef for his share, and the other rations were in proportion. I presume they would have thrown in the hides of the animals, but in the decaying Confederacy, leather commands a high premium just now. This is the first time meat of any kind has been given to the prisoners–not even bean or pea soup has been supplied–nothing but raw meal, or half-done, lime-raised corn bread, has been given to us to eat. Since we have had bread issued to us we utilize some of it for coffee in this way: We cut a slice off the loaf and hold it at the fire until it is well done. Then we put it in an oyster can full of water and boil it. This we call our "coffee." It is a weak substitute for the genuine article, but it gives us a good, warm drink, which is quite a luxury to our poor, cold, shivering bodies.

A visit to the dead house this afternoon revealed forty-three ghastly, emaciated bodies. The deaths are becoming so numerous that the dead wagon is kept busy all the afternoon hauling the dead to the trenches outside the stockade. This wagon is utilized for more purposes than hauling out the dead; it is also used to haul in our ration of bread every forenoon, and the only cleansing it gets is the evaporation, or hardening of the excretions which exude from the dead bodies, during the night when it is not in use. They say the more the wagon hauls out the less it will have to haul in, but they forget that this rule works both ways, because the less amount of bread the wagon hauls in the greater the number of dead it will have to haul out.

November 19th. Our rations of bread come to us with unbroken regularity, but the size of the loaves is gradually diminishing while their strength is constantly increasing. The more I see of this Salisbury Prison bread, the more I am impressed with the belief that lime, as a substitute for the old-fashioned yeast of our mothers is a sad failure. At least, it does not succeed in raising corn cob meal. However, it does make stronger coffee but weaker stomachs.

The mustering officer, representing Jeff Davis' government at this recruiting station, has changed his tactics. Heretofore he has carried on his work of trying to get Union prisoners to prove traitors to their Flag by enlisting in the rebel army, before rations were issued. Now he carries on his work after they are issued. Perhaps he thinks we are in better humor and more pliable after their miserable limed bread has begun to get in its work on our stomachs. Or it may be he imagines we will be willing to enlist to escape living any longer on such miserable, deadly stuff. Whether these conjectures are right or wrong, it is evident he thinks that

125

eating our rations poor as they are, will have some influence in making us more susceptible to his loving appeals and highly-colored promises. He has been trying hard to-day to get a few blacksmiths to enlist in his army, but so far he has not found any who are willing to disgrace their manhood by turning traitors to the Flag they swore to defend against all its enemies.

The location of a tunnel was made known to the officer of the rebel guards by a poor, starved wretch who hoped to profit by the betrayal of his friends. The tunnel was nearly completed to the outside of the stockade, and its discovery was a terrible disappointment to the poor fellows who had toiled so many long and weary nights with the hope of effecting their escape through it. The rebel authorities let the betrayer out of the stockade on parole of honor, because his life was in danger while he remained inside. A squad of negroes were brought in who opened the tunnel from the top and filled it up. So sure were the men who had been working in it that they were beyond the danger point of discovery, and their escape was only a question of a few hours, that they had already to anticipate the sweets of liberty, and speculate as to the line of "under ground railroad" they should travel on. But, alas! what won't a starving man do to sustain life a little longer? The betrayal of these comrades was base and inexcusable, and yet, the man who was guilty of the betrayal to better his own condition, was not low and base enough to consent to save himself by taking the oath of allegiance to the Southern Confederacy. So he had some sense of honor left in him after all.

November 20th. This morning one of the prisoners who was lying out in the mud, having no shelter or bedding to lie on, died, and some one took the liberty of appropriating what few articles of clothing he had on him, which, as may well be supposed, were very scanty. Two of the citizen prisoners died last night. When these are hauled out to be buried we dignify them with the name "funerals," because the bodies of the citizen prisoners are encased in a square pine box called a "coffin" and are taken to their burial one at a time. The rest of the poor fellows, when they die, are piled into the dead wagon as long as the bodies will stay on it, and are buried in the manner described in a former chapter.

Charley Bowen caught a mouse this morning, dressed it, and while boiling his burned bread for coffee, dropped his "fresh meat" into it and had a combination of boiled limed, corn cob meal bread, coffee and mouse soup, which he pronounced one of the most delicious dishes he had ever eaten since becoming a guest of Jeff Davis at his Hotel de Salisbury.

About 2 o'clock this afternoon one of the colored prisoners was shot while walking along the dead line, by one of the young guards. Those who witnessed the tragic event say the unfortunate victim of this young rebel's murderous hate was at least four feet away from the dead-line. The least pretext whatever is sufficient for these young scoundrels to shoot a prisoner, whether white or black.

November 21st. Some of the prisoners had boxes of supplies shipped to them from home and they were delivered to them within the stockade to-day. But before the authorities would allow them to be delivered each one had to be opened and its contents thoroughly inspected, and during the examination the larger share of its contents were stolen. The little that was allowed to remain until it reached its rightful owner, was so helpful that many of the boys have been encouraged to write to their friends to send them aid. If one-half the requests that have been sent out are answered, the inspector of this new department will live fat, as nothing is allowed to go out or come in without being thoroughly examined. All letters received from friends at home are opened and read before being delivered; and all letters sent out from the prison must be confined to six lines, a Confederate stamp attached to the letter, the letter to be left unsealed and delivered to their post office department near the south gate. If nothing objectionable is found in the letter it is sealed up and forwarded to our lines, from whence it is forwarded to its destination, free of charge, by a grateful Government.

CHAPTER XIV.

TUNNEL STOCK ABOVE PAR - BLOOD HOUNDS IN READINESS
HUNGRY, COLD AND HEART-SICK - STILL TRYING TO ENLIST
PRISONERS - BECOMING DESPERATE - A BREAK FOR LIBERTY
BEING ORGANIZED - MORTALITY INCREASING - NO RATIONS
A BREAK FOR LIBERTY - A REIGN OF DEATH AND TERROR
TRYING TO RELIEVE THE WOUNDED
TERRIBLE AND REVOLTING SCENES

November 22nd. The most exciting topic of conversation now is "Tunnels." Tunnel stock is running high. Those who have become stockholders" in these enterprises talk only of the adventures they will have when they have crawled through the opening on the other side of the stockade. Plans are being laid for escaping the terrible blood hounds which are sure to be put on the track of any prisoner who is found to be missing. The rebels are equally prepared for and confident of thwarting any designs or enterprises of this kind. A large kennel of fierce blood hounds is kept near the stockade and outside the camp limits, for the purpose of chasing any Yankee prisoner who may be bold and venture-some enough to attempt to escape from the clutches of these human blood hounds. These dogs are taken each morning in a circuitous route around the stockade and entire camp, and if any prisoner has escaped during the night and has passed outside of, or crossed their route, they very soon detect it and are on the trail in hot pursuit. Then begins a gala day for those who have the hounds and hunting expedition in charge. If the fleeing fugitives are overtaken by the hounds, their only safety is to climb a tree or surrender themselves to some planter where the dogs will remain until the officers, sometimes numbering a dozen or more, arrive and the prisoner is again taken into custody. When the Yank is overtaken and once more in their power, and merriment begins, he is compelled to march back to the prison ahead of the blood hounds, and he is warned that his life depends on his own ability to keep out of the reach of the brutes. His captors are on horseback and making all kinds of threats, telling the prisoner that is the way they bring back runaway niggers and Yankees. This is called "Southern chivalry!" Its more proper name is "Southern barbarity and deviltry!"

November 23rd. The dawning of this morning brought us suffering beyond the power of words to express. We are hungry, cold and heart-sick. For some reason unknown to us we were allowed to go without any rations—nothing to eat since the day before yesterday. This lack of food and exposure to the intense cold, is increasing the number of sick, which, of course, means a large increase in the death roll. The lime with which the rebel cooks attempt to raise the bread they give us to eat is having its natural effect on the prisoners. The stomachs of some have become so affected that they cannot retain the bread, while others have such sore mouths that they cannot eat the bread except by breaking it into very small pieces, soaking and boiling it, and then eating it with a spoon. The teeth of many have become loose, and in some instances, have fallen out. Such are the dreadful results arising from the very food these monsters are giving us to subsist on.

The mustering officer made his appearance again to-day and has been using all his powers of persuasion and flattery, backed up by great promises, to induce the prisoners to enlist in his miserable rebel army. His offers to-day were, one hundred dollars Confederate money, three bushels of sweet potatoes, full rations and twenty dollars per month. This is a strong temptation to men who are starving to death, especially when they know there is no hope whatever of a change in their condition, unless death make it. To suffer day after day, hopeless, starving, perishing, while, by a single act the whole aspect of life might be changed to comparative comfort and plenty is a severe test of patriotism and loyalty. But that act would mean treason to the Flag we swore to defend. And it is wonderful to see with what determination and scorn these slowly-murdered men reject the alternative. Death anytime and in any way! Treason and disloyalty, never!

The day has nearly closed and nothing has been given us to eat. Excitement is a fever heat. The prisoners are gathering in groups all over the stockade and are becoming desperate. The question is discussed, *"Must we yield to this barbarous treatment without making an effort of some kind in our own behalf?"* But what can men in our forlorn situation do? Guarded by men whose greatest delight is to find some excuse, even the slightest, for shooting us down like dogs: loaded cannon trained so as to sweep every part of the camp; in the clutches of men who are deaf to all appeals of mercy and justice; no possible way of letting our Government and friends know of the inhuman manner in which we are being treated– what can we do? Nothing! Only wait, suffer, starve and die, unless a just and merciful God in some way interposes for our relief.

November 24th. This is a cold, disagreeable morning. Starvation, anxiety and suffering are depicted on every face. *"Bread! Bread!"* This is the cry and talk of famishing men by day–it fills their dreams by night. Well, the bread has come at last, but in quantity wholly insufficient to satisfy our hunger. In quality, strong with lime as usual. Poor and poisonous as it is, the poor, famishing men devour it as rapidly and voraciously as a ravenous beast would its prey.

There is considerable whispering going on among the prisoners about making a concerted rush for one of the gates, breaking it down and gaining our liberty if we can, or dying, if we must. Any fate is preferable to living in this way. The great majority are determined to remain loyal to our country and our Flag. If it must be death by starvation or by the bullet, the latter is our first choice. Hence, preparations and plans are being seriously and carefully made for an outbreak. While there is no definite leader appointed, yet a number of the Sergeants commanding the squads, among whom were McBride of the 15th U.S. Infantry; McManus, of New York; Dunnecliffe, of Philadelphia, Pa.; Spillane, of New York; Reys, of the 14th U.S. Infantry; Murray, of a Maryland regiment; Carrol, of the 45th Pennsylvania Infantry; Sullivan, of the 2nd Massachusetts Infantry; D. H. Sheehan, 20th Michigan Infantry; the Sergeant Major of the 27th Michigan Infantry; and others, consulted together and made some plans, but it seemed to be impossible to get any concert of action. The majority of the prisoners look upon the movement as a very unwise one, and the discussion of plans creates so much excitement and discord that the friends of the movement fear the rebel authorities will discover our intentions and take measures to defeat us.

Night brings its shadows and darkness, but instead of bringing rest and relief to suffering men, it only intensifies their miseries. One can see groups of men, containing a dozen or more, huddled together in the trenches for mutual warmth, or crawling under the frame hospital hoping to find shelter from the terrible cold of these winter nights.

November 25th. The dawning of this morning ushered in a dreary, cold day. Desolation and misery reign supreme. The naked and ghastly forms of dead men are taken to the dead house from all over this desolate camp. Some of them are actually frozen stiff. The list at the deadhouse yesterday numbered fifty-eight, and it is constantly increasing. No rations have been issued to-day, so we are doomed to lie down another night foodless and shelterless. *Just think of it, ye who are rejoicing in plenty!* One pound of coarse corn meal bread the only food for forty-eight hours, and the probability is for even a longer time than that! Is it possible that our friends in the North, and especially the Government at Washington, has forgotten us? If not, we cannot help asking why some measures are not adopted by which we can be released from these conditions?

Today, at noon, the crisis came. A mere handful of poor, weak, but desperate men resolved to break away from this awful captivity or perish in the attempt. A rebel relief of fifteen men entered the stockade at noon. Forty-eight hours have elapsed since we have tasted food. The men were weak and faint, but desperation gave them superhuman strength. All felt it was better to die by the swift bullets of the guards than to longer endure their fiendish, systematic murder by starvation. These desperate prisoners, armed only with clubs, sprang upon the rebel soldiers, who, taken by surprise, were quickly disarmed. One rebel guard resisted, but a quick bayonet thrust soon put an end to his resistance. Another raised his musket to shoot down a prisoner, but before he could pull the trigger, his brains spattered the fence behind him. The guards were all killed

> The November 25, 1864, uprising and escape attempt by the Salisbury prisoners was the most famous in the history of the prison. The plan was to overpower the guards at the time a change was being effected of the guards inside the prison compound. Though the prisoners did succeed in overpowering the guards and taking their guns inside the prison, the one shot they had in the rifles was of little use in combating guards posted around the stockade. Additionally, the cannons were turned upon the rioting crowd and fired canister into them (one was loaded with pieces of punched-out boiler plate). Also unknown to the prisoners, the uprising occurred just minutes before the 67th North Carolina Infantry–composed of Junior Reserves–was scheduled to leave by train. These young men were called forward to assist in putting down the uprising. Those prisoners that found themselves in a position to make a break and run for freedom were so weakened by their impoverished condition that they were easily overpowered. Major Gee indicates in his records of the event that 13 prisoners were killed, 3 were mortally wounded and 60 were injured.

but one. His life was saved by prisoners.

The prisoners, now aroused to the most desperate frenzy and determination, made a rush for the big gate, hoping to reach the arsenal, which was located just north and west of the railroad depot, and arm themselves sufficiently to whip the small detachment composing the garrison, then march to the east and intercept Sherman's army, which was supposed to be operating in that direction. After the prisoners had seized the arms of the guard, they found, to their great disappointment, that they carried only one load of ammunition each. The muskets were used as clubs, but in this they were ineffectual, so that only a few got through the gate and these found themselves powerless to go any farther because they had no ammunition. In a short time every rebel musket was turned on the fighting prisoners. Three field pieces were hurling grape and cannister shot into the struggling mass of human beings. It so happened that a train loaded with rebel soldiers was lying at the depot at Salisbury, and these were rushed forward and opened a deadly fire on the prisoners, so that only a few of those who succeeded in getting outside the gate lived to be driven back.

Thus the first insurrection in Salisbury was a dismal failure. It could not have ended otherwise. There was no leadership, no well matured plans, no concert of action. The desperate men acted solely on the impulse of the moment. It was an ill-advised, futile attempt. It lasted but a few moments, nevertheless, in that short time, eighty-one were killed and as many wounded. The enemy were so enraged that they kept up the firing long after the prisoners surrendered.

~ ~ ~ ~ ~

The material used by them for canister and grape shot on this occasion, was pieces of iron punched out of boiler iron, about the size of the pieces usually punched out to admit the rivets in making steam boilers. Two of these pieces I have carefully preserved as a memento of this terrible day. This was the only attempt to insurrection in any southern prison during the war, as far as I have been able to learn

THE ATTEMPTED ESCAPE FROM SALISBURY PRISON

~ ~ ~ ~ ~

November 25th (continued). A day of greater distress and suffering I never saw before. Nothing to eat for nearly forty-eight hours; eighty-one of our comrades shot dead and double the number wounded. It is useless to expect that any surgical aid will be given to the wounded men, hence, most of them will soon follow those who were killed outright. How can men live in the midst of such surroundings?

After quiet had been restored, two Confederate officers came into the pen and began an investigation for the purpose of finding out who were the leaders of the mutiny. At first they offered to release whoever would give them the desired information but finding all their efforts fruitless, they asked a man belonging to a Pennsylvania regiment if he would tell them who the leader was, promising to reward him with a parole and transportation to the Federal lines. The brave man told them he did not know, and even if he did know he would die before he would betray them to his enemies. This so enraged the officers that one of them struck the soldier on the side of his face with his sabre, knocking him down and cutting a great gash along the side of his cheek. After the officers had re-tired, those of us who remained uninjured went to work to do what we could to relieve the terrible sufferings of the wounded. As we had no bandages, no medicines and no surgeons, we could do but little for the care of the poor fellows. About 4 o'clock two surgeons came into the prison with their instruments and appliances to dress the wounds and amputate the limbs of those whose condition required it.

Many such were found–two having each an arm and one a leg taken off. These operations were done in the crudest manner imaginable. A rough table was placed inside and close to the little gate, and on this the unfortunate men were placed. The surgeons claimed they had neither chloroform nor ether, so the operations were performed without anes-thetics, and the cries and piteous appeals of the poor fellows were heard all over the camp. So terrible was the sight and sounds that there was scarcely a man who was not in tears. One man who was badly wounded in the arm refused to have it amputated preferring, as he said, to die with his arm on his body, rather than be butchered as his comrades had been. His friends entreated him to submit to the operation in order to save his life, but he resisted all entreaties and would not submit. After the opera-tions were performed, the men were removed to the hospital, which is only one stage nearer to the dead-house. The hospital is over-crowded with the men who were wounded in the break. A great many are being cared for by their comrades outside the hospital. Many a man who en-joyed a comfortable hole in the ground, gave it up to a wounded com-rade, while he tramped on the outside the long, weary night, glad to know that by this act of self-sacrifice the life of a brave, but unfortunate, comrade might be saved. The dead who were killed in the break for lib-erty were piled up outside the gate, and were not counted in the list kept at the dead-house, but were hauled direct to the trenches.

~ ~ ~ ~ ~

There is abundant testimony to corroborate, beyond a doubt, the awful fact, that one man was hauled to the trenches with the dead while the blood was still running from his wounds. Some say he was allowed to die before he was thrown in, but two respectable citizens of Salisbury, men of good standing, testify that he was buried alive.

Perry, Iowa, Oct. lst, 1898

B. F. Booth

Dear Sir:

Have read the book you sold to my wife and I wish to add my testimony to the truthfulness of its contents as I was born and partly raised near Salisbury, N.C. In the statement you make regarding the burial of the dead in Chapter 14, you say one man was buried alive. Now as to the facts in the case. On November 25th when that out-break was made, I was a boy eleven years old, and my mother being a widow, I was trying to make my living and at this time, November 25th, 1864, I was working for a man by the name of Wm. Lockart, who was at that time one of the ten guards at the Salisbury prison. I remember well how on that eventful evening he came home to supper -- he lived near the stockade -- and while the family were all around the table, and I numbered with the rest, this man told how the Yankees tried to break out and how they shot them down right and left, and how two men were hauled to the trenches with the blood still running from their wounds and were thrown in the trenches and buried alive. He described how these men tried to brush the dirt out of their faces as it was thrown on them by the merciless brutes who buried them. This was so revolting to me that it fired my young heart with indig-nation and I resolved never to live among such speci-mens of humanity. I watched for an opportunity and soon it came -- I was taken care of by Company G of the 129th Indiana, acting as cook, and soon obtained the good will of the Company and was fitted out with a suit of blue, and let me say to you I was proud to wear it, and inside beat as loyal a heart as ever wore the blue. I came home with the regiment and ever since have lived among what they term the Yankees and never have I regretted the change I made. I find many incidents in your book that are yet fresh in my mind but none more vivid than these two prisoners being buried alive. Your book is a true record of facts and should be in every library in the land.

Yours truly,
J. H. Merritt

CHAPTER XV.

November 26th. Another cold, wet, dreary night has closed, it rained all night, and the weather was so cold that ice formed on the trees so thick that large limbs broke under the great weight, making it dangerous for the men to seek shelter under them. The wind is piercing cold and snow is falling; all the prisoners and especially of those who have no place of shelter from the pitiless storm and of this class there are a great many, suffer terribly. No rations of any kind were issued to us yesterday, and owing to the great excitement the dead were not hauled out. The sight is a sickening one to behold and one that ought to make even a savage hide his face for shame. Rations were issued to-day, but we could easily see that the fiends from whom we receive them would much prefer to let us starve. It is the same old limed corn bread. A large number are unable to eat the stuff until they first soak it and boil it in water, and then they eat it with a spoon. In hundreds of cases their stomachs are so deranged by the lime in the bread, that it is impossible for them to retain the stuff we are compelled to call "bread."

The men who were wounded yesterday are in a terrible condition. Nothing is being done for their relief and no food is given them to appease their terrible hunger. Poor fellows! It is painful to hear them talk of the nice bread their mothers and wives at home could make; how delicious beefsteak and ham tasted when fried by them. So constantly are pictures of home and plenty before them, that no effort to change the conversation can succeed. The home pantry and its contents is the only subject of their conversation by day and by night. Two rebel officers made their appearance in the prison and have taken out six of the sergeants commanding the squads, swearing the vengeance on them and claiming they were the ones who incited the outbreak yesterday.

The dead wagon had to have an extra team of horses to-day in order to do its awful work of hauling out the dead bodies of those whom God has mercifully released from their sufferings by death. Never did death seem more appropriate and welcome than now.

November 27th. To-day reveals many deaths among those who were wounded two days ago. The death list among the sick is also increasing very fast. The diseases most prevalent now are Scurvy, Bloody Diarrhea, Running Ulcers, Gangrene and Fever. A simple change of diet, or even a sufficient quantity of any wholesome food, would check most of the cases of scurvy; but such a humane act on the part of these inhuman men is not to be thought of. Rather would they do all they could to increase the fatalities instead of decreasing them. To add to the terrible plight of the sick in the hospital, there is hardly a square inch of floor or wall free from the terrible vermin of which I have so often written. The poor fellows who have a little strength left are always fighting them with desperation, but the poor helpless sick wounded men suffer tortures beyond the power of language to describe. The foul vermin are literally devouring them alive. To see these men, the heroes of many hard-fought battles, men who left happy homes and loving friends to defend the Flag of their country, now weak and helpless, covered with mud and filth of all descriptions, writhing in unspeakable agony, while maggots, worms and lice are crawling all over their poor bodies, and even creeping from mouth and eyes, and ears, was a sight well calculated to numb the brain, and chill the heart of the most indifferent beholder.

The stock in tunnels is now at a high premium, the guards who have been stationed inside the stockade having been removed, thus giving the operators in these popular enterprises a better chance to carry on their work without being observed and disturbed.

November 28th. Since the outbreak of the 25th inst., many cold blooded murders have been committed by the guards. Prisoners have been shot down at the mere will of these murderers, and no rebuke has been administered by the authorities. The negro prisoners are the special objects of their hate, but black and white alike suffer. It has been currently reported that for every prisoner shot and killed the guard was promised a furlough for thirty days as his reward. I cannot vouch for the truthfulness of this report. The fact that many prisoners have been killed without the slightest provocation, I do know to be true.

November 29th. The victims of the outbreak have helped to swell the numbers in the dead-house to-day. As they receive no attention of any kind they are fast dying off. Many of these poor boys might have lived if their wounds had received proper treatment, but the surgeons attached to the prison gave them no care whatever. As a result, the death list numbers from fifty to sixty a day. The increasing severity of the cold and the continued lack of shelter, is adding daily to the already intense suffering of the prisoners in this stockade. Oliver Crocker, one of our hut-family, froze both of his feet last night to such an extent that he can scarcely walk. Quite a number of the prisoners have become insane, being so reduced in strength by constant exposure that the mind is no longer able to bear the strain and endure the anguish. The poor fellows wander here and there through the camp, yelling as loudly as they can for "Bread! Bread!" This one word, shouted again and again, is the only word, they utter. It is pitiful to hear them. The prison is fast becoming an insane asylum.

November 30th. One result of this long period of confinement, with its accompanying misery, hunger, exposure and degradation, is that many prisoners are losing all sense of right, justice and honor. Petty thieving is practiced to an alarming extent, adding to the general misery. If a man happens to leave any of his effects out of his sight, and even out of his reach, they are speedily picked up by some sneak, and the rightful owner has no assurance of recovering his property. We dare not leave our hut without leaving some one to guard it. Rations must not be kept longer than we can devour them. If put away, no matter how secretly they may be hidden, some poor fellow sufferer is sure to find them and appropriate them to his own use. We dare not even go away from the presence of our friends to eat the little that is doled out to us. If a piece of bread is displayed in some parts of the prison pen, and the fortunate possessor is alone, two or three poor famishing fellows are sure to attack and take it away from him. The number of deaths for November registers 1043, an average of over thirty-four for each day.

December 1st. A sad accident happened to one of the unfortunate maniacs last night. Some time during the night he fell into the sink on the east side of the prison pen. As there was no one near when the accident happened, he was not discovered until this morning. The poor fellow was too weak to extricate himself, and so he died under these horrible conditions.

Rations have been issued to us quite regularly since the 25th of November, but they have consisted solely of the regulation corn bread. To-day a welcome change was made by the addition of some meat, the second we have had since taking up our abode here. As may well be supposed, it was very scanty in quantity and very poor in quality. The amount allotted to two men would not exceed one-fourth of a pound, and the meat consisted of livers, lungs, hearts and heads of beeves killed for the rebel soldiers guarding this prison and garrisoning the post of Salisbury. Still it is meat, and is relished as only starving men can relish it.

December 2nd. The sutler is still in business but his trade is not thriving, owing to the scarcity of money among the men who would be his patrons if they could. He has to contend against the competition of the citizens who wait along the road to the creek, where we get our water, and among whom a good deal of trafficking is carried on by the men who go out on the water detail. They prefer to take trade of almost any description rather than Confederate scrip, for whatever they have to sell. They do not have faith in their own money, and, at heart, I am sure they have just as little faith in their bogus government and their dying cause. To-day I received from one of these outside peddlers a large plug of tobacco, three sweet potatoes, a corn dodger weighing fully one pound, all for one finger ring. I also have a promise of a pound of butter tomorrow afternoon for another ring like it. What a treasure for so small a thing!

December 3rd. A most heinous crime was perpetrated by one of the guards to-day. A prisoner saw a piece of wood just across the dead line that had in some way been split from one of the stockade logs. While he was in the act of reaching over the line to get the piece of wood a guard shot him dead. The ball crashed through his head, killing him instantly. Many believe that the guard purposely split off the piece of wood and threw it where he knew some poor fellow would be tempted to reach for it, and all for the purpose of getting an opportunity to kill a Yankee. What brave soldiers they are, indeed!

The scurvy is fast spreading among the prisoners, many being already doomed by it. How easily this could be remedied by a change in the stuff they call food, but no step has been taken, or is likely to be taken, in that direction. And to make matters worse, the men affected by the disease receive no medical treatment whatever. The diarrhea is also raging to an alarming extent. Men suffering from this terrible disease are also left without treatment except such as they may be able to provide themselves by peeling the bark from the oak trees inside the enclosure. This bark is steeped in water and a strong tea made and drank for a remedy. So numerous have been the cases of this disease that many of the trees are peeled of every bit of bark as high up as a man can reach while standing on another man's shoulders. Then the squad of men detailed to go into the timber for wood get blackberry roots, which gives us the best remedy we have found. Unfortunately the supply is very limited, as we can only get the roots occasionally.

To-day I again went with the water squad and found my man awaiting me with his roll of butter. I gave him the ring and became the proud and fortunate possessor of one pound of butter, which I found to be a valuable addition to my "pantry." Instead of spreading it on my bread—my lime-raised corn bread—as common people would do, I put a piece about the size of a walnut in my cup when making my coffee, which imparts a better flavor to it.

Cold blooded murders are of nearly every day occurrence. To-day a guard fired into a crowd of men that had congregated together, but with no wrong intent. After he fired he commanded them to disperse. Since the insurrection of the 25th of November the prison authorities have been very watchful. The guards have strict orders to prohibit any number of men from congregating together in any part of the prison grounds, fearing they may be devising plans for another outbreak. And the cruel guards are not slow to take advantage of every opportunity offered to put their cruel orders into execution, even though the facts do not call for

143

such summary measures.

December 5th. The prison is in a state of great excitement this morning. By some providential manner a rebel paper found its way into the prison, and it contained an editorial saying that the next week we were to be paroled. While some were very hopeful that the editorial was true, others prophesied that it was only a ruse of our enemies to keep us quiet, because their actions have given evidence that, notwithstanding their superior advantages; they are afraid of us, and this paper was sent into the prison for the purpose of keeping the prisoners in good spirits in hope of a near release. The paper was printed on the plain side of wall paper.

December 6th. This is a very cold and disagreeable morning. Last night the weather was so cold that it snowed and froze. It is sad and painful to see the poor barefooted fellows walk around in the snow as long as they can stand it, and then, brushing the snow from their bare feet, sit down on them to try and put some warmth into them. In many cases the joints of their limbs are swelled to twice their natural size, while the vermin have eaten sores from their hips to their ankles, so that when they bend their limbs the sores crack open and bleed, causing intense pain. I have seen several bones exposed, caused by the poison infused into them by the graybacks. The irritation produced is so great that it is almost impossible to refrain from scratching the sores, which increases the irritation and suffering.

~ ~ ~ ~ ~

Kind reader, let me draw upon your imagination to create a picture that will give you a faint idea of what life in Salisbury Prison means. Imagine, if you can, a cold, raw, December day; the ground covered with snow and slush; a cold, drizzling rain falling; fully one-half of the prisoners without covering or shelter of any kind, not even a hole in the ground; hatless, shoeless; with no clothing save a light blouse, or shirt and pants, and these all tattered and torn, tied up with strings to hold them together; no food save a small piece of corn bread raised with lime, made out of musty meal, only half baked, and that given only once a day. This is not a picture, a dream, a fancy—it is a living, terrible fact, as thousands of Union soldiers can testify. Do you wonder that it keeps a four-horse wagon and several men busy to bury the dead each day?

144

WINTER COSTUME IN SALISBURY

~ ~ ~ ~ ~

December 7th. Since the weather has become so cold we have made a very valuable addition to the comfort of our hut in the shape of a fire-place built of mud, and as both ends of the hut are open the smoke is easily carried away. In this fireplace we can boil our coffee with a very small amount of wood.

December 8th. It is a sad thought that many who saw the sun go down last evening are not alive to greet it this morning–no less than twenty-one poor, suffering men died during the night and were taken to the dead house, from thence to be carted away and thrown into a trench with as little respect as one would throw a dead animal into a refuse-pit.

Many a poor fellow who yet lives is only too glad of the privilege of getting the scanty clothing which the dead had on. Some will take the legs of pantaloons and draw them around their ankles, thus making a comfortable pair of moccasins which, to a man destitute of shoes, and compelled to walk on the snow day and night, is a great relief.

December 9th. This morning I was again so fortunate as to be permitted to go out with the water squad. I had an opportunity to trade a ring for a corn dodger. One of the old guards informed me this was the coldest morning he had ever known in this region, and he was an old resident of the place, having lived here for over twenty years. *You, dear reader, can imagine what the prisoners must suffer, being destitute of shoes, clothing and shelter.*

December 10th. The weather has moderated somewhat. The snow is melting, and consequently the mud is deep all over the camp. One misfortune attending the melting of snow and the falling of rain is, that the loose dirt covering of many of the dug-out's allow the water to run through, causing the dirt to cave in and thus ruin the only shelter many of the poor fellows have. People in good, comfortable houses cannot realize what an irreparable misfortune it is for a man to lose even his poor dug-out. To do so means that he must stand out in all kinds of weather absolutely shelterless.

To-day our ration of corn bread was accompanied by one pint of soup having about one dozen beans and two dozen maggots in it. But we are not fastidious enough to object to the quality, it is the lack of sufficient quantity that causes complaints to be made. We are willing to take the soup and beans and not make any fuss about the maggots.

CHAPTER XVI.

A GREAT MISFORTUNE - A GOOD MEANS OF RECREATION
VISIT THE HOSPITAL - A DEAD HORSE - FOOD A LITTLE
BETTER - DEAD, 1252 - GRAYBACKS GALORE - THE TRADE OF
MARKET SQUARE - RUMORS OF EXCHANGE - ESCAPED
PRISONERS - DISLOYAL GUARDS - A PRISONER KILLED
COLORED PRISONERS DYING - A SIDEDISH - THE BREAKY-
BONE FEVER - TWO ESCAPED PRISONERS CAUGHT - HEAVY
SKIRMISHING(?) - TERRIBLE SUFFERING
CONTRAST BETWEEN REBEL AND UNION PRISONERS

December 11th. A great misfortune occurred last night which blasted the hopes of many poor fellows. A tunnel which was nearly completed, the outer end of it having been carried beyond the stockade, caved in last night, just outside, and so close to the stockade that three or four of the posts settled into it, completely ruining the tunnel and carrying dismay and sore disappointment to the poor fellows who had toiled so long and so hard to complete it, hoping thereby to effect their escape. The disaster was caused by the ground becoming soaked with water from the melting snows. While digging tunnels has not been very successful, the enterprises have not been altogether valueless. The work gives relief from the monotony of prison life, keeps the bodies of the operators warm, and encourages them with bright hopes and expectations of success in gaining their liberty. Alas! how few of those who have gone through the one successfully completed, lived to reach the land of freedom and of home!

December 12th. A visit through the hospital to-day revealed the sad fact that the last one of the wounded placed therein has died of his wounds. There are only five of the victims left inside the stockade, and these were among the number who were slightly wounded. The loss of that awful day must number between two and three hundred. As the dead-wagon was hauling out its load of precious freight to-day, numbering about twenty dead bodies, the road being very muddy, one of the horses balked inside the stockade. One of the guards became angry and attacked the poor brute with his bayonet. In doing so, the hammer of his gun caught on his leg in such a way that it was discharged, the ball striking the horse just behind the front leg, killing him almost instantly. We thought now was our opportunity to get some fresh meat, and we united in asking the prison authorities permission to dress the dead horse, but they refused the request. We then tried to buy the carcass, and more money was offered for it than the horse was worth while living. At this point an officer stepped to the gate and put a stop to all further negotiations by ordering the teamsters to haul the dead beast out immediately. One man asked the officer why he would not let us have the horse. His answer was:

"I do not want you'uns to go home and tell the folks up thar that we'uns fed you'uns on dead hoss."

But what a luxury a piece of nice, clean, dead hoss' would have been, in comparison to lime-raised, half-baked corn bread and maggoty soup.

December 13th. Our rations come with more regularity and with some improvement in their quality. The meal is ground finer, if any lime is used in raising the bread, it is so little that its presence is not easily detected. The quantity is about the same. The bread which has been issued up to this time has had a terrible effect on our stomachs. This, together with the scurvy, which is very prevalent, is making great inroads on our numbers. From the 13th of November to the night of the 12th of the present month (December) the dead numbers 1252. These figures were taken from the book at the dead house, which registers the correct number taken out to the trenches for what they are pleased to call "burial." These trenches, with the brutal scenes enacted in and about them, makes the darkest spot on the character of this nation, and will be remembered as the infamy of the leaders of the rebellion as long as time lasts.

December 14th. The weather is so cold that it has been impossible for us to take off the few rags we have on our poor bodies to skirmish for graybacks. As a consequence, they have become so numerous that they are literally eating us up. There is not a vessel inside the stockade large enough to boil a shirt in. The only way to exterminate them is to take off the garment, or what is left of it, sit on one end of it while the fighting is carried on at the other end. But under the present conditions of the weather it is impossible to remain naked so long. This gives them a chance to multiply with fearful rapidity, which they do.

PRISONERS PICKING LICE FROM THEIR CLOTHING— "SKIRMISHING" AS IT WAS COMMONLY CALLED.

"Market Square," as it is called, is getting to be a place of great notoriety. It is located just west and south of the wooden hospital, and is the nicest piece of ground in the stockade. Anyone having anything to sell or trade can always find a market for it by going to this place and letting the fact be known. Brass buttons command a price ranging from two to three dollars each; a cup of water for a chew of tobacco, and vice versa. An old soup bone that has been gnawed for twenty-four hours, will usually sell for five dollars. This, if it has a porus end, is broken into pieces, placed in a tin can and boiled for an hour or two, then bread crumbs are added to it and boiled, making a dish which brings great satisfaction and delight to the fortunate possessor. The articles for sale on "Market Square" are as numerous and assorted as the contents of a boy's pocket. The bone jewelers will pay as high as two and three dollars for an old, dry bone.

December 15th. Encouraging news was started in prison to-day. It is rumored that an exchange of prisoners is soon to be consummated, and we are to go home. Some are ready to catch at every rumored hope of release from this terrible torture, as eagerly as a drowning man is said to catch at straws. Others put no credence whatever in such rumors, believing them to be started by our enemies that the pain of disappointment might be another ingredient in our cup of bitterness.

When the blood hounds were taken on their customary tour around the stockade to-day, at a certain point they began baying and started out on what their keepers call a "hot trail of an escaped Yank." The entire herd of blood hounds were let loose to find the fugitives. It is supposed one of the guards was bribed to let the prisoner escape. A careful search was made for tunnels, or breaks in the stockade, but none were found. The only possible means of escape was over the stockade, and that could not be accomplished unless the guard were asleep or bribed. The latter is not improbable, as the old guards are on duty, and they are much more favorable to us than the young ones. Woe be to the poor prisoner who should approach one of the youngsters, or "Junior Guards" with a proposition to let him escape. He would escape, but it would be by a ball crashing through his heart or brain.

December 16th. The secret of the escape of the prisoner the night before last was discovered this morning. It seems that five of the prisoners bribed one of the old guards to let them escape, and he did so. They went out at the big gate. The discovery of this transaction has caused great excitement among the prisoners and rebel authorities. The escape was discovered and reported to the prison commander by one of the "young bloods." As a result, the old guards are under arrest. No tidings of the fugitives or their pursuers have been received up to this time. The authorities have become very strict. No gathering of the prisoners in any considerable number in any part of the prison is allowed. If a crowd does gather they are ordered to disperse at once, and if the order is not quickly obeyed they are fired into. In many instances the shot has been fired before the order has been given. Such was the case to-day in the northwest part of the prison. A crowd had congregated when a ball was sent crashing among them, followed by the order to disperse. This time there was not much pity wasted on the unfortunate man who was killed.

The murder took place in the famous, or infamous, "Devil's Den," the victim being one of their own convicts. It would have been the same if the crowd had been composed of Union soldiers. No favors are shown to any.

> Devil's Den was the top floor of the main building of Salisbury Prison. It came to be occupied by a class of prisoners known as rebel convicts or muggers among the prison populace. They consisted of Confederate convicts and Union felons who had escaped to the south. Among the prison population at Salisbury they were regarded as the lowest class of humanity.

December 17th. The colored prisoners are fast disappearing, death cutting them down every day. They are a pitiful lot to behold. Their sufferings are even more intense than the suffering of the white soldiers. All ambition to live seems to have died out in them. They become so despondent that they will tumble down almost anywhere, give up the struggle, and die. I was allowed to go out with the water squad to-day. One of the guards informed us that the rumor of an exchange of prisoners was freely talked about on the outside, and he believed it was true. But it will never do to build any hopes on these rumors, because when they prove to be false, as they always do, the effect of the disappointment is highly disastrous to the prisoners.

Our rations to-day had another side-dish composed of the same as has been given us on one or two other occasions, and which is dignified with the name "meat." The amount given us is very small. Only about three or four ounces to each man. It serves to intensify rather than satisfy our hunger.

December 18th. This is a cold, rainy Sabbath day. Mud ankle deep, and not a dry place in the stockade. The suffering of the naked and shelterless men is beyond description. The deaths are as numerous outside as inside the hospital. The scurvy is on the increase, and a disease called the "Breakybone Fever" is attacking nearly all the men. All this comes from the extreme

> What Booth refers to as "Breakybone Fever" was apparently a slang term for the disease known as dengue. Dengue is a painful disease that affects the entire body. It particularly affects the small joints of the body and occurs only under the most extreme unsanitary conditions. Body lice are the common vector of the disease. Though requiring a long period of convalescence, the disease is seldom fatal.

exposure and the lack of proper food, from which all are suffering. Both these diseases are very contagious and fatal, especially among those who are reduced in flesh and vitality. The limbs swell to an enormous size, causing excruciating pain, especially in the joints. The pain is even more severe than the pain of neuralgia.

December 19th. This morning two of the escaped prisoners were re-turned to the prison. They report that the other three got separated from them and the hunters were unable to discover their tracks. They entertain a good hope that, having eluded their pursuers, they have made good their escape to our lines. The two men captured were kept at Major Gee's headquarters all night, where every effort was made to extort from them the manner in which they escaped, and which of the guards aided them. But to the honor of the men, they would not reveal anything to the rebel commander.

> On December 20, 1864, twenty-four-year-old Edward H. Goodison from Company H of the 22nd Iowa Infantry died in Salisbury Prison. Goodison was from Jefferson, Iowa, and had mustered in on August 27, 1862. He was serving as third corporal when he was taken prisoner at the Third Battle of Winchester.

December 20th. The weather having moderated, we are skirmishing for "game." The prisoners are taking advantage of the mildness of the day and are engaged in the laudable and necessary duty of hunting graybacks. And they do not have to hunt long or go far, to find them galore. While the men are in a nude state it is painful to look at them. Many are so poisoned by the vermin that running, ulcerated sores cover their limbs from the hips down to the ankles. They receive no medical treatment and have no means of cleansing their poor bodies. The extreme filth and poison intensifies these ulcerous sores, which soon re-sults in blood poison and a slow, but sure, death. However, when death comes their sufferings are ended, so that after all, death is the best friend of the poor fellows and is longed for by many.

For several days a Catholic priest has been visiting the pen, hunting up the sheep of his flock, and offering all who will go out with him better quarters and more wholesome food. This offer is made only to those of the Catholic faith. Many of his own flock are suspicious of his motives. So far only a few have accepted his invitations.

It is wonderful how ready the prisoners are to appreciate and make merry over a good joke, notwithstanding their extreme suffering. A good one has just come to our knowledge, and is causing many smiling faces, and much sharp, but pleasant, bantering between the guards and our-selves. A correspondent for one of the New York papers, named [Albert D.] Richardson, has been in the pen for some time, but has also been busily engaged in maturing a plan for his escape. Day before yesterday he carried his plans into execution by assuming the role of a hospital physician, and as such, he boldly walked up to one of the gates and passed out, the guard showing him all the respect due one of their own physicians. His plans succeeded admirably and he is now breathing free air, while he is making all speed towards the Federal lines, followed by our earnest prayers that he may succeed in escaping the rebels and their blood hounds. His absence was not discovered until late to-day. We are joking the guards over this exhibition of Yankee ingenuity deceiving their authorities and throwing even the blood hounds off the trail. They wince under it, but have to admit it.

December 21st. Great suffering prevails among the prisoners, caused by the breakybone fever, nearly all of whom are affected by it, myself among the number. My ankles and knees are badly swollen. About 4 o'clock every afternoon the torturing pain begins, and continues with such severity that it is impossible to sleep or rest. The excruciating pain continues until about 8 o'clock in the morning when it disappears, only to return with increased vigor when evening again appears. The only way in which the affectected men can gain any relief is to set close to a hot fire, almost roasting the knees and ankles, but owing to the scarcity of wood, and the limited number of fires, few of the sufferers can avail themselves of this remedy. The rest have to keep walking, painful though it is, to keep the blood in circulation. When exhaustion comes on, as it surely does, they are compelled to sit down and resort to the measure of chafing the limbs and parts affected. The hospital surgeons make no effort whatever to give us medicine, or afford us relief of any kind.

December 22nd. I had a talk to-day with a rebel soldier who has been in the military prison at Rock Island, Illinois, and has recently been exchanged. He says that while the southern leaders are anxious to effect a general exchange of prisoners, the authorities at Washington are opposed to it, claiming that to do so would be to very greatly reinforce the armies of the Confederacy, and increase its fighting strength and prolong the horrors of the war. What a wide contrast exists between the condition of the rebel prisoners in the northern prisons and Union prisoners in the prison pens of the south. The former, being well-fed, clothed, sheltered and cared for, when exchanged, returns south stronger and more able-bodied than when they were captured, and are ready to return at once to their regiments in the field. But what a sorry lot of soldiers the victims of southern prisons, the victims of starvation, exposure, cruelty, neglect and disease would make! Even when they are exchanged and permitted to go north, it takes months of the most skillful medical attendance and careful nursing to restore them to health, and many thousands of the poor fellows are so diseased and broken down that they never will recover, but must eke out a poor, miserable existence until death comes to their relief. We would a thousand times rather fight them in honorable battle, in open field, than satisfy their fiendish delight in seeing us compelled to endure such wretchedness as they heap upon us.

ROCK ISLAND PRISON

Rock Island Prison was located in the Mississippi River between the cities of Rock Island, Ill, and Davenport, IA. The island, about 3 mi long and a half-mile wide, had the disadvantage of poor drainage and was partly swampy. Federals approved construction of the prison in July, 1863, and in August the quartermaster general instructed the builder that "barracks for prisoners on Rock Island should be put up in the roughest and cheapest manner, mere shanties, with no fine work about them." The 84 barracks, each 82 ft x 22 ft x 12 ft, were all enclosed by a high fence. A cookhouse was at the end of each barrack. All barracks were poorly ventilated and inadequately heated. An artesian well on the island supplied some water for the prison, but most was drawn from the river. Inside the prison, water was always scarce and sometimes nonexistent. In Dec., 1863, about 5,000 Confederate prisoners were sent to Rock Island, though the installation was not yet completed. Until the end of the war it held between 5,000 and 8,000 prisoners. Many of the first to arrive had been exposed to smallpox and the disease spread rapidly. In Jan., 1864, of 7,149 prisoners, 173 died; in Feb. 331 died; in March 132. Thousands of others were ill but survived. Commandants of Federal military prisoners had been authorized, at their discretion, to reduce prisoners' rations and to use the money saved on improvements deemed necessary for the prisoners' health. At Rock Island a thirty-thousand-dollar hospital was paid for out of funds issued for rations. Though there were complaints about the food, the hospital was needed. The total number of Confederate prisoners held at Rock Island throughout its history was 12,192. Sixteen percent (1,964) of those prisoners died. Today all that remains of the prison is a cemetery containing the graves of the 1,964 Confederate plus 125 Union guards who died at Rock Island.

CHAPTER XVII.

A GLOOMY CHRISTMAS - MY CHRISTMAS DINNER
WORKING WHILE SUFFERING - LETTERS - NEW PRISONERS
A ROYAL(?) VISITOR - LIBBY VS. SALISBURY - HELL AND
PURGATORY - DEATHS INCREASING - FROM THE DEAD TO
THE LIVING - A GRUESOME KIND OF TRADE - THE EFFECTS OF
SCURVY - THE LAST DAY OF 1864 - A GLOOMY NEW YEAR'S
DAY - A SICKENING SIGHT - FALL OF THE BAKERY CHIMNEY
A NEW MODE OF BURIAL - PUNISHED FOR DISOBEDIENCE
CITIZEN PRISONERS - TOBACCO AND FOOD

December 23rd. The Christmas season is again drawing nigh. What a great contrast there is between this and other Christmas seasons I have spent. What preparations for merry-making we used to indulge in before the years when the terrible war-cloud settled down upon the land! But no preparations are being made now, at least not by the "citizens" of Salisbury prison pen. Although so close to the great festal day, there are many who are alive this morning, who will not be living when Christmas morning dawns. It is enough to touch the hardest heart with pity to see groups of starved, suffering Union soldiers, now the victims, as prisoners, of southern deviltry and hate, and hear them talking about the good things in their mother's pantries at home–the roast turkey, mince pies and the other delicacies so common in northern homes at Christmas time. Their suffering is increased by the consciousness that for them there can be only hunger and misery, unrelieved by any ray of hope for the future. God only sees and understands the full meaning of the contrast to the men who are passing through it.

December 24th. Last night was one of excruciating torture to me. My feet are so badly swollen this morning that I cannot wear my old, patched up shoes, while my knees and ankles are so weak and painful that I can scarcely walk. Such pain as I endure is beyond description. I sat in the hut all day and improved the confinement by making a ring, hoping to be able to trade it for some bit of food that will make my Christmas a little more happy than the ordinary days of the year.

December 25th. Christmas is here, but as I was unable to get out with the water squad I was unable to procure anything extra to eat. It has been a dismal day to the prisoners of Salisbury. There was not enough joyous feeling in the whole prison to prompt a man to say as much as "Christmas Gift!" The only talk is of home and its good Christmas cheer. No matter to what group of men one may go, or what kind of conversation one may introduce, it will not be to the old, but pleasing, subject, of how their mothers used to cook. We are slowly but surely dying of hunger! Our talk is the only way we have of satisfying the unspeakable craving of our famished bodies for food.

As the day advanced I went to the sutler and succeeded in trading him the ring I had made for two corn meal biscuits, a small piece of boiled beef, not to exceed four ounces, five potatoes, about the size of walnuts, and sixteen grains of black pepper. You cannot realize how rich I felt. The meat I put in an oyster can, cut the potatoes fine and put them in, then added the pepper, filled the can with water, placed it on the fire, and watched the process of cooking my Christmas dinner. I soon found that my can was not large enough to hold it all, so I borrowed another can and divided the mess. In due time it was cooked in fine shape, and never did prince, potentate or king eat his sumptuous feast with such relish and delight as I ate my Christmas dinner of 1864 in Salisbury Prison.

December 26th. This morning finds me unable to walk, my feet being so tender I cannot bear my weight upon them without suffering great pain. Oliver Crocker is my companion in tribulation and retirement, his feet being so blistered from being frozen that he is not able to walk. We two occupy the hut all day. This gives us an opportunity of making rings, for which I am thankful. If it were not for my good fortune in the ring trade I must certainly starve. Fortunately anything made by a Yank is considered by the citizens of this region to be a great prize, invaluable to them as mementos, and for which they are willing to trade food of such kinds as they have, when they would not sell it for rebel scrip.

A number of the prisoners received letters from home to-day, but as I was not acquainted with any of the fortunate ones, I heard no news of interest to me. It is impossible to get any news of importance in the letters from the north, as nothing is allowed to come into the prison except news of a purely family character.

December 27th. We had an addition of five prisoners to our number this morning. They had escaped from Andersonville during the early part of the month, and after much wandering around, through the country, were finally recaptured near Raleigh and brought to this prison for confinement. They report having endured terrible suffering while wandering through the swamps and rivers in order to hide their tracks from the bloodhounds which were put on their track.

A rebel officer of high rank, said to be General Winder, accompanied by his staff, reviewed the prison to-day. His face is a good index to his base heart. He was promoted by the Southern War Department to be Commander-in-chief of all the prisons in the south because he possessed the qualifications necessary for such a position—a brute nature in human form.

December 28th. The weather continues to be very cold. I am still suffering great agony from my swollen limbs—am unable to sleep at night or walk during the day. My condition is becoming

JOHN HENRY WINDER

John Henry Winder graduated from West Point in 1820, 11th in his class, with a commission as 2d lieutenant in the artillery. He served capably in the U.S. Army, and by 1860 was a major of artillery. Winder resigned his commission in April, 1861, and accepted a Brigadier General's commission with the Confederacy. Assigned some of the most difficult and thankless tasks associated with the Confederate war effort, Winder was charged with responsibility for Federal prisoners of war and for the internal security of the Confederate capital in Richmond. In carrying out his duties he received praise from his superiors and scorn from the public. Winder took his duties seriously and received severe criticism for his seemingly high-handed methods. Some Union prisoners complained of poor treatment at Winder's hands, but others termed his administration fair-minded, and at least one carved a bone pipe as a present for the Commandant. In June, 1864, Winder received orders placing him in charge of Andersonville Prison in Georgia; in July he was given command of all prison facilities in Alabama and Georgia, and in November he became commissary general of all prisons east of the Mississippi. His abrupt manner and attention to rules and regulations, combined with the dwindling resources of the Confederacy, hampered him in these assignments. On Feb. 8, 1865, he died in Florence, SC, from strain and fatigue.

deplorable. How little we know what the future has in store for us. We often sing, "It is Better Farther On," but such has not been the experience of those who were removed from Libby Prison to Salisbury Prison. Bad as the former prison was, it was a palace compared to the prison we are now in. There we had plenty of food, pure water, good shelter from the cold and storms, and a fair quality of bread for our rations. Here, thousands of the poor fellows have no shelter whatever, while we often suffer for water, and always for food. We were all anxious to get away from Libby—we would now rejoice to be permitted to return to it.

December 29th. I had a talk to-day with one of the recaptured Andersonville prisoners. He reports the treatment and the suffering of the men there about the same as here. However, they have one luxury given to them there which we do not get here—bean soup. With this exception, he says Andersonville and Salisbury stand related to each other as hell and purgatory.

The deaths are constantly increasing. Our clothing is becoming more and more dilapidated by the constant wear and tear to which it is subjected. If Jeff Davis does not send a corps of tailors here very soon to replenish our wardrobes, we will be in much the same conditions we were in when we first opened our eyes on this wicked world. Those who can get hold of a "stiff s" (the dead are called "stiffs") clothes, are considered to be fortunate. How inhuman even honorable men can become under the terrible power of suffering! It is a frequent occurrence for the men who are detailed to gather up the dead, to find bodies in different parts of the prison pen. They were dragged there from their huts, or places of shelter, after they had died, to be stripped of their clothes by the living. They are left lying where they were stripped, are gathered up and delivered to the sergeant in command of the dead-house. In other instances the dead bodies are sold as articles of commerce by those who find them, the value of a body being estimated by the quantity and quality of the clothing it has on. The clothing becomes the property of the one buying the body.

December 30th. This morning is the first time I have been able to walk since Christmas Day. I can walk but very little yet, my feet being swelled to a great size. This is the condition of nearly all inside the stockade, many of whom are unable to move about at all. The prisoners, and they are many, who are affected with scurvy are in even a more terrible condition. They present a ghastly appearance—mouth open, teeth loose, many of them gone, and the inside of the mouth so sore they are unable to swallow anything unless it is in liquid food. These poor fellows are among the greatest sufferers.

A CASE OF SCURVEY

December 31st. This is the last day of the year 1864. It also marks the last day on earth of thirty-five brave and patriotic soldiers who preferred to die amid the tortures of Salisbury Prison than enjoy the comforts of the Southern Confederacy by proving disloyal to their Government and its Flag. They leave about 8,000 comrades behind them who give notice to the bogus Confederacy that they too are determined to walk in the footsteps of these noble martyrs, and will help to fill trenches under the shadow of the stockade rather than give any aid or comfort to their unholy cause. The atrocities perpetuated within the stockade by the rebel authorities, will be a strain on the reputation of this country that can never be wiped out.

January 1st, 1865. What strange and radical changes a few months will sometimes bring to pass. What a wide contrast I see between my surroundings on the opening day of 1865 and those of one year ago! This has been a dismal, gloomy day to the prisoners in this stockade. There is nothing going on to raise the drooping spirits of the thousands of men who have been hoping against hope. All operations in tunnel digging have ceased; exchange stock is way below par–indeed there is none at all in the market now. The only interest that continues to hold its place in our minds is the one great fact of hunger and something to satisfy its cravings. Groups of starving men, reduced to mere skeletons, may be seen huddled together talking of what they would have to eat to-day if they were at home. The very thought of home, its plenty and pleasures, seems to impart strength to the poor fellows who have nothing else to feed on.

January 2nd. The weather has become warmer. A heavy mist, almost equal to a rain, fell to-day. A horrible thing was brought to light some-time during the day. A dead body, badly decayed, was taken from one of the sinks. From the appearance of the body it must have been buried in the depths of the awful filth for a week or more. No effort was made by the prison authorities to remove the putrid remains from the prison grounds. They said they would have nothing to do with it until it was removed to the dead-house, so there it will have to go or remain unbur-ied.

January 3rd. This morning the big hospital (or "Slaughter house," as it is justly named), presents a sad spectacle. When the chimney was erected, it was placed on the inside of the hospital wall. The material used was a very poor quality of soft brick. It was built up from the ground without any foundation being placed under it and the result is, the lower courses of brick were crushed and the whole structure fell the full length of the building, killing ten men and wounding several others. It can scarcely be called a disaster–rather let it be called a kind act of providence by which poor, suffering men are released from their misery.

January 4th. The weather has become very cold again. There was a severe frost last night. The ground is frozen hard and a cold and the northwest wind is blowing, all of which increases the sufferings of the exposed prisoners.

The dead list is climbing up at a rapid rate. Large numbers of the men are suffering from badly frozen feet. The intense cold also increases the agony caused by the breakybone fever. I am again unable to walk, my feet swelling so badly that I am really alarmed. Large blue spots, painful as boils, are making their appearance on them. My poor stomach is in such a state that I cannot retain the corn bread without soaking and boiling it into a liquid form. My stomach seems to be gradually shrinking as I can now eat only one pint of this corn bread gruel in half a day, and even this causes me great suffering.

January 5th. One advantage gained by a residence in this prison is, that we are being trained in new experiences as well as in new observations. To-day I witnessed a new method of removing dead bodies for burial. Two negroes were brought into the prison having a rope with a great hook attached to it. They went to the place where the dead body taken from the sink yesterday was lying and throwing the hook over the body, dragged it out to the burying ground. It was in such a decomposed condition that had it not been for the few rags which covered it, it would have fallen to pieces before it reached its last resting place.

We were punished to-day for not removing the dead body ourselves by having our rations withheld from us. Thus it will be seen that every excuse they can possibly find to make the starving process more complete and sure, is improved by them.

January 6th. To-day I visited the citizen prisoners and hospitals. It seems unreasonable that their own men should be kept confined in this prison and away from their families, without any charge whatever being made against them. At least no charges are made public. The condition of these citizen prisoners is somewhat better than the condition of the soldier prisoners. They are kept by themselves, have much better rations, and are favored with good shelter from the storms and cold. The hospitals remain in the same terrible condition heretofore described. There is no change in either the surroundings or the sufferings of the sick. The-dead-house registered thirty-four dead to-day.

CHAPTER XVIII.

IN NEED OF FUEL - A SAD DEATH IN OUR HUT - WOLF IN
SHEEP'S CLOTHING - SOUP AND SALT - THE SECRET OF THE
SALT REVEALED - REBEL DEVILTRY - MORE TOBACCO
AWFUL SUFFERING - A DREAM - A VISITOR - RED PEPPERS
ESCAPED PRISONERS RECAPTURED - TERRIBLE SIGHTS
A TUNNEL OPENED AND ABOUT A HUNDRED GO OUT
THE ESCAPE DISCOVERED - MEAT
WEARING DEAD MEN'S CLOTHING

January 7th. Another very cold morning and consequent suffering. The ration of fuel allowed us is being reduced in proportion as our bodily strength is reduced, as all we are allowed is the amount three men can carry for each squad. We select our stoutest men for detail on the wood squad, but as it is difficult to find three men who are not affected with breakybone fever or scurvy, the amount of green pitchpine they can carry such a long distance is very small, but it is all we get. Crocker and myself are able to walk around some now, but my ankles are still very sore and my feet are so tender the pain is very great when I put them on the ground. Crocker's frozen feet have healed sufficiently to enable him to walk a little, but, as they were frozen into a solid blister, which caused the skin to peel off, they are in a terrible condition. Just think of men being left in such a state and no remedy whatever given them! Who can find any excuse whatever for such brutal treatment?

A member of Co. H, of my regiment, and an occupant of the south end of our dugout died to-day. A strange thing about this death is that it is the man who, when we decided on this location for our dugout, remarked that it was so handy to the dead-house our "friends would not have far to carry us, when," as he expressed it, "we handed in our checks." Poor fellow! Little

> Alexander Miller of the 22nd Iowa Infantry Company H, who was twenty-one years old, died at Salisbury Prison on January 7, 1865. He was one of those who were captured at the Third Battle of Winchester on September 19, 1864.

did he think that he would be the first one to be carried out. It is sad beyond expression to see a comrade and friend dying in such a shameful manner and his comrades powerless to aid him. But such is the fate we must all expect unless relief comes to us very soon.

The Catholic priest is still making his daily visits. He seems to manifest more interest in the prisoners of foreign birth than in Americans. It is generally believed that he is a rebel recruiting officer in disguise. If he is, and is picking on foreigners as his easiest victims he will be left as badly as he will be when he knocks for admission at "The Golden Gate."

January 8th. We had another addition to our rations to-day–a pint of spotted bean soup, but, as usual, containing more worms than beans. Still, a luxury of this kind receives no adverse criticism because there happen to be worms in it. It is soup! The worms are the trimmings–we wish it would come oftener, worms and all. We also got about four ounces of salt. But, what in the name of common sense is the salt for? We have not a thing in the world that we can use it on, in, or with. We are a little like the Irishman who, when asked what he had to eat, replied; "I have potatoes and salt for breakfast; salt and potatoes for dinner; and salt without potatoes for supper."

We are having the Irishman's supper. But we had one painful lesson in "salt" taught us when we ate the salt codfish in Libby Prison the night we started for our present residence. Can it be they are arranging another pleasure trip for us? I really hope so. It matters not where they take us, it cannot be worse then this place in which we are now confined.

January 9th. This morning Connely went out with the wood squad. I would like to have the double rations given to the wood men, but I could not chop much wood. This morning reveals the secret of these barbarous wretches in giving us the salt yesterday. We were informed that we must do without water to-day, owing to the fact that they were unable to furnish soldiers to guard the water-carriers, a detachment of their force having been sent away on other duty. Our only resource for water to quench our raging thirst is the filthy stuff contained in the wells which act as catch-basins, for all the filth from the living and dead of this prison-pen. Some of the men are so nearly crazed for water that they resort to scooping out holes in the ground, and as the snow thaws in the middle of the day, the water runs into the holes and is eagerly drank by the poor fellows. This is filthy enough, but is not quite as bad as that taken from the wells. This, is rebel chivalry. Could Satan himself devise more ingenious plans for murder by slow torture?

January 10th. I have been out of tobacco for two days, but to-day I was fortunate to procure a plug for a ring I finished a few days ago. Not being able to walk sufficiently to go with the water squad, Connely went and made this happy trade for me. He also brought in some blackberry roots, which we boil and drink the tea as medicine, which is all we have. Connely seems to endure the hardship and privations of prison life better than most of the prisoners. I do not know what I should do if he was not here. He takes such a reasonable view of the situation. He does not get despondent himself and will not allow Crocker and myself to brood and complain over our troubles, which we certainly would do if this happy, cheerful comrade was not with us. He is the counselor, advisor and comfort of our little party. Sad would be the day if he should be taken away from us. He is a noble fellow.

January 11th. I am suffering terribly with my feet and ankles this morning. My feet are swollen so badly I cannot walk and my ankles and legs are as blue as indigo. My mouth is also very sore while my teeth are so loose that it is difficult for me to eat. The meal of which our bread is made is much coarser than formerly, and they are putting more lime in it. How men, professing to be human, can persist in giving poor, helpless creatures such stuff to eat, is beyond comprehension. I am convinced that I cannot stand the suffering much longer; I feel this morning as if the end must come soon. The bread being only half baked, sour and poisoned with the lime, only aggravates my hunger. My stomach is so weak it is not able to do the work the millstone ought to have done. I am convinced this is all done for the purpose of killing the prisoners by a slow but sure process.

January 12th. Last night was one that I shall long remember, it being one of excruciating suffering. I slept but little, and even that was disturbed by dreams. Should God grant my dreams would prove to be realities, what joy would be mine! The Salisbury town clock can be heard striking the hours, and last night I heard it strike every hour up to 1 o'clock. Then I went into Dreamland. I dreamed I had just returned to my old home. The family were all seated around the table for supper. I remarked that I was fortunate in coming home just in time for supper. All looked amazed to see a stranger, as they supposed, no one having recognized me, making himself so familiar. Seeing this I spoke to my father and said:

"Father, is it possible you do not know me?"

He gazed at me steadily for a moment, then got up and came to where I was, and taking me in his arms, said:

"Frank, is it possible this is you?"

I replied, "This is what is left of me."

Soon all the family were gathered about me, and after a general handshaking and greeting, I informed them we would do our handshaking after supper, because I was very hungry just then. My sister immediately placed a plate on the table for me. I quickly perceived there were twelve persons seated at the table and I would make the thirteenth. Being of a superstitious nature, I believed the number thirteen to be an unlucky number, so I refused to set at the table, and seated myself on the floor by my father. I told them that was the way soldiers eat their meals. They all remonstrated against my position on the floor, and a half dozen offered me their places at the table. I was persistent in refusing all offers and made them keep their places. I asked for a plate of beans which was given to me. My mother then handed me a cup of coffee, and as I took it from her hand the cup slipped on the saucer, turned over, and its precious contents, almost boiling hot, fell over my ankles and knees. This caused me to awake. The excruciating pains in my limbs, and the more intense pain of disappointment at my heart, can be better imagined than told. What a painful awakening that was! From the plenty, comfort, love and solicitude of home, to find myself almost frozen with cold, my knees and ankles aching as if they would burst, while the hunger growing in my stomach was terrible. Here I was in a rebel prison, and only God knows when or how I will get out of it. In the darkness and stillness of the night I imagined I could almost feel my naked body on the dead wagon, jostling along towards the grave yard. There was no more sleep for me that night, so I lay on my pallet and studied over my pleasant dream until it became so vivid and so deeply impressed on my mind that to forget it will be one of the impossibilities of my life.

January 13th. The long, weary night has passed away and the

morning has dawned, but the day brings no relief, either from hunger or pain. My knees are swelled to twice their natural size. Our suffering is increased by the intense cold, as we have had no wood for two days. Connely is out with the wood squad now, but he will not be in until nearly dark, and I am unable to move about.

Louis Auringer, of the 81st Pennsylvania, came to see me to-day. He manufactures bone Bibles. He sat and worked by me the greater part of the day. We talked of home, friends, prospect of exchange, and other things, which made the day pass away quite pleasantly. I cannot feel as hopeful of exchange as he and some others do. But perhaps I am too much disposed to look on the dark side of things. Still I cannot avoid facing facts, not as I would like to have them, but as they are.

January 14th. I am feeling somewhat better this morning. My limbs do not pain me so much. Last evening when Connely returned he brought with him two of the largest red peppers I ever saw. I made a strong tea of one and drank half a pint of it, which greatly helped me. I slept quite well, so this morning I feel more encouraged and have greater hope of recovering.

The three prisoners who escaped on the 12th of last month were re-captured and returned to the prison to-day. They had almost reached our lines when they were betrayed to the enemy. They report having suf-fered a great deal during the cold nights. If they had been a little more cautious they would have reached our lines the next night, but becoming hungry, they approached a negro at a farm house to ask for food, but in-stead of giving food to them he betrayed them.

~ ~ ~ ~ ~

Very many of our men who escaped from the prisons of the South were re-captured through the treachery of the house servants, for they were treacherous. But it is the testimony of every escaped prisoner that none were ever betrayed by the "field hands," or common negroes. They could always be approached with perfect confidence, and would give the Union prisoners all the aid within their power, often acting as guides through unknown regions, as sentinels to warn them of danger, or as providers of food. These poor fellows often rendered the service to the prisoners at the imminent risk of their own lives, but it was given cheerfully.

~ ~ ~ ~ ~

January 15th. I am still improving both in health and in spirits. I now begin to cherish a reasonable hope that I may yet live to see "God's Country." I am now able to eat my corn bread by breaking it up and soaking it in water. I have not been able to walk for four days, but this morning, with the assistance of a cane, I am able, though with much pain, to walk to Market Square. In walking among the poor prisoners in this pen, it is no uncommon sight to see men whose hands and feet are rotting off them. The weather, especially the nights, has been so intensely cold, that the naked, shelterless bodies of the starving men were unable to endure it, or escape without being badly frozen. Indeed, thousands had their extremities so frozen as to destroy life in these parts, which superinduced a rotting of the tissues by a kind of dry gangrene. The rotten flesh frequently remained in its place for many days, a loathsome but painful mass. It finally gradually sloughed off, leaving the sinews which passed through it to stand out like shining, white cords. Such objects are to be seen everywhere, but more especially in the gangrene ward, in the big hospital. The surgeons do not make any effort to check the disease, but simply allow it to run its course until death, or permanent disfigurement results. The sick are increasing to such an extent that every building in the stockade is filled to its utmost capacity.

January 16th. The prison is in a state of great excitement this morning. A tunnel which has been under headway for about two weeks, was opened some time during the night and about a hundred prisoners went out to temporary freedom, through it. The company digging this tunnel has been the best organized of any yet engaged in this work. The number of operators was limited to twenty-five men each of whom was bound by the most solemn oath not to reveal the movement until it was completed. The tunnel being done, a meeting was held yesterday and it was agreed to open it up last night at "low twelve." It was agreed that each man belonging to the organization could have the privilege of taking two of his friends with him through the tunnel. The provision was included that the men who had done the work should go through at 12 o'clock, then their friends to follow at 1 o'clock, thus allowing the originators of the movement to gain their exit and have one hour's start before the crowd should rush through, and thus endanger the safety of all.

January 17th. This is the eagerly looked for slaughter day, and our regular ration of corn dodger is accompanied by some meat, consisting of the offals of the beeves. Disgusting as such meat would be to us at home, here it is hailed with delight, and is eaten with an eagerness and a relish that is astonishing. But men dying from starvation and exposure will eat anything that gives promise of sustaining life.

Good fortune befell me to-day. I came into possession of a pair of trousers which I converted into a pair of moccasins, which adds greatly to the comfort of my poor, sore feet. What a power there is in circumstances to enable one to overcome his prejudices. How heathenish a man would be considered who would take a pair of trousers off a dead man and put them on his own person, or cut them up for other purposes! But here it is different. When men die in this prison pen they are taken to the trenches naked. Some poor fellow considers himself in good fortune if he can appropriate to himself the few articles of clothing the dead man may have on him. Personally, I have laid aside all the repugnance to wearing dead men's clothes. My chief, and indeed, my only regret is that the dead man had suffered his wardrobe to diminish to such scanty proportions before I made his acquaintance. If the treatment we are suffering continues much longer, I fear we shall be led to appropriate not only the clothes, but also the bodies of the dead.

For the first time in a whole week, I make a trip to the east end of the prison to see some of the comrades who are situated near the east side. I find the same suffering there that prevails everywhere. They are without clothing sufficient to keep them from extreme suffering. More than half the squad are barefooted, and many of them have badly frozen feet. Connely has resigned his position on the wood-squad, and is reduced to regular prison fare. The weather is very cold again. About three inches of snow fell during the night, and the wind is cold and piercing, all of which adds to our distress. Many of the prisoners are yielding up their lives to the terrible torture.

169

News has reached us this evening that the tunnel has been discovered and hunters, accompanied by blood hounds, are in pursuit of the escaped prisoners. The report was brought in by one of the boys who went out this evening with the wood-squad. God pity the poor fellows; they can scarcely hope to escape capture, or death by the terrible blood hounds!

CHAPTER XIX.

LONELY AND SAD - NIGHT SOUNDS - A VISIT - CONNELY
LEAVES THE WOOD SQUAD - A WRATHFUL COMMANDER
A MAN SHOT BY THE GUARDS - THEIR IDEAS OF A YANKEE
SOME OF THE ESCAPED PRISONERS RECAPTURED
TRADESMEN IN DEMAND - SAD CASE - MASONIC CHARITY

January 18th. Major Gee is out of humor this morning. He came into the prison followed by about a dozen guards, called the prisoners to "Attention!" and demanded them to inform him where the tunnel was opened last night. He informed us that no rations would be issued to us until we gave him the much-coveted information. None of the men seemed to know where the tunnel was started, in fact, they professed entire ignorance of the whole affair. He ordered his guards to institute a careful search for it, which resulted in finding it near the west side, which was directly south of Gee's headquarters. It seems that after the escaped prisoners went out, the hole through which they made their exit was closed so completely that the tunnel was not discovered until late in the evening. This piece of Yankee ingenuity has so completely outwitted the Major that he is cursing and storming around like a crazy man, and his wrath is heaped on our poor heads. He swears we will get no more rations until the fugitives are brought back. My earnest prayer is that they may all reach our lines and then our true condition will be made known to the people of the North who will rise up and demand that our Government shall send an army here to release us and destroy this accursed place.

The excitement outside must be intense judging from the commotion. One-half of the garrison is under marching orders, and we can distinctly hear the tread of many horses.

The most awful threats are being made as to the fate of the escaped prisoners, if they are caught, which God forbid. But it will certainly be a sorrowful time for any poor fellow if he should be caught, especially while the excitement is raging as it is now. Many of the citizens from the town of Salisbury are on the walks with the guards, and exulting that we were where we could not run away their "niggers" and burn their barns. What debasement of humanity that such low and contemptible insults should be flung in the faces of helpless men by those who are ranked among the "blue bloods" of the South!

January 19th. This day witnessed another foul, unwarranted and cold-blooded murder. One of the men belonging to a Michigan regiment, was shot through the body while wandering near the dead-line. The man was seen by a dozen or more of the prisoners and all declare he was not over or near the dead-line. He was shot by one of the South Carolina Reserves. They have two regiments here composed of boys under military age. These young fellows who have grown up since the war began, imbibed the idea that a "Yankee" was not a human being, and that it was not any more harm to shoot one than it was to kill a wild beast. Their passions had been inflamed by wild and terrible stories of the cruelty and depravity of the Yankees, until they believed it was a meritorious thing to improve every opportunity to exterminate them. Evidently the young murderer who committed this crime had no more idea he had committed a crime than if he had killed a venomous reptile. We are also convinced that the commander of the prison takes the same view of the case, because the young scoundrel was not even relieved from duty. But this man Gee, the commander, is more guilty than the guard. His method of murder is more hideous and barbarous than death by the rifle ball. He intends to starve us to death, as we have gone without rations of any kind for two days, and a good prospect to go the third day in the same way.

January 19th. The result of this attempt to reach "God's Country" is a reduction of rations and a resort to every restriction which could possibly be conceived by a rebel. While in Libby I imagined that the deeds of villainy were well nigh exhausted. I had thought that the catalogue of crime was nearly filled by the incarnate Turner and his hosts.

But alas! You have only to see the heartlessness and intrigues of the authorities here of Major Gee and his associates Johnson and others, and you have only to witness the suffering, the frenzy and the fever and you will then say, that these are the deeds of pitiless monsters.

172

January 20th. This morning about a dozen of the escaped prisoners were recaptured about forty miles northeast of the prison. The hounds ran them into an old planter's house and there they were taken. The rebels and hounds are still in pursuit of the rest of the fugitives. The returned men report that after they got away from the stockade they divided into squads of about ten and twelve and traveled in different directions, hoping by so doing to make the escape of some at least more possible.

During the excitement of the last few days I have been on my feet more than I have since Christmas. It is a great pleasure, and affords me great happiness, to be able to walk around once more. The exercise is very beneficial to me. It is difficult to get around because the mud is very deep, which is a poor condition of things for old, woolen moccasins. The Major has either relented, or is feeling rejoiced over the return of a part of the escaped men, as our rations of corn dodger came to us again, for which we are very thankful.

January 21st. The irrepressible recruiting officer is plying his vocation with renewed energy. The scarcity of mechanics of all kinds, and the pressing needs of the bogus Confederacy, have influenced them to hold out all kinds of inducements to the mechanics among the prisoners to go out and enter the employ of the Confederacy. Shoemakers are especially in demand; next to them are the blacksmiths, machinists, moulders, metal-workers, harness and wagon makers. There has not been a week since we came to this prison that a rebel recruiting officer has not gone among the prisoners seeking to induce men of these trades to give their service to the rebel government. Such men can go out any time on parole and are promised fabulous wages.

Being a harness maker by trade, I have been approached by several officers who have tried by all kinds of promises to induce me to give them the benefit of my knowledge of harness making. I have been offered thirty or forty dollars a week, good board, plenty of tobacco free of cost, and a comfortable Confederate uniform. But the pay was to be in rebel scrip, worth from ten to twenty cents on the dollar; and wearing a rebel uniform was far more repugnant to me than wearing the clothes of the dead, but loyal, true and brave Union soldiers. The labor of the large numbers of skilled workmen of all kinds to be found among the prisoners, would have been valuable to the needy Confederacy. Our shoemakers, machinists and railroad men could have done more to help the rebel cause by making shoes for their barefooted soldiers and repairing and running their railroad trains, than a division or two of our army could have done to injure them. Never before did the South feel the lack of skilled laborers as it does now. They had plenty of men at their command, but the men who were competent to go into their railroad shops and put their old rolling stock in order; and run their trains after they were made ready, were very scarce. And the same is true of all other classes of skilled labor.

~ ~ ~ ~ ~

The contrast between the armies of the North and the South in the matter of skilled workmen, was very great. Salisbury Prison contained among its thousands of prisoners many, very many, of the best and most competent mechanics of all kinds—men who, by education, training and experience, were competent to carry on any business, run machine shops, railroad engines, and everything else that was needed. The rebel authorities not only realized but openly acknowledged this state of things, by holding out such great inducements to our skilled workmen to enter the service of the rebel Government. But all their solicitations, inducements and promises were spurned with indignation. Our men were determined to die rather than gain their liberty at the expense of disloyalty to the old flag. The almost invariable reply to all solicitations was:

"No sir; I will stay here until the maggots and lice devour my carcass, before I will lift a finger to aid your infernal Confederacy and its army!"

Of course, there were a few exceptions to this rule, but only a few. I remember one comrade of my regiment went out as a mechanic, and three days after deserted them. In the early part of December he reached home but was a complete mental wreck. The untold hardships of his homeward journey; sleepless nights, foodless days, evading blood hounds and rebel patrols—was more than he could endure, so that when he did reach his home, it was found that the light of reason had fled, and he ended his days a total wreck.

~ ~ ~ ~ ~

January 22nd. One of the most notable features of our brutal treatment by the rebels and citizens of Salisbury, is our complete abandonment by all religious denominations. The only visit we have had from a minister of any religious denomination has been a Catholic priest who has visited us occasionally. We are treated as if we were brutes without souls, moral instincts, or spiritual needs.

~ ~ ~ ~ ~

The only interest manifested by these rebels in the welfare of any of the prisoners, was shown by members of the Masonic and Odd Fellow Orders. I mention this as it was the only recognition manifested by any of our foes to the claims of human kinship. Members of these orders among the rebel soldiers and citizens interested themselves in securing details outside the stockade, in the cook house, the commissary department, and elsewhere, for their brothers among the prisoners, who would accept such favors at their hands. Some of the more favored ones were out on parole of honor, and enjoyed certain liberties under certain restrictions not granted to others. Such of the fraternity among the prisoners as did not feel inclined to go out on parole received presents in the shape of extra food, especially of vegetables, which were worth their weight in gold. Material was also furnished them out of which to construct huts for their use. Such as made themselves known before they died, were buried according to the rites and customs of the orders. The prison surgeon, and probably all the assistant surgeons, were members of these fraternities, and the wearing of a Masonic or Odd Fellow emblem by a prisoner, was sure to be recognized, and to be the magic amulet that would procure for the wearer the tender of their professional services. These prisoners are detailed in the hospitals as nurses, ward-masters and such like, as a recognition of fraternal obligation and friendship. In one instance I personally know of a Mason divulging the secrets of the order to a comrade (on the conditions, and solemn promise, that if he lived to get home he would join the order) which secured him a parole of honor, and was the means of saving his life.

I was not fortunate enough to belong to either of the Brotherhoods (but I often wished I did belong to them), so that I missed the advantage of these fraternal friendships and the benefits they procured. I take special pride in emphasizing one fact, that during the entire long period of my imprisonment, I was not brought under any obligations to any of Jeff Davis' followers for a single favor of any kind. No scoundrel of the whole crew lives, or ever did live, who can say that he ever did me the slightest favor of any kind, not even the gift of a kind word. From first to last I received nothing but my regular rations (and even these were often withheld from me), except as I would receive extra food, or tobacco, from private citizens in trade for rings of my own manufacture. I owe no man in the Confederacy any debt of gratitude—and I am glad of it.

CHAPTER XX.

January 23rd. We are still without tidings from the men in pursuit of the escaped prisoners. Companies of citizens from the adjacent country and a part of the garrison, accompanied by numerous blood hounds, have been in pursuit, but so far only one small squad has been brought back. The effect of this is to inspire encouragement in the hearts of those of us who remain. If good wishes and earnest prayers will assist the brave fellows to succeed in reaching our lines, they will never be apprehended and returned to this den.

The number of negro prisoners has diminished to an alarming degree. Out of about 300 who were brought here, I do not think there are fifty left, and they are in a fair way to follow their comrades. They receive the same rations the white prisoners get, but they fare worse in other respects. They do not seem to have the energy and grit of the white men to provide themselves with shelter. They will also dispose of the last garment they possess for a sweet potato or a bite of bread. I saw one negro this morning trade his shoes for a sweet potato, a small piece of bread and a chew of tobacco, turning his pedals out naked to the weather. This means one more victim for the deadwagon, because a negro is like a young turkey, when he gets chilled through he turns up his toes, froths at the mouth, then all is over with him.

Our rations came to-day as usual. It is amazing how much husk there is in the corn in this forsaken country. The bread we get to eat is nearly one-half husk, or corn-bran, or something of that nature. I know if this kind of corn was raised up North, Yankee ingenuity would bring about some kind of transformation in the seed so that it would produce more corn and less husk.

January 24th. When we were received in this vile prison there were no sick or wounded men among the prisoners, but there are not to-day five hundred well men among 8,000 inside the stockade; this is a lamentable fact and the rebel surgeons coincide in this belief. The mud is ankle deep all over the prison and no dry place to be found but under the wooden hospital and that is filled overflowing all hours, day and night.

I borrowed a pair of shoes from Comrade Strawser, one of our boys, and went out with the water squad. I wanted an opportunity to trade a ring for something to eat, but to my disgust, our guards were some of the young tarheels (North Carolina Reserves), who were mean and devilish enough to prevent us from trading with the citizens, who were waiting and anxious to exchange tobacco, sweet potato pies, and sweet potatoes for any kind of relics made inside the prison. But these young bloods would not allow it, giving as an excuse, "It is 'ginst odahs to 'low it!"

That such orders had been given them we have no doubt as a commissioned officer accompanied them to see that the "odahs" were obeyed. He was a pitiful second lieutenant, who assumed all the dignity and authority of a Major General. From his general appearance and demeanor if he could have been sold at his own estimated value, the returns would have paid off the entire war debt of both sections, leaving the country free to do as it pleased. We returned to camp with water, but no rations.

January 25th. This morning the weather is much warmer than it has been for several days. With a drizzling rain and a heavy atmosphere, the odor from the sinks is beyond description. One of the guards said the citizens could smell it three miles away and then remarked:

"*I didn't know you all smelt so; why, you Yanks smells worse than niggers!*"

Comrade Judson, of Co. H, of our regiment, who is one of the stockholders in our dugout, is very low with malarial fever and scurvy. The probabilities are we will have to carry him to the dead-house.

I visited the citizen prisoners headquarters to-day and find the same suffering there that prevails everywhere within this prison hell. Their despondency and hopelessness are plainly visible in their haggard faces. A great many of them have died, while others are terribly afflicted with scurvy, and are unable to walk.

An interior view of this prison presents a picture of misery and despair which has never been paralleled on God's earth. One must go through the prison pens of the Southern Confederacy to see sights and conditions which cannot be seen anywhere else.

I wrote a letter to-day for D. W. Connely to his sister, Mrs. Frank Wade, who lives in the neighborhood where my wife lives. I enclosed a few lines to my wife. All letters must be confined to six lines, and nothing derogatory to the Confederacy, or the management of this prison, must be written therein. It is vexatious to be compelled to write to our friends that we are all right; and perhaps, according to the standard of prison conditions we are all right—at least we think so if we are only able to walk.

January 26th. Market square is a central meeting point for all inside the prison and is gaining great notoriety. All who are able to walk are certain to meet here at least once a day to exchange gossip and eagerly listen to the latest reports pertaining to our exchange and most of all, to curse the rebels and the bogus Confederacy. Their wrath was raised to a high pitch to-day when an emissary of the Confederacy made his appearance with all the pomp and dignity his bald-faced impudence could inspire, and placed on the market Confederate skin plasters, five dollars for one greenback, his stock of trade being so low no business was done. Greenbacks commanding a high premium, he finally offered fifty to one, when he retired amid the curses and derision of the prisoners.

This evening about a dozen of those who escaped on the night of the 16th were brought back to the prison. They report having been traced by blood hounds and were recaptured by citizens. Every able-bodied man not in the Southern army is patrolling the country for rebel deserters and escaped prisoners, which makes escape almost impossible.

January 27th. The weather is again cold; the ground froze last night, but the sun has come out bright and full of a genial warmth this morning. Would to God it might pour some rays of hope and sunshine into our poor, hopeless hearts. I am happy to say my feet are improving so I am able to take my customary morning walk. About one-half of our boys are stationed near the east side, the rest are quartered near the center of the grounds east and west, but south of the center north and south. There is little motive for motion of any kind, and no room for exercise, however strong our desire might be in that direction. Many of the prisoners yielded unresistingly to the despondency which naturally arose from the dull, routine life we are compelled to live. It requires great determination and exertion to take exercise here. The tendency is to lie still, fret and die. The ground is all preempted, or homesteaded, and is so full of holes and other devices for shelter, that it requires considerable time, patience and care to pick one's way through the narrow paths between the different parts of the prison. I usually walk over to the dead-house and from there to the east side, to hear the gossip of the day. Then I visit the hospital and render what assistance I could to my sick comrades. I then returned to Market Square, where everything in the stockade is bought and sold. Here I trade for rubber buttons and rubber combs, the material out of which I made my finger ring. This daily trip, attending roll-call, making bread-coffee, skirmishing for "game" among the dilapidated clothing, and the rest of the day making finger rings, constitute the daily routine of my life within Salisbury stockade.

January 28th. Great excitement prevails among our boys at the south side this morning. It is the general belief that the day of our release from this prison is near at hand. The report has reached us that terms of exchange have been agreed upon, and we are to leave here during the coming week. The news came from one of the old guards who says he has been in a position to learn the facts. Whether true or not, the report has acted like magic on the prisoners. They are showing their hopes in their cheerful faces and expressions of joy. All are hoping we are not being deceived as we have been heretofore.

January 29th. The weather is moderating and the suffering from cold is decreasing. If the terrible diseases and vermin would only abate likewise, life would become more tolerable to us, but there is no sign of diminution in either of these plagues. The sanitary condition of the prison becomes worse and worse. It is almost impossible to endure the terrible effluvia which is constantly arising. The news of exchange is having a good effect on the sick as well as on the well.

January 30th. We would judge from the joyful demonstrations at the Sergeant's headquarters last night that we had already received orders to go to "God's Country." The hope of a speedy exchange is given so much credence that the Sergeants were having a jolly time. Patriotic singing was kept up until a late hour at night. The most astonishing part of the whole matter is, that the guards did not fire on them as they have done heretofore; no effort of any kind was made by the rebels to stop the hilarity. This goes far towards confirming our belief that the report is not without some good foundation. The excitement is such that we begin to think there is not much difference between intoxication excited by wine, and that produced by good news, especially when it brings a hope of release from such torture as we have been enduring in this prison. The boys all act as if they were really drunk—handshaking, greeting, singing, and some actually crying for joy. There have been five or six maniacs here who lost their reason from hunger, and who were constantly shouting for "*Bread, Bread!*" but now, all seemed to have gone crazy and are shouting "*Glory, hallelujah!*" singing "*Home sweet home,*" "*We'll Rally Round the Flag, Boys,*" each group having a good time of its own. To our delighted astonishment, the prison authorities allow all this to go on without any remonstrance or interference whatever. What can it all mean?

We are now demonstrating our ingenuity by representing the dead men as still in the land of the living and drawing their rations as when they were living in fact. These extra rations we divide among the actual living, giving us a handsome increase in our rations. This has been done for about two weeks, unobserved by the prison authorities, and now it is done at a wholesale rate, which causes the authorities to congratulate themselves that the death list is diminishing. Poor fools; they are woefully deceived! But we are willing that they should be deceived as long as it gives us more food.

January 31st. I was up all night with Comrade Judson. He seems to be much better this morning. We secured some medicine from the hospital surgeon in the shape of sumach berries, to be boiled like tea and drank. It is a very simple remedy, but we hope it will be beneficial to the sick man.

The one employment of the prisoners now is speculation on the truthfulness or falsity of exchange rumors. The report is now abroad that the sutler brought a paper into the prison and showed it to some of the boys, which contained an editorial to the effect that next week we would be taken out of here. If this report should prove to be false, the effect upon the prisoners will be very disastrous, and will result in an increase of the death rate, and, I fear also, of the number of maniacs.

There are no further reports from the hunting parties who have been after the fugitives. No captives have been brought in since the 26th of this month. It does seem incredible that so many could escape the dogs and the hot pursuit of their enemies. Perhaps some were captured and left lying where they were taken. These ghouls are capable of committing any degree of atrocity their murderous hearts move them to commit.

Some of the old guards are in charge of the water squad to-day. I was one of the detail in the afternoon, but the officer in charge would not allow any trading to be done, and so I had to return without accomplishing anything. I have been out of tobacco since yesterday morning, and but for the interference of the officer, I could have secured a plug of tobacco while out after water. The squad detailed to get wood has to pass so near headquarters that it is impossible to do any trading on that route; even the guards are watched so closely that we cannot do any trading with them.

CHAPTER XXI.

I SUCCEED IN GETTING TOBACCO - A HIGH-TONED PATRON
HOPES ARE RISING - A SALE, AND AN ENCOURAGING
INTERVIEW - WE ADOPT A JOHNNIE - PLANNING HIS ESCAPE
PRISON PRAYER MEETINGS - RELIGIOUS DESTITUTION
THOUGHTS OF EXCHANGE - OUR FIRST ISSUE OF CLOTHING
ROBBED BY MAJOR GEE - MAKE MY LAST RING - VISITED BY
MAJOR GEE - HIS BRUTAL CHARACTER

February 1st. Nothing unusual has transpired to day. Judson is better this morning, the universal excitement over the exchange is helping to restore his health. George Edmonds, of my company, went out with the water squad to-day. I gave him a ring to take out with him and trade for tobacco if an opportunity offered. He was successful, and now we are the happy possessors of a treasure beyond price—a plug of tobacco. What joy it brings to all our hearts as we roll the sweet morsel under our tongues!

February 2nd. While I was at the sutler's tent this morning, a Lieutenant of the young "tar-heel" regiment was there inquiring of the sutler if he had any of them Yankee-made finger rings for sale. Being answered in the negative, I told him I would make him one tomorrow. After a few preliminaries were settled I received the contract to make a ring for his royal nibs. What an important contract that was! The price was to be ten dollars; the ornaments on it were to be two hearts. After taking the size of his finger, I went to my dugout and was unkind enough to allow myself to think that he needed more brains than hearts. Judging from his appearance and conduct he needed both, but not of the kind my poor skill could manufacture. It was amusing as well as disgusting to see him lay down a $1000 bill and ask the sutler to give him small bills in exchange. He seemed to do it with such disdain and with as little concern as a small boy would banter another to trade marbles.

February 3rd. Nothing occurred to disturb the quiet and peace of the "stockade family" yesterday. The usual routine of prison life went on. Judson is feeling much better. Hopes of exchange are rising, as rumors are numerous that negotiations are going on, and prisoners from other rebel pens are constantly leaving for our lines. We have received tidings that we are to leave here as soon as transportation can be furnished.

I finished the ring to-day, and this evening the young dandy "tarheel" Lieutenant met me at the sutler's tent after roll-call, according to agreement. He paid me the ten dollars like a man. I made bold to ask him if he would give me any information about the rumors of exchange now being circulated among the prisoners. He replied that the rumor was correct and true, that we would leave here as soon as transportation could be furnished us. I remarked that these rumors had been quite frequently circulated in the prison, but had always proved to be false, and I had become skeptical about putting my faith in them, because when they proved to be untrue the disappointment was a great shock to men as weak mentally and physically as we were.

"Well, sir," he said, *"this one is true. I give you my honah on that."*

This gave me some good encouragement. With the ten dollars I got from my "tar-heel" Lieutenant I purchased three small sweet potatoes and about one-half of a ration of bread. The bread kept by the sutler for sale is of the same quality as that issued to us for rations. His stock-in-trade is bread, potatoes, onions, black pepper, boiled beef, rice and cow-peas, all of which he sells for an enormous price. Owing to the scarcity of money he does not carry on a very thriving business.

February 4th. To-day one of the rebel convicts—a mere stripling of a boy, came to our dugout and told Connely and myself that he had been conscripted in the rebel army, had deserted twice, and while being taken the second time he had stabbed a rebel officer, and he was here awaiting trial. He was confident the Union prisoners were going to leave very soon, and he was afraid he would be handled roughly after we left. He asked us if we could not in some way aid him to get out of the Confederacy. He was not to exceed 18 years old, and was an innocent looking youth. He was blind in one eye. We put all confidence in his veracity and honesty, and told him we would see what we could do for him. We were afraid the disfigurement of his blind eye would make it hard to effect his escape without being detected, and we might get ourselves into trouble. But he pleaded with us so earnestly, assuring us that if he was detected we would not be implicated. We finally told him we would consider the matter. It was arranged that he should come back the next day and we would decide what we would do in his case. After he left we decided to do what we could to help him get away, and finally hit on the plan of naming the kid "Jacob Berry." This was the name of a member of our company who was killed on the railroad while going home on a sick furlough, near Joliet, Illinois, August, 1863.

February 5th. The weather is quite chilly this morning, but the excitement runs so high we forget all about the cold. The belief is becoming fixed in our minds that this will be the last Sabbath day we shall spend in this miserable den. Every Sabbath Day prayer meetings have been held in different parts of the stockade, but on this Sabbath all praying people have assembled near the west end of the ground. The meeting was largely attended, and great interest was manifested. Many prayers from true contrite hearts went up to God in faith, believing that He would hear and answer us. During this prayer meeting the young "tar-heels" near the assemblage ceased to walk their beats and became interested hearers. Since we entered this stockade there has not been a single minister of any sect to visit us, except the Catholic priest. It appears that we are not even counted worthy to have the comforts and help of Religion extended to us.

February 6th. Out Johnnie came around this morning to see what we had concluded to do in his case. We told him we had decided to aid him all we could, but he must be very cautious, and if he was detected by the rebel authorities he was not to let them know that we were aiding him. We told him to trade his cap for a broad brimmed hat, which would help to disguise him as well as to hide his blind eye. We also told him he must adopt the name of "Jacob Berry, Co. I, 22nd Iowa Infantry," and be paroled under that name. We wrote it down on a piece of paper and gave it to him, so he would become familiar with it, and when he was around us we would call him by that name. We also told him where we were from, where we enlisted, who was our Captain, all in order that he might be somewhat familiar with our history in case he was questioned. We cautioned him not to be seen in our company too frequently, for fear his associates might suspicion him. When the time came (if it ever did) when we should go out, he was to fall into ranks near us, and if questioned as to where he belonged, to answer that he belonged to the 22nd Iowa Infantry. In this way our plans were laid to help a brother man to gain his freedom and escape the cruelties of his own kindred.

February 7th. The night has gradually worn away. Our expectation of what is to take place during the next few days makes the nights long and wearisome. It is natural for men to hope, especially when situated so unfortunately as we are. Comrade Judson is slowly improving, and under favorable conditions he may recover sufficiently to reach our lines, but if this rumor should turn out like the others the disappointment will no doubt hasten him to the grave. It is difficult to control our thought. Fancy runs wild and dwells upon scenes of pleasure and comfort from which we are now excluded. When the strong spirit returns from its wanderings week and weary, how natural it is for the body to sympathisize with it. Such are the wearying struggles we engage in until we sink into a kind of despondency, which scarcely cares whether we live or die.

February 8th. Rations of bread were issued to us earlier than usual this morning. The Sergeants of the different squads were ordered to report at the north gate, where they were informed that the Federal Government had sent us some clothing and for them to take charge of it and issue it out to the men. On November 10th muster roll for rations was 12,500; our number last night at roll call was 6,050. Each squad was counted and clothing issued to squads according to number. It was then issued to the men of each squad as far it would go. Those most needy were first supplied–there being one blanket for every three men. Seven pairs of pants and twelve overcoats were issued to our squad, which numbered sixty-nine men. There were no shirts, drawers, blouses or socks allotted to us. Our allowance of shoes consisted of three pairs. I was barefooted, my feet being wrapped in a pair of old pants legs, but it seems that others needed shoes worse than I did, so I got none. I was thankful we were so fortunate as to procure a blanket for Connely, Crocker and myself. This we gave to our sick comrade, Judson, which he needed so much.

It now penetrated my cranium where all those new clothes our barbarous, murdering guards were wearing came from. All through this long and severe winter, while we have been nearly naked and suffering untold agony from cold and exposure, these scoundrels have been wrapped in our blankets, shod with our new shoes and comfortable in new Union clothing, all of which our government sent here for our use, having shipped an abundance of clothing here early in the winter, expecting that the rebel authorities would be honorable enough to give the articles to us, but which they did not. Instead of that, they put them on their own troops, who were shooting our poor fellows to their death, in cold blood, and heaping all manner of indignities on us. There is not a shadow of a doubt but that the rebel authorities promised our government at Washington they would give the prisoners whatever was sent to make them more comfortable. But they lied and stole from the men they were killing and mutilating with blood hounds. *Can my readers imagine anything more barbarous than this? Savage Indians are possessed of more honor and mercy.*

February 9th. Comrade Judson continues to improve. He was able to sit up awhile to-day. We feel very anxious to have him recover strength sufficient to enable him to move with us when the time for exchange comes. We are all certain that under skillful medical treatment and nursing he will be restored to health.

To-day I exhausted my stock of rubber. I shall keep this ring and take it home with me as a present for my wife and as evidence of my skill and industry while an inmate of Salisbury Prison. I suppose my wife has long ago given me up as dead, but if I had just one month's diet of our old-fashioned hard tack and "sow bosom," with a generous supply of Uncle Sam's good coffee thrown in, I believe I could make these "tar-heels" believe I was the liveliest corpse they ever handled. It would be so sweet to take revenge on them for wearing the clothing they so maliciously stole from us during the winter. I often imagined I had met with grievances which made me mad–real mad–but never before in all my life have I felt towards any human being as I do towards these "tar-heels" from North Carolina. I am compelled to watch them day after day wearing the clothing which ought to be covering our poor, naked, shivering bodies. It is more than human nature can bear. But this only indicates what southern rebels are at heart.

February 10th. Many anxious inquiries were made to-day as to the probable time when we are to be relieved of this great mental strain concerning our exchange, but no definite or satisfactory answers were elicited.

Major Gee entered the prison to-day, accompanied by three of his understrappers and held a short conversation with the sutler. Then he walked around the stockade as if he were looking for some one he had lost, and finally made his exit at the little gate. No one could muster up courage enough to ask him for information concerning our release. The very sight of the man is repulsive. It is easy to read the true character of the brute by the cast of his countenance. The very features of the man's face portray his inwards depravity. To one who comprehends the capabilities of the human soul, there is something terrible in its perversions. The higher and nobler the purpose to which the life is devoted, the darker and deeper the infamy into which the soul may be plunged when it is sold into sin, and is dominated by viciousness. Demons grow from germs that might have brought forth angels. Such is the character of Major Gee. It seems as though he is dead to all the better feelings of humanity. He is prepared to commit any crime against God and man, or both. The evil passion of his depraved nature is so strong and active that he is ready to use every means within his power to increase and intensify the sufferings of his helpless victims.

CHAPTER XXII.

Friendship gifts - Hope and fear - An inquiry and its
result - Hope brightened - A preacher and his
sermon - An unappreciative congregation - Great
anxiety - Trying to make a maniac understand - Rain
and mud - Bad tempered men - Excitement, hope and
fear - A trade and ring making - Seeking for news
Auringer's death - How news spreads - Terrible
condition of the hospital - Death rate decreasing
Wood sergeants to report their men - Our day of
deliverance arrives - Exciting scenes - Our johnnie
happy - The dead list.

February 11th. About dusk last night L. K. Auringer, of the 81st New York, came to me and gave me a pressing invitation to join a party of which he had means of escape to-night. I courteously declined his kind invitation not wishing to run the desperate and almost hopeless chance of escaping the ever-watchful guards. Then I knew I would have to battle against the ferocious blood hounds which would certainly be put on our track as soon as our absence was discovered. Much as I desired to taste the sweets of liberty, and grateful as I felt to the kind comrade who out of the goodness of his heart was willing to give me the opportunity of realizing my earnest desires; yet, situated as I was, barefoot, almost naked, worn and wasted with long and severe suffering, I know I would not be able to make my way through an unknown country abounding in bitter enemies. All these considerations, to which was added the dread of being devoured by blood hounds, as some of our poor fellows in their efforts to escape had been, made the probability of final escape so small that I had to decline the privilege offered to me. I wished him God-speed, and hoped he would be greatly successful. Comrade Auringer, as I have already stated, was a skillful worker in bone, making bone bibles, rings and other trinkets. As he turned to go, he handed me a beautiful little bone Bible, and said to me:

"Comrade, take this home, and when you look upon it, remember me."

In return for his beautiful gift, I gave him one of my finger rings, made of rubber, and said to him:

"Comrade Auringer, our friendship since our acquaintance was formed here, has been mutual. I will always remember you. Take this ring, and if you live to get home, put it where you will often see it, and when your eyes behold it, remember me then."

Discouragement is beginning to invade the prison; many are beginning to think there is no foundation for the report of our exchange and release, therefore, we are again doomed to be disappointed. Our adopted Johnnie came to us this morning and told us he had heard all the Federal prisoners had left Andersonville on exchange, and that we would soon be released from this prison. However, we surmise that the advance of Sherman's army has had a great deal to do with the removal of the prisoners from Andersonville. We have not had any information concerning his movements, as no "fresh fish" (the name given to new prisoners), have been brought here since the colored prisoners came in early in the winter. We want it distinctly understood that Salisbury Prison is open only to distinguished and selected company, viz., colored troops and "barn burners from the Shenandoah Valley." I determined to make a desperate effort to learn something of our prospective destiny, so I went to the hospital, took my station at the door, and waited until the rebel surgeon came out. When he appeared, I mustered up courage enough to ask him if he would be kind enough to tell me if he knew when we would be paroled. He answered me that he did not know just when it would be done but that we would be released as soon as transportation could be had. I replied that if they would grant us the privilege, we would willingly march and live on the wind. All we craved was the privilege of getting out of this place. Here our conversation ended. That there is some prospect of our going out is certain, but when the day will come is all too uncertain for comfort.

The news that Andersonville prisoners had been released was false. Andersonville prisoners were not released until April, 1865.

The memory of last night's parting with Comrade Auringer still lingers with me. I feel lonesome since he is gone. Our acquaintance began in this vile prison and we soon became warm friends. We had aided each other in many ways, but now he is gone and I am left. I laid awake all night expecting every moment to hear the rattle of musketry and the shrieks of wounded men. The night was very still. I could distinctly hear the steady tramp, tramp of the rebel guards as they walked their beats, eagerly wishing for an opportunity to distinguish themselves by shooting a Yank. I could hear them cry out in genuine southern dialect:

"Post number f-o-a-h; f-o-a-h o'clock and all is well."

This was taken up by post number five, and so on all around the stockade. This was repeated by the guards every half hour in order to let the prison authorities know they were on the alert.

February 12th. Judson is much better this morning. Exchange stock is at a high rate of premium again. The rate was raised by a minister of the Gospel who came in this Sabbath day to preach to us "barn burners." We have been in this prison over four months and not until to-day has a single minister come to us to preach the Word of Eternal Life to give us comfort and strength. I did not hear the text from which this one preached. His harangue was simply an apology for our captors. He excused their barbarous treatment of us on the ground that the Confederacy was not in a condition financially to provide us with better quarters and food. *"But now,"* said he, *"before another week rolls around you will be within your own lines, or, at least, on the road there."* He hoped we would carry no animosity with us, *"for, my friends,"* said he, *"we have not had the means to supply your wants as we should have done, if we were able."* The impudent hypocrisy of this fellow who disgraces the sacred office of the ministry by calling us "friends," and apologizing for the barbarous treatment we have received from our enemies, aroused within me a feeling of intense indignation. If we were friends, where had he been that he had not come to preach to our needy souls the Word of Eternal Life which we needed so much? I seriously disturbed his peaceful soul by asking him where the clothing was that Uncle Sam had sent to us? That, certainly, has been "available" to the Confederacy, from the way the guards were dressed. Someone in the rear of the audience yelled at him that *"The animosity of both rebels and the graybacks would be apt to stick to the Yankees!"*

His sermon failed to have its desired effect, and when he discovered

191

that fact, he brought it to a speedy close by bidding us all a very Christian(?) and affectionate farewell. However, his sermon had one good effect, it confirmed our hopes of exchange and release, not because he was a so-called minister, but because we believed he would not have made us this visit, and said what he did unless the day of our departure was near at hand. Every man who can walk is on the move, so that the inside of the stockade has the appearance of a bee-hive. Notwithstanding a heavy snow is falling.

February 13th. The terrible anxiety we are enduring is a very great strain on the nervous system of men whose vitality is already greatly reduced by long starvation, sickness and suffering. Anxious eyes are momentarily looking for the gates to be opened to admit the messengers who are to bear to us the glad tidings that the obstacles which have so long stood between us and liberty are at last removed. How eager we are to hear the welcome message that will give ease to aching hearts and food to empty stomachs! The suspense is terrible.

Only two of the maniacs are now living. This morning a comrade was trying to make one of them understand that we were going to leave here soon, and then we would go to where there was plenty of bread. But the effort was a failure. No change of mental condition was visible in his countenance. The cry of the poor fellow was:

"Bread, Bread!"

His eyes had a wild, staring gaze. His countenance was a true index to his mental and physical agony.

Bread was issued to us to-day. For some reason there is more activity on the railroad than usual; trains are coming and going more frequently. They seem to be heavy freight trains, but the nature of them we cannot tell.

February 14th. The weather has become quite mild. A hard rain fell during the night, but the morning is clear and bright, making it quite pleasant overhead, but very muddy and disagreeable under foot. Notwithstanding the mud, every man who can be on his feet and able to walk, is on the move from place to place, hoping to hear some bit of news that will confirm the hopes we have been cherishing for so many days. One thing is quite noticeable among the prisoners, viz.: the estrangement which seems to prevail between the eastern and western soldiers. There is not much social life between them. The New Yorkers occupy the extreme east end of the prison ground, and are almost constantly fighting among themselves. It is nothing unusual to see a fight in that quarter every hour in the day, and they often take place between those who are the best of friends. The fact is, every one feels so ill-natured that

> There seems to have been considerable animosity between eastern and western Union troops during the Civil War. Reasons in many circumstances were nothing more than petty jealousy and simple "boyishness." When troops of the east and west gathered in Washington DC after the close of the war for its greatest spectacle—The Grand Review of the Army—numerous fights broke out between soldiers of the Army of the Potomac from the east and Sherman's troops, most of whom were from the western states.

it does not take much to get a fight started on short notice. To say they all are cross is to use a mild expression.

February 15th. Judson can now sit up a part of each day. Crocker cannot walk very much, his feet are so tender. The rest of our squad are in reasonable health. The chief topics of conversation this morning are, the evacuation of this place and bread. The rebel preacher said last Sunday we would be within our own lines, or on the road, before the next Sabbath day would dawn, but if either be true a move will have to be made very soon. Excitement runs high, mingled with grave doubts and fears, but the uneasiness which seems to prevail among the guards, and the moving of so many trains, means something. The anxiety can be easily discovered in the face of every rebel we see, but the cause we cannot tell as they will not divulge it to us.

February 16th. This morning I made another trade. I traded two brass buttons for the back of a rubber comb, and spent the day making another finger ring. There is so much excitement that it is difficult to do any kind of work. One wants to sit still and see the excited groups of men going from one part of the pen to another, seeking to learn the latest reports. A man may start a favorable report and in a half hour's time go to another part of the prison, when he will be sure to hear the same report told with such emphasis and candor that he concludes it came direct from good authority. Thus hope is kept alive in the hearts of men who would otherwise sink under the load of despair.

February 17th. This morning I took a stroll over the east side to see the boys of my regiment who are stationed there. The same state of excitement is manifest there that prevails in other parts of the prison. A report started at the east side will speedily sweep westward, gathering many additions as it moves along. It is not like the traditional "rolling stone" which is said to gather no moss, because a very slight camp rumor concerning our exchange gathers great crowds of eager listeners who attend to all that is rehearsed and then carry their own versions of it to others just as eager to hear.

I walked through the brick hospital on my return, and the sights which are presented to the eye are appalling. It is not so cold outside the building as it has been, and the vast hordes of vermin are literally eating up the poor, helpless victims who are confined there. The vermin are so numerous that the dust and straw on the dirt floors seem as though they were literally alive, while the fragments of clothing which partially cover the poor, emaciated bodies of the sick men are so covered with them that it is impossible to tell the color of the garment. If one stands still in one place, for even a few moments, they will crawl up his legs like ants from an ant hill.

February 18th. This is the last day of the week and the prediction, or promise, of our preacher has failed to materialize, because we are neither in "God's Country," nor on the way there. One thing is sure, the close of each day brings us nearer the time when we will go out from here, but the question is, how will we go out? The manner of our going is what we are the most deeply concerned about at present. To march out to liberty would be much more preferable than to go out by way of the dead-house; and yet, how many poor fellows must go by the latter route before the blessing of the former is made available to them.

Owing to the favorable weather the death rate is becoming somewhat smaller, but the prison authorities are not entitled to any credit for it. They have made no exertion towards diminishing the death rate. I am quite sure if it was within their power, they would increase rather than decrease it. I visited the citizen prisoners to-day and find their numbers are diminishing at about the same ratio as the other prisoners. This evening as the wood choppers came to the gate they were halted and the officer of the guard informed them that their services as wood choppers would be no longer needed. He requested each man to hand him his parole by which he was allowed to pass out of the stockade to cut and bring in wood. Two days supply of wood is generally kept on hand, and as these wood-men are not discharged it certainly means that the time of our departure is not far distant.

February 19th. When we are to leave here and where we shall go is the theme of conversation all over the prison grounds. A report has been started that an army is marching towards this place, and we are to be shipped farther south. This is not generally believed, and would be a disastrous thing if it should prove to be true. The report has been brought in by the water squad that we are to be taken to Wilmington, N.C., and there exchanged. One thing is certain, we are going to leave this place but when we are going time alone can tell.

The rebel preacher did not put in his appearance to-day. I suppose he discovered from the treatment he received last Sunday that his visit was not very acceptable. As a consequence we got no rebel sermon to-day, and I fear we have lost the friendship of one minister of the Gospel—such as he is.

February 20th. Our rations came to us this morning, in quantity the loaf being much smaller than usual. Our adopted Johnnie came over to our dugout to-day in a state of great excitement. He said a rebel officer was in the "devil's den" last evening counting the convicts, and he is afraid the convicts will be taken out before the soldier prisoners go, and if they do, they will get him sure. He said one of the guards informed him we were to leave to-day or tomorrow. Trains are coming and going, and on the arrival of each train, the boys are ready to bet that is our train. The suspense we are enduring is painful; hope has been the only staff on which we have leaned, and by it men who are walking skeletons have been kept up and saved from breaking down and dying; while others have become despondent and, according to the vernacular of the prison, have made "fat corpses."

This evening I made a visit to market square to hear the latest reports and imagine my surprise when I saw Gilman, Auringer's brother-in-law, who made his escape on the night of the 10th with him and others. He informed me that they were tracked in the snow on Sunday night, the 12th, and he was recaptured. The others ran in different directions and in the chase one man was killed and he believed it to be Auringer.

Thus another noble spirit was ushered into the presence of his Maker, sent thither by the brutal hand of a murderer. How long, oh God, how long will such fearful atrocities be allowed?

~ ~ ~ ~ ~

The tidings of Auringer's death was sad news to me. I was fortunate in forming a very close and happy acquaintance with this comrade in the early part of our imprisonment. He was a whole-souled genial fellow, of a happy disposition, always looking on the bright side of things; seldom despondent himself, he always had a word of cheer for his associates. When we bade each other farewell on the night of the 10th inst., he had great hope of reaching our lines. We spent an hour together that evening building "castles in the air." When we parted he promised me if he succeeded in reaching our lines, he would write immediately to my wife, and added in a jocular way:

"I'll be making love to her before you get home."

To which I replied:

"All right."

And then in the darkness we parted, he to escape, only to die a horrible death—I to live a little longer, and still suffer what is worse than death. The bone Bible which he presented to me when he left, I carefully preserved through the remainder of my imprisonment, and on my return home gave it to my wife. While I am copying these lines from the original bits of paper on which they were written while I was in prison (thirty years after the tragic incident took place) it lies on the desk before me, and is one of the most dearly-prized treasures of our household. The ring I gave poor Auringer never reached its destination. I am convinced that it became the property of some heartless, murderous rebel.

~ ~ ~ ~ ~

February 21st. Rations were issued to us earlier than usual. The commanders of squads were ordered to report to the officers at the gate promptly at 12 o'clock noon. When they had reported they were ordered to make a report of the number in each squad who were not able to march, in order that transportation might be furnished for them, but all who were able must march to Greensboro, a distance of about sixty miles, from which place transportation will be furnished us to our lines. Our departure is to take place tomorrow. When the Sergeants came in

196

and announced the welcome news, the commotion began. Such shouting and singing! No tongue nor pen can describe the joy and happiness this welcome message brought to the prisoners. Handshaking was the order of the hour, reminding one of an old-fashioned Methodist love-feast. Crocker's feet were too sore to permit him to walk, and Judson was too weak, so they were both put on the list for transportation. The rest of our little dugout family were willing to undertake the overland route. Our Johnnie was as happy as the rest of us, and kept clear of any rebel officer who chances to pass through the stockade.

After receiving the joyful news of our release tomorrow, Connely and I went to the dead-house and copied from the register a list of the dead from October 6th, 1864 to February 21st, 1865, at noon. The number of deaths for the 138 days aggregates 3,800. There has been a large number taken to the hospitals outside the stockade from time to time and the number of deaths there we have no means of obtaining, but from the best information we have from the death list there will be added to the following number five hundred more, making a total of four thousand and three hundred.

In the hospitals there are several hundred who are so emaciated by long starvation and suffering that are too weak to be moved, and unless speedy relief comes to their aid they, too, must soon follow their dead comrades who sleep in the unknown graves of Salisbury Prison, victims of a barbarous foe.

~ ~ ~ ~ ~

In the month of April following our release, when General [George} Stoneman captured the town and prison, the rebels burned the books to prevent them from falling into the possession of our Government and their terrible crime be discovered. The following (table 1, page 198) is the only record now in existence, so far as I know, and that covers only the short space of 138 days, and inside the prison only.

TABLE 1

DAILY DEATHS IN SALISBURY PRISON FROM OCTOBER, 1864 THROUGH FEBRUARY, 1865, AS RECORDED FROM THE PRISON'S REGISTER OF THE DEAD BY BENJAMIN F. BOOTH

October		November		December		January		February	
Date	Deaths	Date	Deaths	Date	Deaths	Date	Deaths	Date	Deaths
1		1	19	1	58	1	40	1	23
2		2	28	2	48	2	40	2	20
3		3	34	3	37	3	33	3	25
4		4	23	4	29	4	34	4	43
5		5	34	5	40	5	34	5	14
6	1	6	19	6	29	6	28	6	24
7	1	7	22	7	37	7	39	7	20
8	2	8	17	8	34	8	26	8	29
9	2	9	26	9	28	9	34	9	17
10	1	10	19	10	36	10	16	10	26
11	3	11	23	11	48	11	22	11	23
12	1	12	32	12	34	12	40	12	24
13	3	13	37	13	35	13	23	13	18
14	3	14	19	14	34	14	39	14	24
15	2	15	29	15	40	15	31	15	24
16	11	16	19	16	29	16	34	16	20
17	13	17	23	17	34	17	26	17	19
18	12	18	36	18	28	18	36	18	8
19	8	19	19	19	38	19	29	19	16
20	12	20	26	20	26	20	19	20	19
21	7	21	37	21	36	21	18	21	11
22	12	22	37	22	42	22	27		
23	12	23	31	23	48	23	32		
24	29	24	34	24	48	24	18		
25	19	25	53	25	65	25	26		
26	13	26	59	26	24	26	29		
27	19	27	52	27	37	27	39		
28	29	28	59	28	39	28	36		
29	23	29	46	29	31	29	23		
30	10	30	57	30	55	30	37		
31	19	31	35	31	27				
	267		969		1,164		942		458

GRAND TOTAL = 3,800

PART 4

FREEDOM & BACK HOME

Finally on February 22, 1865, came the day Booth and his comrades at Salisbury Prison hoped for–release from the confines of "Rebel Hell." Their return to freedom began with those emaciated and dejected souls who were the most ill. Booth and those who were with him were received with open arms as heroes by Union troops once they were back inside Union lines. Their misery was not over, however, as the effects of months of confinement and deprivation which had worn them to nearly nothing made recuperation difficult. For some, the trip home would be not only their last Civil War adventure, but also the last adventure of their life. It was nearly so for Booth.

On April 13, 1865, as Sherman's troops made their way across North Carolina in the waning days of the war, Salisbury Prison was officially liberated and burned by General George Stoneman. At war's end the Union had captured 462,634 Confederates. Of this total, 247,769 were parolled on the field, principally in various surrenders as the war wound down. Confederates had captured 200,000-211,000 Union soldiers. An estimated 25,976 Confederate and 30,218 Union soldiers died in prison.

CHAPTER XXIII.

THE DAY OF JUBILEE HAS COME - THE SICK REMOVED TO THE
CARS - MAJOR GEE ANNOUNCES OUR RELEASE AND
DEPARTURE - A CRAZY LOT - MARCHING OUT OF HELL
"FAREWELL YE NOBLE DEAD!" - PEN PICTURE OF MYSELF AND
CONNELY - THE MARCH TOWARDS FREEDOM AND HOME
OUR FIRST CAMP - THE WOLF LIES DOWN WITH THE LAMB
PEACEFUL SLEEP AND A JOYFUL AWAKENING - ON THE ROAD
AGAIN - I TRADE A RING FOR "SOW BOSOM" - A PERILOUS
CROSSING - TWO MEN DROWNED
OUR SECOND NIGHT'S CAMP

February 22nd. This morning the prison was in commotion at an early hour. Three days' rations were issued to each man—one loaf for each instead of for two, as it was in the prison. One-half of the guards were taken from the stockade, the big gate was opened, and the sick that were able were ordered to be moved out. They were moved to the railroad and placed on the cars, their intimate friends rendering them all the service they could. Crocker walked out and was put into a stock car. Each car was filled to its utmost capacity; some of the poor fellows had to stand, others were piled around wherever room could be found for them to lie down. The sick were loaded by 11 o'clock (leaving a great many who were too weak to be moved at all). A guard lined the road on either side, taking great care that none should escape. Poor fools, this precaution was entirely unnecessary; not a man of us, sick or well, desired to remain in this accursed country any longer than he had to.

Between 11 and 12 o'clock Major Gee climbed on the stockade, took his position at a sentinel's stand, and informed us that we were now to start on our journey to our lines, and owing to the amount of business being done on the railroad to Greensboro, it was impossible to furnish us transportation, but it would be furnished to us from that point to our lines. Here let me digress long enough to say that during the last three months there have been from one to four maniacs in prison. Then the number was reduced to two, and on last Saturday one of them died, leaving only one. But judging from the scenes that took place after he had ceased talking, one would have good reason to say that all had gone crazy. Some would curse him, some sing, while others would pray. The confusion of tongues was as great as at the building of the Tower of Babel.

About half past 12 o'clock the men were formed into column and marched out at the north gate, protected on each side by a heavy guard of rebel soldiers. What a splendid opportunity this was for some artist to gain renown by drawing a picture of this ragged, emaciated army. It looked more like an army of skeletons than an army of men. But little did we care how we looked. We were at last, Thank God, outside the awful living hell–Salisbury Prison pen. The joy of our release; the knowledge that we were on our road to freedom and to home, and the bright anticipations of the future made us perfectly oblivious to so many brave comrades who were near and dear to us by the close association of prison life, with its mutual sorrows and sufferings. We may leave you behind, brave, noble, loyal comrades, but as long as memory survives we will never forget you! Brave and true soldiers ye were indeed! Every man might have saved his life and procured his release by accepting the seductive inducements of the rebel recruiting officers who so often invaded the prison. But no; ye preferred honorable death to a dishonorable life, the price of which must be treason to our flag. We shall ever remember your noble heroism and unswerving fidelity to your country. That holy Flag for which you have died will yet wave triumphant over treason and rebellion–the Flag of a united Nation–the land of the free and the home of the brave. Your names will be enshrined in the affections of a loyal and grateful people, while the names of your murderers will be a foul stench in the nostrils of all the peoples of the earth. With profound sorrow we leave you behind. Your resting places will be unknown to men, but they will be known to Him whose eye sees the flight of a sparrow, and whose love has counted even the hair of your heads. Comrades dead and beloved, farewell, when we meet again it may be to hear from Him who deals out justice tempered with mercy to all, and welcome, "Well done, good and faithful servant, enter thou into the joy of thy word!"

~ ~ ~ ~ ~

Perhaps my readers would like to have me give them, as well as I can, a description of myself as I looked when I marched out of Salisbury Prison this memorable day. It will be a difficult task, but I will make the attempt.

First, as to my cooking outfit. It consisted of an old fruit can, a wooden spoon, a case-knife, and a long-handled frying pan. The frying pan was a partnership utensil which we had smuggled through Major Turner's revenue office when we removed from Libby Prison without his stamps of approval being placed upon it, and which we were now keeping as a relic of that event. I was also in possession of two rubber finger rings which I made during the last few days I spent in the prison, and which I wanted to take home to my wife. In order to overcome the temptation to trade them off, I put them on the third finger, on which they fitted very tightly. In this way I hoped to succeed in getting them home, knowing how well my wife would treasure a relic of this kind, especially as it was made by myself in the prison. For shoes, I wore a pair of moccasins made out of the legs of an old pair of pants, taken from the dead body of a comrade. My shirt was so dilapidated that it was not strong enough to hold a patch, while the left sleeve had disappeared altogether. My pantaloons, or what, out of respect and courtesy, I called pantaloons, were a monument of carefull, but hopeless, patching. The lower extremities were some considerable distance above my ankles, while their general condition provided my body with plenty of fresh air. My blouse, much the worse for long and continuous wear when I was captured, was now a hopeless mass of ruins, and was of the seventeen year locust pattern, split up the back. What there was left of it, was held together with strings, and unfortunately, the same sleeve was gone that was missing from my shirt. For this reason I was compelled to turn my blouse wrong side out, that I might treat both arms with some sort of fairness. Thus, neither naked nor clad, barefooted nor shod, hoodwinked as to our destination, with an old regulation cap covering my head, which gave me a heathenish appearance, I went out from Salisbury Prison in a condition that would have been a lasting disgrace to a third-class tramp of our day.

Perhaps a partial description of my friend Connely's appearance is needed to finish the picture. His shoes could scarcely be called "good," especially would they be accounted scarcely serviceable if the roads were muddy and wet, owing to the fact that he had used his knife on them too freely when captured, as he did his hat, in order to impress his thieving captors that they were scarcely worth taking from their lawful owner. The crown of his hat had long since departed into "innocuous deseutude," which gave the graybacks a fine opportunity of crawling out at the top to take a sun bath when their health and the weather would permit them to take such healthful exercise. His shirt had been on the grayback skirmish line so often that it required an assistant to help him adjust it on his noble frame (the frame was all that was left of him). His blouse, following the fashion of the day, was without a button, and almost sleeveless, and more holy than righteous. His pantaloons had shrunk until the two ends were trying to embrace each other.

In the condition I have tried to describe we started to take a regular old-fashioned, spread-eagle tour through a part of the Southern Confederacy, traveling with all the speed possible for a better "country," expecting in days to come to reap the reward to which we were fully entitled by reason of the terrible suffering we had endured.

~ ~ ~ ~ ~

February 22nd (continued). As night approached, the officer in charge conducted us to one side of the road and into the timber, where we went into camp. We soon had fires burning and prepared our burnt-bread coffee. We had three days rations and felt the necessity of governing ourselves accordingly–the temptation being very strong to eat it all at this first meal taken on the road to liberty and home. Blessed words! How sweet thy sound in the ears of a poor captive! After we had eaten sparingly of our scanty store, we gathered leaves and prepared our beds for the night. Not expecting any one to attempt to escape, and not caring if they did, rebels as well as Union men were soon wrapped in the silence of sleep. This was one instance, at least, where the wolf and the lamb lay down together. How blessed it is to be out where we can breathe the pure air of God's own giving. What a wonderful change from the stifled, foul smelling, disease-laden air we have been inhaling for nearly five months! It is glorious to be here and not there; new life and strength are coming to us already.

February 23rd. The dawning of this morning was hailed with inexpressible joy that we are not amid the disgusting, heart-sickening scenes and surroundings of the old stockade. We are beginning to feel like new men. Fires were blazing and we were soon enjoying their genial warmth. The nights are quite cold, and having very little covering for our bodies, we were quite chilled and the fire does us good. We prepared our usual burnt-bread coffee, and by eight o'clock were again on the road, with our faces and hearts turned towards home. My hunger being stronger than my discretion, I find I have already consumed the larger portion of my rations, and fearing I would run short, I started out to try and trade one of my rings for food.

In marching part of the guards are in the lead of the column, the rest bringing up the rear. Much to our astonishment we are allowed to travel as we please, and even to visit houses along the road. While we were passing a house this forenoon two ladies were standing in front to see the Yankees. I approached them, showed them my rings, and proposed to trade them one for some meat. One of the ladies went to the smoke-house and returned with a piece of "sow bosom" about four inches square and two inches thick, for which I gave her one of my rings. When I tried to take it off my finger I found just as I had hoped, my finger had swelled and it seemed very doubtful about my coming into possession of that much-coveted piece of dead swine. I tried soaping the finger, but that would not work. The lady was not going to be deprived of her "Yankee relic" so easily, so she told me to wait a moment and she would get the ring off my finger. Going into the house, she soon returned with a spool of thread and wrapped some of it about my finger below the ring. Her genius succeeded, and in a few moments the ring was in her hand, the "sow bosom" in mine, and two more souls were made happy. But it took the skill of a woman to do it.

About noon we came to the stream which, owing to recent rains, was bank full and the current running with terrible swiftness. The only way we had to get across was by walking on the railroad bridge which, under the most favorable conditions, was a dangerous undertaking. It was doubly so now owing to the slippery nature of the mud. The railroad bridges in this country are different kinds of structures to any I ever saw before. Generally they consist of a frame work built across the stream, on which timbers twelve inches square are laid and fastened. The rails are spiked in the center of their cross timbers, leaving only three and a half inches of space on either side of the rails to walk on. The danger of walking on such a narrow strip, over a swollen and rapidly flowing stream, is apparent to all. About one thousand men had to cross before I reached the bridge. Some would "coon" it across. Others would walk the stringers, placing a foot on each side of the rail and joining hands, would thus assist each other in the difficult task. I tried the latter plan, but concluded if I fell in I wanted to go by myself. After getting about half way across, I became dizzy and got down on my knees and "cooned" it the remaining distance, much to the delight of others, but with perfect satisfaction to myself. After reaching the other side of the stream, I stepped to one side and waited for Connely to cross, and while waiting, I heard a cry from the middle of the bridge. I looked in that direction and saw two men fall and strike the water together. They came to the surface and started for the shore near where I was standing, but the current was so strong and swift they could not make any headway, and so drifted down the stream. Every effort possible was made to rescue them, but to no purpose; they soon went down to rise no more. It was sad to think just as the poor fellows were on the threshold of liberty, and expecting soon to meet their loved ones, they went down to a watery grave. Thus their long-cherished hopes were blighted, and two more homes were left to mourn for the loved ones who would not return.

The column succeeded in getting across the stream without further accident, and wended its way through a dreary, desolate country. To our great delight and comfort the weather was fine, the sun was warm and shed its bright rays on our poor, half-clad bodies, which filled us with good cheer and hope, in spite of our general wretchedness. Our progress was very slow, the roads being quite muddy. My moccasins were in such a dilapidated condition that I was compelled to abandon them, and failing to find a substitute, I had to continue the journey barefooted. Owing to the fatigued condition of the prisoners, we went into camp quite early in an open field, or clearing, where we soon built up fires, and once more drew on our scanty rations. I had eaten about one half of my "sow bosom" raw during the afternoon, and a part of the remainder I put into the can in which I made my burnt-bread coffee, which made a rich cup of coffee, or soup, for my supper. After eating supper, we again prepared our beds and lay down for another night's rest under a clear sky, and in a pure atmosphere.

CHAPTER XXIV.

RATIONS ALL GONE - IMPROVISED SHOES - SICK AND DEAD
HUMANE OFFICERS - MY LAST RING GOES FOR BREAD
ON THE WAGON ROAD - CURIOSITY - FORAGING FOR FOOD
FLOUR AND SOUR MOLASSES - "WHO STOLE MY CORN?"
SUPPER AND A SLEEPLESS NIGHT - A STRANGE DISCOVERY
INTENSE SUFFERING - A TERRIFIC STORM - MY "SHOES"
ABANDONED - KEEN SUFFERING - GREENSBORO AND
RATIONS - OFF FOR RALEIGH - THE TOWN - NO RATIONS
A NOBLE DEED OF A NOBLE CHILD - OFF FOR
GOLDSBOROUGH - A POOR RAILROAD - GOLDSBOROUGH
HOME ANTICIPATIONS

February 24th. The night has passed and morning has again dawned. We are alive, but thoroughly chilled, the night having been very cold. We are now drawing on our last day's rations, and they are so reduced in quantity that it almost requires a magnifying glass to discover them. Fires are lighted and our scanty meal is soon prepared and eaten. We are now facing the painful fact that our rations are all gone and we are still two days distant from Greensboro, where, they tell us, they will take up our "tie passes" and allow us to ride the rest of the way. My feet are so sore this morning that it causes me great pain to walk barefooted. They burn as if they were frozen. Having no further use for the tent in which I have been carrying my food, I tied pieces of it about my feet as best I could, hoping in this way to protect them from the gravel roads over which we travel.

We started out between 8 and 9 o'clock, eager to reach the end of our journey. The good hope of reaching home acts as a stimulant to many who, under other circumstances, could not endure the fatigue of marching. After camp was cleared, five men were found who could not travel, being sick, with a very high fever. In addition to these, ten were reported

211

as having died during the night. The officer in command left one comrade and one guard to stay with the sick, giving them instructions to signal the first train passing and put them on board. It is evident our old friend, Major Gee, is not in command of this detachment, or such favors as this would not be shown to the sick. We are under the command of a Captain, who has two Lieutenants as his assistants, and so far, they have been kind enough to give us all the liberty we could ask for. This afternoon I was compelled to trade my last ring for bread and a piece of tobacco two inches square.

During the afternoon we left the railroad and began traveling on the wagon road, which is not so crooked, thereby saving about two miles of travel. The route along the public roads is thickly settled, and at every house we pass the doors and front yards are filled with women and children eagerly scrutinizing the Yankees. Many comical, and not very flattering remarks are made concerning our appearance. Some are afraid to come out of the doorway, and are ready to retreat in case a Yankee should move towards the house. During the day we crossed several streams on the railroad bridges and succeeded in crossing without any accident. We also crossed one stream on the wagon bridge, which is much safer and speedier than using the railroad bridges. We marched to a later hour to-day than usual, and consequently we are a tired and discouraged lot of human beings. The rations were all consumed in the morning. The slippery ties of the railroad, when we walked there, made to-day's march one of very intense suffering.

Before we went into camp for the night Connely and myself had all our corn bread eaten up, and we were still one day's march from Greensboro. It was thought we could cover the distance in three days, but we got such a late start on the 22nd, and the roads being so muddy, that it took us longer to make the trip. During the day stragglers were visiting farm houses in search of something to eat, but owing to their destitute circumstances the people were able to give them but very little. However, we succeeded in getting some sweet potatoes, corn and corn bread. Many persons came in from the plantations with pockets full of sugarcane seed, which made the best substitute for coffee we have found in Dixie. I found one generous lady who gave me two sweet potatoes. At another place I procured two good sized ears of corn. It was nearly dark when the head of the column halted and went into camp. The outlook was dreary and so disheartening. We were tired, hungry and foot-sore. About one hour after we went into camp, plantation carts were driven up loaded with flour and sour molasses. This was issued to us at the rate of about one pint of flour and about four ounces of molasses to each man. After we had received our rations Connely went out in search of water, and while he was gone I sat down on our blanket with the flour and molasses in front of me, and the sweet potatoes and corn under the blanket. When Connely returned with the water I mixed our flour into a sort of mush, and while he was boiling it I was going to parch the corn so we could enjoy some genuine corn-coffee. Imagine, if you can my feelings when I looked under the blanket to get my corn and found it was gone. When or how the two nice ears of corn were taken I could not tell, as I had not been away from the blanket a single moment. My disappointment at the loss of our treasure was so great, that the words uttered would scarcely be appropriate for these pages. I was certain I knew who had stolen the corn, but when, with many harsh and bitter words, I accused him of the theft, he stoutly denied the charge and strongly protested his innocence. But his protests and details neither satisfied my feeling nor appeased my appetite. The man was a member of my own regiment, but he was in such a wretched condition that I was certain he would not live to reach our lines, and for him to eat it was simply a waste of good food. What wretched, selfish, almost inhuman creatures starvation, abuse and suffering will make of men! We were cheated out of our coffee, but when our mush was cooked, we poured the sour molasses over it and, with our wooden spoons, made short work of it. We then ate our sweet potatoes, after which, the hour being late, we lay down on the wet ground, covering ourselves with the blanket, in which manner we passed a sleepless, wretched night.

February 25th. I find myself very weak and exhausted this morning. I am very feverish and my whole system is tortured by pain, Yesterday was one of the worst days I have passed since I was taken prisoner, and I am feeling the effects of it to-day. The suffering caused by the wet condition of my clothes was greatly augmented by consuming hunger.

Our adopted Johnnie came to us and gave us some sugar cane seed, which we parched and with which we made some coffee. We drank the coffee and ate the seed which, in a small way, served to appease our dreadful hunger.

The early morning was beautiful to behold, but the sky was soon over cast with dark clouds and a severe thunderstorm broke upon us. I think it was one of the worst storms I ever saw. It was accompanied by a drenching rain, which lasted three hours. We were without shelter or fire, and so were compelled to keep moving to avoid being chilled. The pieces of tent with which my feet were covered became so wet and heavy with water and mud that I could not keep them on my feet; I was compelled to abandon them and continue my journey barefooted.

After the rain ceased it remained cloudy and chilly until about 1 o'clock when, to our great delight, the sun came out bright and warm.

We are now nearing the end of our journey and are anxious to get the first glimpse of the town. Trains were running to and from it and we were often compelled to get to one side of the track to give them the right of way. About 2 o'clock we came in sight of the town, and a hearty hurrah was sent up from one end of the column to the other. A young "tar heel" asked if we were cheering their flag? One of our boys said that the people of Goldsborough saw us coming and thought it was Sherman's army approaching, and they had pulled down their old rag, and it would not be long until it was pulled down at Richmond.

Our progress was very slow and our suffering intense. While we could see the town and were so anxious to reach it, yet it was with the greatest difficulty we could muster strength enough to go on. Some were so fatigued and discouraged they felt like lying down by the roadside and giving up the struggle, but they were encouraged and urged forward by more hopeful, determined comrades, who reminded them that the fair land of freedom and of home was not far distant, and the victory would soon be ours. The officer in command also helped to encourage us forward by telling us that when we got to the town we would be served with rations, and ride the rest of our journey.

About 5 o'clock we entered Greensboro, more dead then alive, and were camped in the outskirts of the town, with a guard all about us. A good many of the boys were left by the roadside during the last few miles of our march, they being too weak to keep up. Some guards were left behind to accompany them as they became able to travel. Rations of corn bread were issued to us. The loaves were supposed to weigh one pound each. When the stragglers were all in and had eaten their corn bread, we were put on board the cars, destined for Raleigh, North Carolina. Our train pulled out of Greensborough at 9 o'clock p.m. We were piled on flat cars, there being only two or three box cars, and they were filled to their utmost capacity. It was my misfortune to be assigned to a flat car, and there were so many crowded on it, that those who sat on the edge of the car were in constant danger of being crowded off. I sat on the edge of the car, but took the precaution to place one foot against the iron stake and thus braced myself, making my position more safe. The speed of the train was very slow and the night air quite cold. Sleep was out of the question, especially to those who were situated as I was. The men who were seated on the floor of the car could get some sleep by putting their backs together, but sitting on the edge of the car was too dangerous a position to admit of going to sleep.

February 26th. We reached Raleigh about 8 o'clock this Sabbath morning, having passed through a night of great suffering. Soon after reaching the town we were unloaded and were soon surrounded by the citizens, who were anxious to see what a Yank looked like. We were interviewed and reviewed by both black and white, male and female, and if they formed their opinion of us from our present appearance, I am sure we would not be flattered by them. But it was brutes and demons of their own like who brought us into the condition we are in. When I got off the train my feet were so sore my knees and ankles ached so severely, I could not walk without assistance. We remained here until about 1 o'clock pm. Having eaten up all the bread issued to me at Greensborough I am now without any food to satisfy my hunger. If I had any money, or any relics to dispose of, I could have purchased food, but the only relics I have left are wrapped up in my piece of tent, and nothing could now tempt me to part with them. Some of the boys took a walk around town, but I was not able to walk, and even if I had been able to, I would not have gone, because I have seen all of this doomed Confederacy I want to see. I would be supremely happy if I could see the whole country falling into Hades!

When the command started for the depot it was with very great difficulty that I could stand on my feet, but the fair and beautiful homeland of which I had so often dreamed by night and by day seemed so near that I used my utmost exertions to walk. Connely came to my help by telling me that tomorrow we would see our flag once more. This put new strength into my aching limbs, and enabled me to march to the depot to take the train for freedom. The depot was four or five blocks away, and while we were marching along the street, and passing a small cottage, a little girl some five or six years old, came running towards me with a pair of old boots in her hands having the tops cut off at the instep. She reached them to me, saying:

"Here, soldier, is an old pair of boots; they are not very good ones, but they will keep your feet off the stones."

You may imagine my joy as well as my gratitude to the dear child. I immediately put them on, and from that day to this, I have never had any footgear I appreciated as I did those old boots. I thanked the little girl; placed my hand on her head and prayed for the blessing of God to rest upon her. In my haste, and the excitement of the moment, I forgot to ask her name, which I would be glad to have enshrined in my heart, as I have her kind act to me, in my destitute condition. When she accosted me she did not say, as all Southerners do, "Yank," she said "Soldier," a royal term of which I was never more proud than at that moment. Does it not indicate that in her home there were hearts that beat affectionately for the Stars and Stripes, and for those who had suffered in defense of that dear Flag? We reached the depot and were soon aboard the cars bound for Goldsborough, where we are to be paroled. Our train was composed of flat cars, and by making great exertions, I was on board in time to get a middle berth. The train pulled out and bore us away toward our lines, where we shall regain our freedom and then–home.

The country through which we passed looked so desolate and for-saken that I wondered if the sun thought it worthwhile to shine upon it all. But God is so merciful that He maketh His sun to shine upon the bad as well as upon the good. I am sure He does more than man would do– especially men in our condition. The speed of our train is very slow, at least it seems to us. The road is very rough and much out of repair, and from the clatter made by the engine and cars, they are not in better shape than the road-bed. Usually the grades are quite steep, and on one grade the engine failed to reach the level. The train was backed down and we were compelled to wait an hour until steam sufficient to take us up the grade could be made. We reached Goldsborough just at dark, and were marched a quarter of a mile out of the city, where we entered a clearing and camped for the night. Connely and myself found a dry spot, or as dry a spot as we could which was near a large pine stump. Here we lay down on the bare ground, pulling our blanket over us, this being the only piece of bedding we now possess. We talked of home and the comforts we would soon be enjoying and already anticipated the joyful welcome we would receive from those who, no doubt, have long since mourned for us as dead.

CHAPTER XXV.

DISAPPOINTED AND DESPONDENT - HOPE AND FEAR - MORE DEAD - RUMORS OF PAROLE - SICK AND SAD - BRIGHT ANTICIPATIONS - PAROLING BEGINS - OUR JOHNNIE PAROLED - BOUND FOR FREEDOM'S LAND - "GOODBYE CONFEDERACY" - RAILROAD ACCIDENT - A DESOLATE REGION - FRIENDS IN SIGHT - THE LOYAL BLUE AND THE OLD FLAG - A STRIKING CONTRAST - HOT BLOOD - FREEDOM

February 27th. This morning brings sadness to the prisoners. The usual quantity and quality of dodger was issued to us, and at the same time we received the information that the paroling could not proceed until tomorrow owing to the failure of the paroling officer to reach here. He was due to be here this morning, but had not arrived, and no word had been received from him. It was thought certain he would arrive sometime to-day. They have pledged us their honor that we shall be paroled from this place just as soon as possible. Honor, indeed! That the great body of Salisbury prisoners have very little faith in the honor of the Southern chivalry might well be understood from the mutterings of distrust and fear heard on every hand. Many are of the belief that it is only a ruse to allay our fears and keep us quiet, while they push us on to another prison pen. Some are aroused to another outbreak if their fears should be realized. Others are sad, weary and despondent, and almost ready to give up and die. Is it not strange that men situated as we are, starved, sick and worn out, can stand so much mental and physical suffering? The day is chilly and dreary, but fortunately for us there is plenty of wood here and good, brisk fires are kept burning, which brings comfort and warmth to our bodies.

February 28th. This morning the sun looks cheerful, and as the weather is much more pleasant than it was yesterday, the spirits and hopes of the prisoners were greatly revived. We were on the road to a day of happiness, but when our rations were issued, the commanding officer read a letter purporting to have been written by the paroling officer, to the effect that he would be here on the noon train and paroling would begin as soon as possible. He requested that all preliminary matters be attended to at once, so that the work of paroling might be carried on as soon as he arrived. Notwithstanding the seeming assurance of the letter, a good many relapsed into a gloomy, discouraged state of mind.

Quite a number of our poor boys answered to roll call last evening for the last time. During the night seven or eight died and were buried this morning. The great wonder is that the number of prisoners, who if they do not speedily reach our lines where they can be properly cared for, will not need to be paroled. The report has reached camp that the paroling officer has arrived and tents are being put up for the occasion. This report was brought in by a colored man, and corroborated by him, saying:

"Me help to stake the tents."

The word of this colored man has more weight with us then the "honah" of any rebel in the Confederacy. While I have been very despondent, Connely has been all aglow with bright hopes. He says we are surrounded by our own men and they have to parole us as there is no place they can take us to but our own lines. I feel I must die soon unless I get relief. The "breakybone fever" is having a deep hold on me, and it is only a question of a short time which will conquer. David says:

"Cheer up; there is a better time coming."

I hope it may speedily come. If it does not, I am afraid I will not be here to greet it.

March 1st. This morning we were up early, not from choice, but because we were so cold we could not lie on the ground any longer. Several fires were started in the camp, at one of which I warmed myself. My condition is deplorable. My stomach is empty of food, my knees and ankles tortured with excruciating pain, my whole body weak and feeble; but I hope soon to be within our lines and then farewell to rebeldom, hunger, misery; all hail to cheer, plenty, friends and happiness.

Rations were issued to us as usual, after which we were ordered to fall into line and march to headquarters to sign our parole papers. We marched to where four or five bell tents had been pitched, when an officer called out:

"Here, some of you'uns come in here and write out the parole papers for

them."

Connely insisted that I should go for one, which would expedite matters, and we would get away sooner, as they had informed us a train was in waiting to convey us to our lines as soon as the work of paroling was completed. I reluctantly consented to act as Secretary pro-tem for the bogus, and now nearly defunct, Confederacy. All the parole papers were written by our men. Why, I know not, unless it was because they did not have men who know enough to write their names. I worked hard, hoping we would get done by noon so we could get out of there, but it was a larger task than we could complete in so short a time. Dave had found our adopted Johnnie and brought him up to sign his parole. He was paroled as "Jacob Berry." (Berry was my brother-in-law, a member of my company, who was killed by the cars near Joliet, Illinois, in the fall of 1863, while enroute for his home on a sick furlough.) He seemed to breathe freer air after he had signed his papers. One officer was stationed at each tent and as fast as the men signed their names, they were marched off to themselves, counted, and kept separate until the work was all done, which was not until late in the evening. Just at dark all were marched off to the depot and again loaded on the train. This run was to be the last and was to take us out of rebeldom, for which we were truly thankful. Two of the men who were on the same car with me died during the night. It seemed so sad to witness the death of these poor fellows just as they were on the point of reaching home; but the suffering of body and mind was more than they could endure and two more victims of rebel cruelty were added to the tremendous account they will have to render to God.

We were "making haste" very slowly; the road-bed being in such bad condition. It was impossible to go at a decent rate of speed without endangering the lives of all on the train. In many places the speed did not much exceed that of a good walker. Sometime between midnight and daylight the train parted, three cars running back to the foot of the grade. The engineer pulled the rest of the train fully two miles before the mishap was discovered. The three loose cars went down the grade at a rapid speed and did not stop until they struck an up-grade on the opposite way. Our engine started after the cars and met them as they were returning in our direction, they having run up the grade a distance sufficient to impart great momentum to them as they came back. Seeing that a rear end collision was inevitable, our engineer slowed down, and before he could get started again, the "wild" cars were gaining on us at a rapid rate. Our situation was anything but pleasant. The engine was put to the best speed possible, which did not exceed eight miles an hour, when the cars struck us with tremendous force, scattering us in every direction. Fortunately the only injury done was a severe shaking up of the prisoners.

For many hours we had not seen a living human being in the country through which we were passing, and but few houses, all of which seemed to be destitute. There were no towns nor stations of any importance on the railroad. The country was swampy, covered with heavy pine timber, the only industry carried on being the making of tar, rosin and turpentine. Peanuts were raised by the farmers, and carted to Wilmington where they were sold. It was as forlorn and desolate a region as I ever saw.

March 2nd. At the dawn of day we saw a man on horseback whom we took to be a scout or forager, but being so far away we could not tell whether he was a Yank or a Johnnie. An hour later we discovered four infantrymen out foraging. They were carrying something on their backs, but we could not tell what it was.

However, we could make out their blue uniforms quite plainly, which convinced us we were nearing our lines. Hope took on new life, and the joy of the famished, half-starved prisoners was expressed by cheers. About 7 o'clock a.m. our train stopped and gave a loud, shrill whistle. We were sure this meant something of importance. By looking forward a mile ahead of us we could see rifle pits running at right angles with the track. We could also see the bright guns of the guards flash in the sunlight as they paced to and fro, but they were too far away for us to distinguish whether they were friends or foes. The suspense we were undergoing was terrible. It was evident from the conduct of our guards that we were near the place where the other fellows had the guns and were in power, and their reign was at an end. A little dandy of a Captain who seemed to be in command since we left Goldsborough, walked from the rear of the train to the front. As he passed we could see that his face was pale and his eyes shone as if he was in a state of excitement. When he had reached the forward part of the train he called to the guards in a squeaking voice:

"Here, you fellers, thar, get down heah and form a line."

They obeyed the order, but evidently intended to take their own time doing it. They huddled together more like a flock of sheep than a detachment of soldiers. We took in the situation immediately. The line we saw in our front was the outworks of our glorious army, and the cowardly guards were not certain that even a flag of truce would save them from the punishment their crimes so richly deserved. They were scared out of their senses when brought face to face with Union soldiers who had guns that would shoot. The contemptible, cowardly wretches! There was a vast difference between walking their beats on the platform around Salisbury stockade, and deliberately, and with murder intent, shooting down poor, helpless prisoners, and standing face to face with the comrades of these murdered men, who, if the word had been said, would have revenged the death of their comrades. But they were under a flag of truce, and Union soldiers knew how to honor and respect it. Would they have done as much under the same circumstances? I doubt it.

Our engine gave a loud, long and shrill whistle, and then the train moved along so close to our line that we could see the grand, loyal blue that clothes the line in our front, while a little to the westward we could see the glorious Flag, the stars and stripes, the emblem of freedom, whose stars never flashed so brightly, and whose waving never seemed so majestic as it did this moment. It seemed to me the world could not produce the equal of the men whom our eager eyes were looking at. Well-formed, stalwart, robust, healthy, well-clothed, well-fed—a striking contrast to the scrawny, villian-visaged, diminutive clay-eaters and white trash who had looked down upon us from their sentry boxes at Salisbury Prison. We could now see the white flags on the front and the sides of our engine, and a group of our men were standing on the railroad track in our front, and we knew we were on the inner threshold of our land of freedom. I sprang off the car, forgetting all about the pains in my ankles and knees. Soon others did likewise, and then the getting off became general. Presently the little dandy Captain looked back, and motioning to us said in that old, hateful and brutal tone of voice:

"Git back on that cah, dah."

An hour before this time I would have obeyed that order instantly, knowing if I did not a bullet from a murderous rebel's gun would be sent straight at me; but now I felt I was once more a free man, with all the rights, liberties, and dignity of a Union soldier under the protection of the Old Flag, and in the presence of comrades loyal and true, who had guns and who knew now to handle them. I looked the "tar-heel" Captain in the face, and with all the vehemence I could possibly throw into my voice, said to him:

"You go to h–ll, you white livered son of a b---h; your day of authority is passed. When I get some meat on my bones I hope I'll meet some of your tribe on equal grounds, and we will talk this matter over!"

He passed by me and never opened his mouth. His day of shouting was over; the end of his reign was reached. Descending from the cars, we passed through our lines, a Rebel and a Union clerk checking us off and counting us as we passed through.

CHAPTER XXVI.

A THRILLING SCENE - GENEROUS COMRADES - WELCOME
ADDRESS - THE MARCH TO WILMINGTON - THE DEAR OLD
FLAG - WEEPING COMRADES - GRUB, AND PLENTY OF IT
A GREAT FEAST - DRUNK ON COFFEE - A GOOD SLEEP - EASY
SHOES - FAREWELL TO OUR ADOPTED JOHNNIE - OUR FIRST
NIGHT'S SLEEP UNDER THE FLAG - A GLAD AWAKENING
SAD SIGHTS - PLENTY VS. STARVATION - AN INVITATION TO
DINNER - DRAWING RATIONS - FORCE OF HABIT
ON BOARD SHIP

March 2nd (continued). *I wish I had the power to carry my readers back to the moment and place described in the last chapter. I would show them a scene which lies beyond the power of mortal man to describe; it must have been seen to be appreciated.*

~ ~ ~ ~ ~

The point of our lines first reached was North-East River, a few miles from Wilmington. The outer works were held by colored troops who were true to the trust reposed in them. All the men who were off duty crowded around us and lavished unstinted kindness on us. They gave us blankets, shirts, shoes, pantaloons and other articles we stood so much in need of. They were placed here with only three days rations, and now they had given all to us, and seemed sorry that they did not have more to give. The sick men were carried by willing, tender hands to comfortable beds of leaves and blankets. A great number of huge and generous fires were made, and we were given ample room to stand around them and warm our cold bodies. All who were able to walk were ordered into line to march to Wilmington. At this time a Lieutenant, or Captain, I have forgotten which, stepped to the front and made us a short address of welcome to cheer us up and encourage us to march to the city, where, he said, rations were being prepared for us, promising us all we could eat, and the best the land afforded. He told us that after we had reached Wilmington our hardships would be ended, and a generous Government would remember our loyalty to the Flag, enduring the suffering we did rather than join the rebel army. He spoke very feelingly and lovingly of the poor, famished comrades who could not resist the temptations held out to them by the rebel authorities and goaded by the desperation of hunger, were led away to join the rebel army.

Those who were able to stand marched to the city, where, within a mile of headquarters, the old flag was proudly waving to welcome us home. At the sight of the Flag a great shout swept along the line:
"OUR FLAG IS THERE!"

Then a hurrah went up which told how glad we were to see that Banner for whose defense we had suffered so much. All shouted and cried and shouted, until nature could do no more. The climax was reached when we drew near to headquarters and saw that poles had been erected on each side of the road which were wreathed in ever-greens, and a banner drawn across the road from pole to pole, on which was inscribed, in large gilt letters, these words:

WE WELCOME YOU HOME OUR BROTHERS

A band was standing at its base playing "Home, Sweet Home." This was more than we could bear. The sight of the Flag, the cordial welcome extended to us, the touching strains of the dear old song, unmanned us. Men fell down by the side of the road and wept like children–wept tears of joy; joy that could be expressed only by tears. The band had to cease playing before the column could be induced to move forward. Then the men rose to their feet, cast their eyes up to the banner, when another outburst of joyous tears was indulged in. I noticed old veterans who had been accustomed to scenes of sadness on many a hard-fought battle field, and could look upon them apparently unmoved, who, as they looked upon our emaciated and naked bodies, and into the faces which bore the evidences of extreme suffering from starvation, sickness and cruelty, wept tears of sorrow, showing that their great, true, loyal hearts   sympathized with us and were ready to do us any service that was in their power. It was now high noon, and we had been fasting since early yesterday morning. We soon gathered up strength and marched to the headquarters of the Commissary, where we were bountifully supplied with good, genuine army coffee and plenty of sugar, meat, onions, soft bread and "hard tack." If a prisoner looked wishfully for more, after he had eaten his first supply, more was at once handed to him, the Commissary Sergeant saying:

"*Here, my friend, is plenty of it; take all you can carry.*"

So it was with everything, and it was hard for us to believe it. We had been undergoing the starving process so long that it was difficult for us to understand that there was enough of anything anywhere to satisfy our appetites. Connely and I hungered for coffee, the long-talked of, much-wished for, good, old army coffee. We drank of it until we were filled, and still its delicious fragrance filled the air and intoxicated our senses. I drank so much of it that I was positively and helplessly drunk, and many others were in the same condition. When the Post physician was notified of the state we were in, he ordered watches to be placed over us to keep us from overeating, or serious results would follow. Ambulances were sent out from Wilmington to get the prisoners who were not able to travel; they were brought in and tenderly cared for. Two poor fellows who died on the train last night were also brought in and buried under the Flag, with all the honors due to true soldiers. How often, as men have died in the prison, they have said their only regret was that they would have to lie in southern soil. If they could only be buried under the shadow of the Stars and Stripes death would have no sting for them.

During the afternoon we were surrounded by the old soldiers, who would sit and listen to our stories of grief and woe as long as they could induce the prisoners to talk; and many a cheek was wet with tears as the awful truth was told them, or at least, as we tried to tell it. We were now in need of sleep, as we had little or none on the route here. My stomach being satisfied for the first time since that eventful day when I was captured, October, 1864, I began to feel I must have some rest and sleep. While I was looking for a place to lie down, a comrade of a Pennsylvania regiment told me to come with him and he would find a bed for me. He took me to his own quarters, gave me his own bunk, arranged a good, comfortable bed for me, on which I lay down and had a good sleep. When I awoke it was nearly night. I felt refreshed, bodily and mentally, but my ankles and knees still suffered the torturing agony of the terrible breakybone fever. My feet also were very sore, my old boots being so loose they chafed my feet and made them very painful. I had pulled them off to ease my feet, when a comrade came to me, looked at my feet, and told me not to put the old boots on again, but wait until he returned. While he was telling me this, big tears stood in his generous eyes. He soon returned with a pair of good, easy shoes and a pair of nice socks. He requested me to try them on and if they fitted to wear them. I obeyed his request, found them just the fit, and wore them with comfort to my feet and joy to my soul. God Bless that generous comrade.

I went out in search of Connely, and while looking for him, I met our adopted Johnnie, who was glad to see me, telling me he was going to New York on the first boat he could get away on, and probably would never see us again. He expressed his gratitude to us for the great interest we had taken in him in securing for him his liberty. I took his name, but before I could copy it in my journal, I lost the paper, and thus all trace of him has passed from me. If this book should come to his notice, I would be delighted to hear from him. I found Connely and J. W. Jennings, of Company E, preparing supper. After eating a hearty meal, we began to look for a place to rest for the night, which we found under a porch near the wharf, where we fixed a comfortable bed, and there we three lay down together, with the echoes of the music of the band still ringing in our ears—"Home, Sweet Home." When we awoke in the morning I was dazed and bewildered. I could not for a moment realize that the events through which I had passed, and for which I had so long prayed and hoped, were indeed realities. I feared I was passing through one of those awful, tantalizing dreams that had haunted me during my hours of sleep in prison; dreams in which all the happiness and freedom of home would appear to me so vividly, only to be followed by a wretched, tormenting awakening. But I soon became conscious of the joyful fact that this was no dream, but a glorious reality.

To many who came out of Salisbury Prison with us, and endured the great fatigue and suffering of the march and weary transportation to our lines, the beams of the rising sun brought no gladness, because during the night the "weary wheels of life had ceased to move," and their eyes were forever closed to all earthly scenes, whether of joy or sorrow. The dead lay with teeth showing through parted lips, their faces bearing evidences of the awful suffering through which they had passed; the rotting feet and limbs; their almost fleshless hands clenched in the last agonies of death, all told a tale of horror which chills the blood in one's veins to look upon. Their sad fate, dying within the threshold of freedom's land–almost within sight of home–seemed much more sad to me than the fate of those who had died while yet in the prison. Most of them were so near death that it is very doubtful if they even realized they were once more under the protection of the Flag they had loved unto death.

Connely, Jennings and myself went to work and prepared a breakfast fit for a king. We had a large coffee pot full of good, rich coffee, a pan of well fried bacon, onions, soft bread and hard tack. What a sudden transformation from the customs of the "dining rooms" in Salisbury Prison. Then and there, only one meal a day; sometimes, yes, many times, only one meal in thirty-six and forty-eight hours, the menu consisting of a small loaf of bread made out of meal, into which was ground corn, cob, husk and all, and that raised with lime. Now, three full meals a day composed of the very best Uncle Sam can provide; there it was, in any quantity we wished to take it. We were informed that sometime during the day boats would be at the dock to take us to Annapolis, from which place we would receive furloughs allowing us to go home. Who can describe our emotions as this glad news fell on our ears? As my feet were so sore I was not able to walk around very much, and being eager to get home as soon as possible to obtain the medical treatment and nursing I needed so much, I did not feel like taking as much interest in my present surroundings as some others. A comrade of an Indiana regiment invited me to go with him to his quarters for dinner. His name was William Lucas. I accepted the invitation, and on our way to his quarters, we passed by the Commissary headquarters. Just in front of it was a platform scale used for weighing rations. I stepped on the scales and was weighed, and I tipped the beam at eighty-seven and a half pounds. This fell a good deal short of my fighting weight. One week before I was captured I weighed 181 pounds, so that in some way or other I had left 94 pounds of myself divided between Libby and Salisbury Prisons. If these

229

remnants, wherever they may be floating about, will only haunt and trouble the wretches whose treatment took them away from me, I will not regret the decrease in weight. Comrade Lucas's mess was composed of four big-hearted and robust-looking soldiers. I was introduced to the mess, received a warm welcome, and was made as comfortable as possible. In a remarkably short time a dinner was prepared which seemed to me to be inexcusable extravagant. One of the mess had visited the sutler's tent and returned with canned fruits, sauce and jellies. Besides these luxuries, we had fresh fish (not the kind we had at Salisbury), soft bread, good coffee with plenty of sugar, and in fact everything the market afforded was spread before me at that dinner. And what a dinner I did eat! The contrast was so great and tempting I could not resist. If this thing keeps up much longer I will degenerate into a child of luxury, and will have to ask to be sent back to my old quarters and fare at Salisbury in order to learn abstemiousness and humility. However, I'll try it awhile longer. It is good as far as I have gone. What queer fellows these soldiers are, I do believe they would have killed me by urging me to "eat more." Their enjoyment was as great at seeing me eat as mine was to be permitted to eat the good things their whole-souled generosity had provided for me.

About 3 o'clock in the afternoon we were ordered to fall in and draw rations. This was a bewildering order to us, as we had formed the habit of drawing rations only once a day—sometimes once in two or three days—and only one small loaf then. We fell into ranks and marched to a group of Commissary Sergeants who dealt to each prisoner food to last him three days. One Sergeant handed to each man a loaf of soft bread and two days rations of hard tack; another a large slice of bacon; another a handful of sugar, and last of all came onions and pickles in profusion. We have been inside our lines only twenty-eight hours, have had four good, full meals, and now are loaded down with rations to supply our needs during the three days it will take us to reach Annapolis. This is undreamed of luxury! Our expectations are more than realized.

Some of the prisoners had become so accustomed to trading rations while in the prison pen that a habit had been formed which could not be broken off all at once. And so the old time bartering began. Some traded meat for coffee; others traded onions and pickles for tobacco. We had a good laugh at them, telling them they were not in prison now; that there was plenty here, and Uncle Sam was shipping supplies in as fast as we could use them.

It was sundown when we marched to the wharf and boarded a large steamship named "Sunshine." How appropriate the name to us! It did bring "sunshine" to our poor, weary hearts; something we have known little of during many long months. Wilmington is thirty-five miles from the sea. For that distance the river is calm and flows through the most beautiful scenery. At the mouth of the river are Forts Fisher and Casewell, the strongest seacoast forts in the Confederacy. When we reached the mouth of the river, our vessel anchored for the night.

MY WEIGHT WHEN RELEASED–81 1/2 POUNDS

CHAPTER XXVII.

On the rolling sea - A beautiful morning - A change
in feeling - No time for sentiment - Sea sick
In danger - "Water good to settle mad bees"
Annapolis - Cleansed and made clean - Delightful
experience - Benton barracks - Plenty, but can't eat
Sick - An egg episode - Submission and
reconciliation - Pay and furlough

March 3rd. Never did the sun appear to shine so brightly as when he
arose this morning and poured his resplendent light on land and
on sea. Our ship weighed anchor and we were soon tossing on the wide,
open sea. In a little while we were out of sight of land, as the boys remarked, "We could see no more of the Confederacy!" The rolling of the
vessel, the enchanting sights, and the novelty of our surroundings served
to make this one of the most memorable mornings of my life. I was now
beginning a new life, and it was about to begin in dead earnest. I was
leaning over the bulwarks of the steamer, thinking of the awful monotony of prison life, and contemplating the majesty of the deep, when all at
once I felt as though a one hundred pound shell had exploded in my
stomach. The beautiful scenery, the majesty of the ocean, the graceful
sweep and poise of the sea-gulls, the glinting of the sunlight on the
choppy waves, had no more enchantment for me. I had other business
on hand and I must attend to it at once. I turned to go below when my
eyes fell on the most affecting and wretched sight I ever beheld. Every
man in sight was paying penalty for having indulged too freely in Uncle
Sam's hospitality at Wilmington. Every one was calling out, "New York!"
as if that famous city was the next station and near at hand. The sight
was so overpowering to my feeling that I rushed to the railing and gave
into the bosom of the old ocean all the commissary stores I had accumu-
lated since I arrived inside Uncle Sam's domains. I vomited until I was as
empty as a Salisbury Prison meal sack. There was a vacuum within me

233

that extended clear to my toes, and was clamoring for more territory. I feared that with every overthrow, or output I would bring up my new shoes, and part company with my comfort-giving socks. I started below, thinking I would lie down amid-ships hoping to allay the terrible struggle going on in my stomach. I descended four or five steps of the ladder, when a perfume arose and greeted me which was strong enough to spoil a "limburger cheese." I stepped back for fresh air, and concluded to try it again. Reaching the foot of the ladder, I could not help thinking of our camp-cry, and yelled out:

"Here's your mule!"

This was beyond human endurance. They were as mad as they were sick, and were only waiting for a good opportunity to explode their wrath. My innocent "war-whoop" furnished the opportunity, and they were not slow to seize it. So they began to get up on all sides, curse, shake their fists at me, and threaten to wreak dire vengeance on me, winding up their ferocity by yelling:

"You get out of here or we will knock the head off of you!"

Not knowing what men in such a desperate conditions might be led to do, especially as every fellow was trying to give his "mule" away to some other fellow, I considered that discretion was the better part of valor, and retreated in haste—but in good order. Reaching the deck again I now began to join in the universal call, "New York, New York!" The sailors were now washing off the decks, and having accomplished that feat, started to go below with the hose and brooms to wash out the lower regions from which I had to make such a hasty exit. Miserable as I felt, I could not keep from laughing when I saw them go down the ladder, and expecting to see some fun I concluded to follow them. As soon as they reached the foot of the ladder the hoseman turned on the water, throwing it in every direction. This met with a volley of curses from every quarter, but the curses did not intimidate the hoseman. He threw water all over the men, saying:

"When bees gets mad, the way to settle them is to throw water on them."

It is safe to say the plan worked well in this case, also.

Annapolis, Maryland, March 6th, 1865. Since making my last entry I have been so sea-sick I could not write. We reached Annapolis yesterday morning. Nothing of importance transpired on our trip; any more than we were the worst sea-sick crew that ever landed at an Annapolis wharf.

When we reached our lines a few days ago our stomachs were empty and in bad condition. Then when we were taken into the midst of a superabundant plenty, with hands on every side only too willing to hand it out to us we were not strong enough to resist the temptation to overload our stomachs. Hence, we were good subjects to bestow rich libations on the shrine of the god Neptune. And we did it handsomely, lavishly. We will never do it again.

We were marched to the barracks where breakfast was furnished us. We were then drawn up in line and every man was required to give his name, company and regiment. After this, each man was furnished with a complete suit of clothes, consisting of blouse, pants, overcoat, blanket, two shirts, two pairs of drawers, two pairs of socks, a pair of shoes, and a regulation hat, after which we were conducted to the bath house. At this point I got leave of absence long enough to go across the street to an artist's studio where I had my picture taken, minus my old prison garb. Many other prisoners did likewise. On returning to the bathhouse, we were stripped naked, our old clothing being thrown into a pile at the rear of the building. While I was stripping, my pieces of tent, containing all my valuables, went with the rest. Against this spoliation of my treasures I protested, and naked though I was, I made a spring for the pile, crawled on top of rags and graybacks, secured my valuables, threw the pieces of tent away, returned and deposited my valuables with an attendant until I called for them. I was requested to sit down on a stool, when a barber came and shaved my head as closely as only an expert could do it. Then we were conducted to the bath tubs, into which we went and were rubbed and scrubbed by two strong men. In a few moments every vestige of prison grime was removed from our bodies, enough to be subject for taxation in God's country. We were then passed on to two other men who, with coarse towels, wiped us dry. We then passed into another room where we put on our new clothes and came out full-fledged Yankees. Everything here is reduced to a perfect system. During all the process of our cleansing, not a word was spoken. So rapidly was the work done, that in ten minutes from the time we went into the bathroom, covered with rags, dirt and graybacks, and with a matted shock of hair on our heads, we marched out clean and newly clothed in Uncle

Sam's best brand of clothing. We began to feel that we were really men once more. We were next marched to the barracks where each man registered his name, rank, company, regiment, where and when captured, where and when released. Then we were paid at the rate of twenty-five cents a day for rations while we were in prison. This done in order that we might have money to provide ourselves with such necessaries as we needed. Uncle Sam was very kind to his boys. The officers did everything for our comfort it was possible for them to do. A brass band furnished delightful music every morning and evening. All we had to do was to enjoy the good things and good cheer that were provided for us, and this we were doing with grateful hearts.

As night approached, Connely and I found a bunk filled with straw on which we spread our blankets, undressed and went to bed like human beings, a thing we had not been able to do for many months. How changed our sleeping as well as our waking conditions! Clean blankets; no vermin to eat into our bodies, and torment our rest; no fear of being shot by cruel guards; no tantalizing dreams to disturb our slumbers. I believe this was the best night's sleep I ever enjoyed up to that time. On awakening in the morning, we talked of the contrast of our surroundings now and those of one week ago. How, clean clothes, plenty to eat, and that of the best this fair land could afford, a land where twenty-five cents in greenbacks would buy more than twenty-five dollars in grayback scrip. Surely could we want?

~ ~ ~ ~ ~

Yes, dear reader, do not consider us selfish, ungrateful beings if I say there was one thing more we wanted—home and loved ones. And we were going to both.

~ ~ ~ ~ ~

Benton Barracks, St. Louis, Mo.,
March 13th, 1865.

We reached this place last evening, coming via Baltimore, Columbus and Indianapolis–a long and tedious trip. Owing to our extreme weakness we did not enjoy the trip. We have been industriously accumulating everything we could reach in the shape of commissary stores, and the rich dainties provided for us by the Christian charity of the Sanitary Commission, until our stomachs now rebel against the accumulation of anything more. Quite a number of the boys left us at Columbus, Ohio, and Indianapolis, Indiana, these places being the distributing points of their respective commands. Those remaining with us being Iowa, Illinois and Missouri troops, are to receive two months pay and be furloughed home from this place. A large number are sick and in the hospital. We are here reminded of the Irishman's contrast between a rich man's stomach and a poor man's stomach. He said:

"The poor man has to find a mate for his stomach; and the rich man has to furnish a stomach for his mate."

The good old hard tack, "sow bosom," and army coffee are placed before us in abundance, but out stomachs rebel at the sight of them. Our appetites have entirely failed us. To me, everything eatable is loathsome, yet I am hungry all the time. Home is now the only subject on which my mind dwells; the days seem to be long enough to be weeks. I can almost see my home and loved ones there. When I sleep I dream of home only to awake with aching head and burning fever, my stomach rolling as the waves of the ocean, my limbs aching with the excruciating pain of that terrible North Carolina fever.

March 14th. I am burning up with fever, and my legs refuse to carry my body. I stay in my bunk to avoid seeing the doctor who has ordered me to be taken to the hospital. He gave me some medicine of which I took one dose and threw the rest away. Dave Connely soaked some crackers and fried them, hoping to tempt my appetite. This was once a very favorite dish of mine, but now the sight of it is sickening. I can't eat anything. I drink a little coffee but it tastes as bitter as quinine. My strength is failing instead of increasing. I passed the day in bed, bathing my forehead with cold water, which, at times, gave me some relief from the headache; but it would soon return again with greater force.

March 15th. My fever has abated somewhat, but I have no appetite to eat. I bought half a dozen eggs from a peddler, for which I paid twenty-five cents, and considered them very cheap. I was getting ready to fry them when Connely came in and said to me:

"See here, Boosy, you must not eat them. They are the worst things you can eat."

However, I made up my mind I would eat them, let the result be what it would. When he saw I was not going to be persuaded to desist he told me firmly I should not eat them. I was as rebellious as my stomach, and broke them in a frying-pan, and put them on the fire to cook. He stood by watching me, and as I turned to get some salt, he gave the frying-pan a kick and its contents went into the fire.

"There," he said, "I told you you should not eat then, you damn fool, you!"

My feelings may be better imagined than described. It seemed to me while I was preparing to fry them, they were the only food I cared for, and now they were a mass of ruins. I was mad beyond expression. I took up the frying-pan and threw it at him, and wished for a club to follow it up. He dodged it, and good-natured fellow that he was, laughed at me which only served to increase my wrath and indignation. Then he said to me:

"You could have saved that twenty-five cents if you had minded me in the first place."

He went to the post suttler and bought me a can of cove oysters and some tea. He made me a good cup of tea, which I relished. I ate a few of the oysters, but they had a bad taste; indeed, nothing would satisfy me but eggs. I began to plead with him and said:

"Dave, I know that if I had some soft-boiled eggs they would be good for me."

He still insisted they were the worst thing I would eat, and so I had to yield, but I did it reluctantly, and still craved the eggs. The paymaster came this afternoon and gave us two months pay. We also received our furloughs this evening.

Now our prison life is over, ah!
  It is a pleasant thought;
And here we await our furloughs,
  Ere again our homes are sought;
Farewell South, and all thy deadliness
  Farewell traitors, robbers, too,
Cherished Friends of youth and childhood,
  We are coming home to you.
And will not your smiles and welcomes
  Half repay our griefs and cares
When once more you see us sitting
  In the old, familiar chairs?
But there's One who reigns above us—
  We should give our thanks to Him
For the bright hopes in the bosom,
  Where hope but languished dim.
For His kind and loving Presence,
  That at last we lived to stand
Free from prison-life in Dixie,
  In our loved and loyal land,
Let us pray for peace forever—
  For the Union glad and free—
With a tear for comrades faithful,
  Whom we never more shall see.
Ever trusting One above us,
  Though the clouds may gather fast;
Knowing well our Father's mansion,
  Will receive us at the last.

CHAPTER XXVIII.

WE LEAVE BENTON BARRACKS - ARRIVE AT IOWA CITY
TAKE A CONVEYANCE FOR HOME - SICK AT A FARM HOUSE
TRUE FRIENDSHIP - CONNELY REACHES HOME - A NIGHT OF
TERRIBLE SUFFERING - NEAR DEATHS DOOR - WIFE AND
HOME AT LAST - DOWN IN THE VALLEY - LIVE AGAIN
GOOD-BYE

Lytle City, Iowa, December 20th, 1865.

I will now try and finish my account of my prison life and home coming. I left Benton Barracks, St. Louis, Missouri, March 15th, 1865, and reached Iowa City, Iowa, March 18th. This point was the nearest railroad station to my home. Dave Connely was with me. I had not eaten a bite of food of any kind for two days, so that it required all the effort I could put forth to walk, assisted by a cane. Here we procured a conveyance to take us to our homes, twenty-five miles distant. The roads were very

> Lytle, Iowa, was in Iowa County in the central part of Section 1, Fillmore Township. The town was laid out in 1857. After the establishment of the town of Parnell, and the railroad coming to that town (instead of Lytle) in 1884, Lytle died out.

muddy and our progress was slow. We started early Sunday morning, and when about fifteen miles on our journey, we stopped at a farm house for dinner–the name of the owner was Harrington. When we reached this place I was so weak and sick I could scarcely hold up my head. I had a very high fever, and was very hungry, anticipating the pleasure of being able to eat some food at a farm house table. The kind lady had a good dinner prepared, and tried to find something I could relish. When we sat down to the table I thought it was a grand dinner–everything that could be desired was spread before me. I was helped to a cup of tea, but the sight of it was repulsive. I could not touch it. I next tried to eat some potatoes that were fried brown and looked so tempting, but a rebellious stomach would not receive them. Then I longed for a glass of milk, but

241

Dave remonstrated against my drinking it. I was going to rebel against what I considered an unlawful interference on his part, when the lady of the house told me it would not be good for me. Seeing nothing I desired to eat, or rather, could eat, I got up from the table and seated myself in a large, easy, rocking chair, and being so weak and tired, I soon fell asleep. I slept in that position until the company left the table and came into the room, which awakened me. My stomach was in great pain; my head ached and my knees and ankles were throbbing with terrible fever pains.

Here I was, only ten miles from home. I could almost see it now, although I was so very sick and feared I could not keep strength long enough to reach it. My sufferings, mental and physical, were beyond description. The driver had his team ready to pursue his journey, but my strength was gone–I was powerless to move. I said to Dave:

"You go on home; tell my wife where I am, and they will come after me. I cannot endure the trip."

"No," said Dave, *"I have stayed with you from the beginning, and I will not leave you now, comrade."*

Such was the bond of friendship that bound us together, that the noble fellow was willing to make any sacrifice for me. He had endured the trip better than I had. He had exercised better judgment, and had greater control over himself in the matter of eating than I had, therefore, he was in fair bodily condition. His willingness to stay with and care for me when we were so near home, reminded me of what he had told me when we were first taken to the rebel corral at Cedar Creek. He was taken there before I was, and when I was brought in he came to meet me, took me by the hand, and said, "I am sorry to see you here, but as I am here, there is not a man in the company I would rather see than YOU."

We had often divided our last crust with each other. I, too, was sorry we were there, but as it was so, I was glad to have him with me. I am satisfied I never would have reached home had he not been there to advise, cheer and help me. And now, just as we stood on the threshold of our homes, he wanted to stay with and care for me. I insisted that he should go on home and tell my wife where I was, which would be the best service he could render me. On the assurance of Mr. Harrington that I would be well cared for, he reluctantly left me. He reached home about midnight and told his people where I was. His home was only about a half mile from mine.

After Connely left me I became delirious. Typhoid pneumonia had a firm hold on me. The kind lady of the house insisted that I should go to bed, but I told her we had been covered with graybacks, and although I had tried to cleanse myself from them, there were a few clinging to me yet, and I did not wish to take them into her bedding. But she still insisted that I go to bed, which I had to kindly, but firmly refuse. I spread my blanket on the carpet, and accepted the offer of a pillow which she brought to me. I laid down but could not sleep. At intervals I was delirious. About 2 o'clock a hard rain fell. It came down in torrents. I was suffering so much the people of the house thought I would die before morning. They called up their son, a young man, and wanted him to go for a doctor who lived four miles away. Against this I most earnestly remonstrated, because the night was so dark, and it was raining so hard. I told them I would be better soon.

About daylight my stomach pained me so much I could not lie down. I got up and tried to walk, but my legs could not bear the weight of my body. The lady of the house made me some herb tea which I drank as hot as I could bear it, which eased the pain somewhat. I laid down again and fell asleep. Being so weary I slept until about 10 o'clock, when someone placed a hand on my shoulder and called me by my name:

"Frank!"

This startled me, as I recognized the voice to be that of my wife's brother, William Berry. I got on my feet, took him by the hand, and asked him where Sarah (my wife) was.

"She is here," said he; "We have come after you, and have a bed in the wagon." I started out to see her, and to my surprise it was still raining. I went out to the wagon, shook hands with my wife, then went back and got my blanket, and started for home again. I was placed in the bed, and covered over with rubber blankets to keep me dry. It rained all the time we were on the journey. We reached home in the evening. I became delirious, and about 10 o'clock that night the family physician was called in to see me. Typhoid-pneumonia had such a firm hold on me that for four weeks I was in an even balance between life and death. For three weeks of the time I was unconscious, and at no time could I recognize my wife, who was in constant attendance at my bedside. It was only by such nursing as a loving, devoted wife could give, aided by a Merciful Father in Heaven, that my feeble life was kept from going out in the silence of death, and that I have lived to pen this true, unvarnished history of my life in, and my release from Salisbury Prison.

Out of the jaws of death,
Out of the mouth of hell.

CONCLUSION:

I will here close the accounts of the sufferings of the brave and noble boys who uncomplainingly endured the hardships of southern prison pens to perpetuate and maintain the national honor and integrity of our fair land. The 13,715 [13,702] Union dead [graves] at Andersonville, Georgia; 7,000 graves [dead] at Belle Isle; 6,000 [3005] Union dead [graves] at Florence, South Carolina; and the 12, 137 [12,132] graves at Salisbury, North Carolina prison pen (which only existed during the last year of the war), who preferred to fill honored graves rather than surrender their loyalty and devotion to country and flag.

These figures are startling facts that cannot be realized by those who were babes and those who have been born since those dark days. It will not be surprising if these facts are assailed. But for all such people I am fortified by facts from hundreds of survivors of those scenes and who are still living witnesses of this history, as will be seen by a few letters found in the following appendix.

When I look back over the "Dark Days of the Rebellion," I do not wonder that historians have shrunk from the unpleasant task of making up the record as it would make the darkest pages of our country's history, and remain a perpetual and everlasting disgrace to American civilization.

EPILOGUE

Camp Pope, once an open field, where Booth and the 22nd Iowa Infantry received their first rudimentary training in the art of soldiering before embarking on their three-year journey southward, is part of Iowa City's urban landscape. Ground that soldiers marched over and drilled on is now yards and lawns and part of it is a playground at Longfellow School. A plaque on the school ground commemorates its location.

**PLAQUE COMMEMORATING THE LOCATION
OF CAMP POPE IN IOWA CITY, IOWA**

Libby Prison, which destiny brought Booth to, was dismantled and rebuilt as a museum in Chicago in 1889. The enterprise did not prosper, and the building was finally destroyed.

Salisbury Prison, after being burned, lay in ruins for a time, and then the bricks and whatever could be had from what remained were salvaged. Today the prison grounds are covered by houses. On one occasion when excavation was being done for the basement of a house on the site in 1965, a tunnel that was used in an escape attempt was unearthed. A national cemetery exists at the sight where Salisbury Prison's dead were laid in trenches.

Benjamin F. Booth, or "Reporter" as he was known amongst his comrades at Salisbury Prison, continued a lifestyle after his recovery from Salisbury imprisonment that is not atypical of those possessing such creative minds as writers. He was an inventor, and traveled about the country selling animal waterers and feeders that he invented following the Civil War. He also invented something that had to do with streetcars. It would be interesting to know if any of his business travels after the war took him to the former Confederacy. It is apparent that his bitterness toward the South never left him. Whatever his plight, he is sure to have enjoyed many   discussions with other veterans during his travels.

Booth had married Sarah J. Berry two years before the Civil War. They had one son who gave them ten grandchildren. Booth moved to Indianola, Iowa, in 1903. His wife died there in 1909 and he removed to Springfield, Illinois, to live with a brother. On October 15, 1927, Benjamin F. Booth died at the age of 89 years, one month and twenty-four days. At the time of his death he had forty great-grandchildren and eleven great-great-grandchildren. He is said to have lived a conscientious Christian life and was member of the Masonic Order, attaining the thirty-second degree. His vice of tobacco chewing remained with him throughout his life.

APPENDIX

Letter From Martin Burke, Esq.,
Superintendent of the National Cemetery at Salisbury, North Carolina

The following is a verbatim copy of a letter I received from Comrade Burke, giving important facts connected with the past and present status of Salisbury Prison:

National Cemetery,
Salisbury, N.C.,
June 1st, 1894.

Mr. B. F. Booth,
Medford, Iowa:

Dear Sir: Your communication of the 28th ult., was duly received, asking for a description of the prison pen, etc. General Stoneman captured, and destroyed by burning, the stockade and prison pen. The place is now covered with houses and is called "South Brooklyn," but is a part of the town of Salisbury. Having no photographs of this cemetery, I enclose you a sketch with correct figures as to length, angles, etc. Graves; 437 and 18 trenches, where 11,700 Union soldiers, prisoners, are buried. Surface level. The record shows thus: Known 102; unknown, 12,035; total interments, 12,137. Jacob Miller, Co. "H," 22nd Iowa, is among the "unknown."

You can get a photo of the stockade as it stood in 1864 from Hartranft Post, G.A.R., Charlotte, North Carolina, where they are for sale. Don't know how the population stood in 1864, now it is nearly 6,000—one-half of them colored. On last Decoration Day the Hartranft Post, 8 members, and 3,500 colored people, observed the day here, and strewed flowers over all the graves. Everything passed off quietly and respectfully. Not one man (white) from Salisbury town attended. The rebs have no military cemetery in or around this vicinity as I know of. This cemetery is just two blocks directly west of the stockade (that was), and one half mile from the railroad depot. No sign of a stockade now exists, the whole place is laid out into streets. You may remember the branch which runs through the cemetery and south of the stockade. Now it has the same course, as you can see in the sketch.

The rebel commander of the prison failed to turn over any record of the prisoners, or the deaths, at Salisbury Prison pen. We had to open about fifty feet of trench and count the skulls or bodies, then measure the whole trench and make an estimate according to the number found in proportion to the length of the whole trench. It is supposed by the best of authorities that 15,000 instead of 11,700 are buried in the 18 trenches alone.

Wishing you the best possible success in your undertaking, I am, Very Respectfully,

MARTIN BURKE,
Superintendent.

251

~ ~ ~ ~ ~

Letter From Mr. D. Sheehan, Niles, Michigan.

*I am sure that the following letter received from a comrade who was present and partici-
pated in the break for liberty described in Chapter 14, will be read with great interest by all who
wish to learn the true facts of that most tragic event:*

Niles, Michigan,
June 8, 1896.

B. F. Booth,
Indianola, Iowa:

My dear comrade:
Yours of June 1st at hand. How I would like to meet you that I might give
you a greeting. I can see you now as I look back to those fearful days when it
tried men's souls, and put their loyalty and patriotism to a test. I was captured
on 30th September, 1864, at Pegram's Farm, near Petersburg, Virginia, in making attempt to cut South Side railroad, was sent in to the city, thence to Richmond, to the three-story brick building opposite Libby Prison; thence through
Danville to Salisbury where we arrived somewhat against our will on October
7th, being the first batch of Union prisoners there. I remember well the time,
about October 25th, when the men taken in the Shenandoah Valley were
brought in, and how they were robbed and abused by the cut-throat vandals in
our ranks, and summary treatment we gave them; and how they ran the
gauntlet, and then taken out and sent away. After this no one robbed or abused
our men but the rebels. You also think of the time when a number of our men
went out and joined the rebel army on the promise of good treatment. I recollect
the day the mule was killed on the dead wagon by the guard, and how it was
stated that we had him for dinner the next day. Now, as to the attempted outbreak on the 25th November. It was started by the Sergeants who had charge of
the squads. They made their plans in the 2nd story of No. 14 building, and their
names as near as I can recollect, was as follows: McBride, 15th U.S. Infantry;
McManus, of New York; Kunecliffe, of Philadelphia, Pennsylvania; Spillune,
New York Infantry; Sergeant Keys, 14th U.S. Infantry, who deserted the English
army and joined ours at Ogdensburg, New York; Sergeant Murray, of Maryland regiment; Sergeant Carroll, 45th Pennsylvania Infantry; Sullivan, 2nd Massachusetts Cavalry, a very large man; Sergeant Major, 27th Michigan Infantry,
with myself and others. We did it on the expectation that the 67th North Carolina Infantry, made up of young boys from 16 to 18 years, and who had been
guarding us for some time, and who shot many of our men for the purpose of
seeing them fall, was gone. The regiment was ordered up to Warren, North
Carolina, to oppose General Warren, of the 5th Corps, from making an advance
on the State. We learned that they were to go and a regiment of old men took
their place, which was done about 3 o'clock P.M. When the relief guard came
into the prison yard we drew tickets from a hat, and on each ticket was marked
the part each sergeant was to take, with the men of their own selection. The 67th
regiment was on the train ready to leave, when the rising took place, and they
left the train and ran to the prison yard, where they mounted the platform, and
shot with a vengeance, or as long as they could see a man to shoot at. Keys,

McBride and Dunnecliffe led the assault on the rebel guard, and of the sixteen men in the guard, fifteen were killed and about thirty wounded. I was surprised when looking over the list to find that not one of the participants in that affair was killed, the fatalities being among those who knew nothing of it till after it started. We were misinformed as to the leaving of the 67th Infantry regiment. Had they gone, nothing would have kept us in, as the old men were panic stricken. The day after the rebels took out several of the sergeants, among them the Sergeant Major of the 27th Michigan, who wore a Zouave uniform, and was very conspicuous on that account. What was done with them we did not learn.

The tunnel was started in one of the tents and its exit was to be under the large frame building near the yard. I went into it one night before it was finished and was to be one who was to go out when it was completed. On the day we made ready to go the project was given away to the rebels, and we gave up going, as it was the rebels' intention to surround the building, and when the prisoners made their appearance to shoot every one. Davis and Brown, paper reporters, who were there at the time taking care of the sick, and who had the privilege of going in and out, were told by an outsider of the discovery, and begged them to tell the prisoners and save their lives. Davis, Brown and Richardson were to go out with us. In my journey from prison to Strawberry Plains, Tennessee, I traveled over nearly the same ground.

Now, as to my escape. On the 24th of January, I, with several others, after several attempts to get out of Salisbury Prison, with a crowd that was taken out by a Catholic Priest (the only clergymen who visited the prison to console the sick and dying) to a camp three miles west of Salisbury, named "Camp York." On the night of the 25th, Alexander Hays, 94th New York; John Mahoney, 114th New York; James Sullivan, a resident of East Tennessee, who refused to enter the rebel army, and had been a prisoner for three years; and myself, made our escape by climbing over the stockade. I was lifted up by Mahoney, reaching the top and then pulling myself over, and while hanging over helped the rest to get up. A history from this time until my arrival at Strawberry Plains, would make a book of itself. After thirty-four days of travel through the wilds of western North Carolina, and east Tennessee, on the morning of February 27th we beheld the bright folds of our starry banner as it floated in the breeze. Oh, Comrade, I cannot describe to you my feelings at that moment. I fell on my knees and thanked God for my deliverance, as it was out of the House of Bondage and the land of Egypt. Let me hear from you again.

Yours truly,

D. SHEEHAN

~ ~ ~ ~ ~

A STRANGE DISCOVERY

It will be remembered that in Chapter 24 I mentioned the fact that while on the march from Salisbury to Greensboro, some one stole two ears of corn from me, and I upbraided a certain comrade of my own regiment with the theft. The following interesting incident clears up the mystery, and shows that I was correct in my suspicion of the guilty one:

253

While at a reunion of my regiment at Iowa City, September 10 and 11, 1891, the man whom I accused of stealing my corn came to me and, calling me aside, told me he did steal the corn from me that night, but that it was not wasted, as I declared. On the contrary it had saved his life. He said he saw me put the corn under the blanket, but did not see me put the sweet potatoes there, else he would have taken them, too, as the temptation to get something to eat, being nearly dead from starvation, was too great for him to resist. This was the first time I had heard of him since we left Annapolis, Maryland; I supposed he was dead. My readers may be sure we had a good hearty handshaking over it, my feelings at that time being far different to what they were the night I lost my corn-coffee.

~ ~ ~ ~ ~

FROM THE YOUNGEST PRISONER IN SALISBURY

Dear Comrade Booth:

In reply to your favor of recent date I am pleased to furnish you with the story of my prison experiences in the South.

Of Scottish birth, I came from a family of military antecedents, my great-grandfather having, at nineteen years of age, fought for "Prince Charlie" on the fatal field of Culloden, and one of my grand-fathers having served at Waterloo, under Wellington, and the other under Nelson at Copenhagen. This may in part explain why I enlisted at sixteen, and served under Grant. It was at the battle of Reams Station that, while I had my gun raised firing at the enemy in front, the cry, "Surrender, damn you!" as a Confederate knocked down my gun with his carbine from behind, told me that Hampton's dismounted cavalry had stolen upon us from the rear. It is hardly necessary to describe the scenes which immediately followed our capture–the naked corpses of our men, stripped for their clothing, the midnight march, followed by the march into Petersburg on the following day, and the subsequent night on an island in the Appomattox. Then came the ride to Richmond, where we were searched and robbed at Libby Prison, and then about five weeks at Belle Isle. Belle Isle was a paradise compared with Salisbury, to which we were removed about the first of October. The journey took three days and two nights. We arrived at Salisbury on the third evening, and were marched by a roundabout route to the stockade. I had left Belle Isle without shoes, and the weather at night was frosty and cool. I was assigned to a tent near the cannon at which I should call the southeast corner of the stockade–the corner nearest the railroad depot. The tent was crowded, and I went to stay under the frame hospital, on the ground. We used to "spoon" together to keep warm. There is no need to repeat the awful story, so well known to you and to others who were there – how at first the dead were carried out in coffins, and then we noticed the same coffins came back, and then, as the number grew, no coffins were used, and the corpses were heaped like cordwood in the dead-wagons. Then came the attempt to enlist us, of foreign birth, in the Confederate service. Suffering and hungry as I was, I remember the parting words of my mother–"Die in a ditch sooner than do anything dishonest." I felt that it would be dishonest to purchase deliverance from misery and death at the expense of violating my oath to the Union, and I made answer to that effect when the choice was presented to me.

Every Salisbury survivor remembers the attempted break of November 25, 1864. I regret that the story has never been told by one of the leaders in it. Although I took part in it, it was not until afterward that I heard the details of the plot. I understand the plan was to have a general rising of the prisoners as soon as the able-bodied regiment of

254

guards had started from the depot for the front. The signal was given too soon. I was aroused by the cry, "Prepare to strike for liberty," and I joined in the rush for the big gate. There is an impression on my mind that we expected the big gate to be open for water carrying, but it was closed. Then we turned toward the small gate, and about that time the Confederates open on us with cannon and rifles, and I believe some of the citizens had shotguns.

Many of our men sought cover, but a number of us remained in mass in the market space until all was over. I was in about the center of this crowd. We all dropped to let the bullets pass over. If you ask my feelings at the time I will say that, not having been in the secret of the original plan, I did not know that the plan had failed, and was thinking that we would make another rush in some direction. It was not until the big gate swung open, and the rebels marched in that I saw the affair was over. The number that took part in the break was probably from 500 to 1,000, and the number of our men killed and wounded – eight-one killed, two hundred and sixty-seven wounded–in a few minutes, showed the frightful extent of the massacre. I understood that three or four rebels were killed, one being shot as he stood on the stockade, by one of our men with a gun taken from the guards inside.

The death rate continued to grow, and I would have gone to the trenches too, but for the kindness of a civilian prisoner, Mr. Albert D. Richardson, correspondent of the New York Tribune, who noticed my youth and my emaciated condition, and took me to his quarters. I was of some slight assistance to him, in his escape, being the "little lad" whom he mentions in his book as carrying the medicine chest to the gate.

After the break the guards used to fire into the prison frequently at night, and many of our men were killed in this way, without having given any offense whatever.

I was exchanged in March, 1865, and it may interest Salisbury survivors to know that the representations made by Mr. Richardson in January of that year to the authorities at Washington, after his successful escape, regarding the awful suffering of our men at Salisbury, had much to do with bringing about exchanges.

Major John H. Gee, who commanded the Salisbury-prison, undoubtedly perished some years ago by the wall of a building which was on fire at Jacksonville, Florida falling upon him. Of the fact there seems to be no doubt, as I saw it in the Savannah News. Gee was far more deserving of death than Wirz. Wirz was condemned for, among other charges, having ordered the guard to shoot down prisoners who attempted to cross the dead-line. Gee encouraged, if he did not order his guards to shoot down prisoners who made no attempt to cross the dead-line, and when a murder of this kind was committed, Gee rewarded the murderer with a furlough. There seems to be no doubt also that sick or wounded prisoners were sometimes buried alive.

The war has long been over; its lessons have been taught and learned, and the best interests of our country demand that a union of hearts should support the Union of states; but that is no reason why history should remain unwritten, or be written untruthfully.

Yours ever,
HENRY MANN,
710 Hancock St, Brooklyn, N.Y.

HEINRICH HARTMANN WIRZ

Henry Wirz came to America from Switzerland in 1849. In 1861 he enlisted in the 4th Louisiana Infantry Battalion, which soon saw duty in Virginia. His death bed claim to have been wounded in the right arm at the Battle of Seven Pines on May 31, 1862, has been challenged. He was promoted to captain and assigned to the staff of Brig. Gen. John H. Winder who put him in command of the Richmond military prison. Called "Dutch Sergeant" by prisoners, he was said to be the "essence of authority," "a good fellow at times and a very bad one at other times," and "an infallible dog" who "thought himself omnipresent and omniscient." In March 1864 he was sent as commandant to the prison at Andersonville, GA. Conditions at Andersonville were terrible almost beyond description, and in the North Wirz was considered to be the "monster . . . the fiend" responsible. In May 1865 Wirz was sending the last prisoners north when he was arrested. He protested that conditions at Andersonville were beyond his control and pleaded to be allowed to take his family to Europe; instead, he was taken to Washington and charged with "impairing the health and destroying the lives of prisoners." During his 3-month trial witnesses swore they had seen Wirz "strike, kick, and shoot prisoners in August 1864," a time during which the Commandant was absent from the prison on sick leave. On 6 Nov. 1865, he was condemned to death. Not long before he was taken into the yard at Old Capitol Prison to be hanged on Nov. 10, 1865, a secret emissary from the War Department offered Wirz a reprieve in exchange for a statement that would convict Jefferson Davis of conspiracy to murder prisoners. Wirz calmly answered, "Jefferson Davis had no connection with me as to what was done at Andersonville." The condemned man said to the major directing his hanging, "I know what orders are, Major—I am being hung for obeying them." Wirz remains a controversial Civil War figure. There is no question about the horrible suffering in Andersonville, and Wirz was certainly a harsh man, rough in manner and profane in speech. But his Confederate contemporaries insisted that he did the best job possible in one of the impoverished nation's most poorly equipped, scantily provisioned, and overcrowded prisons—a fact that has prompted many Civil War historians to claim that Wirz was a scapegoat and the victim of postwar hysteria.

~ ~ ~ ~ ~

LETTER FROM LOUIS K. AURINGER

My readers will remember the mention I made of Comrade Auringer, who made me a present of the "bone bible" relic as he was about to take his flight from the prison, and who was afterward reported shot. The following shows that he is alive:

Constancia, New York,
August 10th, 1897.

Comrade B. F. Booth:

Your letter to me was a happy surprise. Your name had slipped from my mind, but now I remember you clearly. You are the one who had the title of "Reporter" on account of keeping a record of the incidents in the prison. Yes, Comrade, I clearly remember your giving me your wife's address, and that I promised to write to her when I reached home, if I should be so fortunate; but if I could tell you of that terrible march of more than 400 miles over the wilds of that mountainous country, traveled mostly by night, you would not wonder that we lost about everything but our lives, and barely escaped with that. However, I succeeded in keeping that ring, and have it yet, the most cherished relic of Salisbury, but your wife's address was lost, together with all papers and trinkets we had about us. This accounts for my not fulfilling my promise.

Gillman was not a brother-in-law but a chum in my company. He was recaptured about fifty miles from the "pen," and there was one other of our squad whom we never saw after our race on that eventful night; and he may have been the man who was killed, as Gillman reported.

I am happy to say that through a kind Providence I am yet alive and "a very lively corpse," but no money could ever hire me to go through another such an experience as we had in Salisbury Prison pen. It seems so strange to me that no history of that prison has ever been written, while Andersonville, Belle

Isle, Libby and other prisons are so well known, while the suffering in Salisbury was far greater and the death rate beyond anything ever known in a prison in the south. It was, I suppose, as Major Gee so often threatened us, that he would have the barn-burners all in the Confederate army, or in hell, in thirty days. But I am proud of the boys who so manfully braved the suffering and privation of the prison, and stood the severest test of loyalty possible or ever imposed on man. I am glad you are going to have your record printed, I rejoice to know that the inhumanity and suffering in that place is to be put in print while there are yet living witnesses to the facts. From your physical condition the night I bid you farewell in Salisbury, little did I think you would ever live to perform that duty. I congratulate you on being alive and wish you success in your undertaking, and if I can be of any service, write me.

I am your obedient servant,
LEWIS K. AURINGER

~ ~ ~ ~ ~

TESTIMONY OF REV. DR. A. W. MANGUM, A CONFEDERATE PREACHER.

To attest the truth of what we have written of the horrors of Salisbury, many other letters might be printed, but we shall be content to introduce extracts from articles of Rev. Dr. A. W. Mangum, printed in the Charlotte Observer, May and June, 1893. He was Professor of Moral and Mental Philosophy in the University of North Carolina in 1880. He was living in Salisbury during the war, and was an eye witness to the events he describes, and though writing to defend and excuse the barbarity of the prison management, bears witness to all the horrors described in our book. He says:

"About the last of September, 1864, Major Gee received a dispatch from Richmond, ordering him to make provisions immediately for a very large number of prisoners. — He was greatly shocked by the order, for he knew it would be impossible to take care of so many, but bad as it was at Salisbury, it was worse at Richmond."

"When the prisoners came they could not be supplied with tents, so suffered greatly from exposure. They resorted to Yankee ingenuity to provide shelter–a few crowded under the hospital and other houses, and slept there in bad weather; but the main resort was burrowing in the earth. The whole enclosure was literally honey-combed by these burrows. They were queer-looking holes, dug some three feet deep, with mud-thatched roofs, a hole being punched through the surface at one end and a little chimney built out of baked earth. The tenant had either to set or lie down, as they were too shallow for him to stand. They must have been wretchedly uncomfortable and destructive of health and life in the incessant rains that fell in January and February, 1865. The hospitals were crowded, and such a number died in them that some preferred to linger and suffer their sickness in these little cells. Consequently they not infrequently died there alone, and were not discovered for days."

This is the testimony of a Confederate Divine.
The Doctor further says:

SICK — FILTHY — RAGGED.

"The Confederacy was in its last struggle – its resources all gone, and therefore, though the condition of the prisoners was wretched and appalling, there was no way to ameliorate it. They were in a miserable plight when they came. Large numbers of them were unable to walk, and had to be carried from the train to the prison. Those who had been confined elsewhere for a long time were pale, emaciated and dejected. Many of them were very filthy and ragged. Some were without hat or cap or any sign of shoes. The clothing of many was very meager and of summer texture. A very large portion had no blankets. Such being their condition it is evident that their suffering in the cold winter were intolerable. Situated as they were the allowance of wood, according to army regulations, was insufficient. Yet as to fuel most energetic efforts were made to supply them. In addition to their other ills, they had to bear the pangs of hunger. Just prior to their sudden advent, Major Myers, post commissary had, in obedience to orders, sent all or nearly all his stores to Richmond, Goldsboro and Wilmington."

CLIMBING OAKS FOR ACORNS.

"They suffered intensely from hunger. They would climb the oaks for acorns, and fish from the filthy sewers the crusts and the bones. The sick especially suffered, as what they got was often so coarse that they could not eat it.

Although such efforts were made to provide water, the supply was insufficient for drinking, cooking and washing. Wells were dug until they drained one and another.

The hospital accommodations were not such as were desired by the prison officials, and were greatly inadequate to the necessities of so large a number of men so unfavorable situated. The buildings were too small, there was a limited supply of bunks and coverings and even straw, and withal a distressing scarcity of medicines."

PESTILENCE AND DEATH

"There was terrible mortality in the prison. From the 1st of October 1864, to the 17th of February, 1865, there were 3,419 deaths among the prisoners. The number of daily deaths varied from eighteen to forty. On one day about sixty-five died. In its worst days the condition of the prisoners was shocking – the appearance and suffering of the prisoners harrowing in the extreme. The red clay soil held the water and under the tramp of thousands became one scene of mud. In December a number of prisoners were detailed to police the enclosure, but so boggy was the whole surface that they could do but little. Ditching would not drain the ground sufficiently. The prisoners were the very personification of forlorn wretchedness. They seemed to grow more and more dejected and ennui congealed the very springs of life. Doomed to inevitable idleness and inactivity, with no sight but such as aggravated the gloom and horror of their shrouded hearts, with hope deferred from week to week, from month to month,

258

many of them sank under the sheer burden of despair, and with a stolid silence and indifference to time or eternity, finished their mortal sorrows in death."

THE DEAD BURIED NAKED — SICKENING SIGHTS.

"There was a small brick building near the center of the prison, which was used as a receptacle for the dead until they were carried to the burial grounds. They were hauled then, without coffins, to the old field west of the prison. A detail, first of convicts and afterwards prisoners of war, was kept day by day, constantly digging the long pits in which they were interred. These pits were four feet deep, a little over six feet wide, and were extended parallel about sixty yards. The bodies were laid in them without covering – there was not material to cover the living, much less the dead. They were laid side by side, as closely as they could lie, and when the number was too large for the space that was dug, one would be placed on top between every two. They generally had very little clothing on, as the living were permitted to take their garments. Seldom does it fall to the lot of man to behold a more sickening and heartrending spectacle than they presented. It was a lesson on the vanity of this life more impressive and eloquent than tongue or pen can describe. It was a picture of the hellish curse of war, in one of its most horrible and hideous aspects. I begged the workmen at least to get some brush to lay over their faces. Sadly have I mused, as I stood and gazed upon their attenuated forms, as they seemed the very romance of the horrible in shroudless, coffinless grave. Those long, bony hands were once the dimpled pride of a devoted mother, and on that cold, blanched brow tender love had often pressed the kiss of a mother's lips. Perhaps while I gazed on their hapless fate, a fond wife and prattling children were watching for the mail that they might receive the longed for tidings from him who was best loved. But I turn from the theme, as I always turned from those harrowing, chilling burials, with a heart full of sadness, and shuddering over the unwritten terrors and calamities of war.

From the congregated evils of imprisonment the prisoners were always anxiously seeking to escape. Gladly did they accept any opportunity to get out, however laborious the duties for which they were detailed. Numbers of them were on parole or detail for various duties. Some were clerks, some in the workshops, some in the shoe factories, some digging graves, some hauling wood on the train, etc. etc."

RECRUITING OFFICER

"A Col. Tucker came there for the purpose of getting recruits from their number for the Confederate army. Only foreigners were allowed to enlist. Nearly eighteen hundred took the oath administered by a Catholic priest. Some may have taken this step in good faith, as it is known they were often recruited by foul means in the United States, but a great number chose it as the only means of escape from their terrible den. They were called "galvanized Yankees" and while most of them made scarcely a show of fighting when the test came, a few stood their ground and fought with true courage."

259

THE DEPARTURE

"About the 20th of February all who were well enough were removed. The sick were carried on the trains. The hospitals were emptied of all who could travel. It was a pitiable spectacle to see the haggard, staggering patients marching to the train. Some faltered along alone; some walking in couples, supporting one another; now and then three would come together, the one in the middle dragged along by the other two; and occasionally several would bear a blanket on which was stretched a friend unable to walk or stand. Deeply was every heart stirred which was not dead to sympathy, as the throng gazed on the heartrending pageant. God forbid I should ever be called to witness the like again! At the train they received refreshments from the hands of several citizens. About 2,800 started to march to Greensboro. A great many who started were unable to make the march. Besides the stragglers, two hundred were left at Lexington and five hundred the next day, were abandoned on the road. About one thousand failed on the way."

NEGROES STARVED AND SHOT SAME AS WHITE PRISONERS

"I have failed to mention that three or four hundred Negroes were brought to the prison, and were treated precisely as other prisoners of war.

After this general delivery about five hundred were confined, some of them from Sherman's army and were hurried to Charlotte just in time to escape Stoneman's raiders in April. The day that Stoneman captured Salisbury his prisoners were penned in the very same stockade which had so long enclosed the hordes of Federal captives. All the buildings and stockade were burned by Stoneman's orders on the night of the 12th of April. A number of his men had been imprisoned there, and doubtless some of them were in the detail to which was assigned the avenging torch.

Having written thus frankly of the dark history of this great reservoir of misery and death, I now ask, Who is to blame?"

* * * * *

We have quoted only such statements from the articles of Dr. Mangums as bear upon the actual condition of the prisoners. The apology and defense offered by the learned Doctor can never excuse the Confederate officers, for the most unexampled barbarism ever practiced by a people making pretensions to civilization. No nation or people have any right by the laws of war to take prisoners whom they know themselves to be unable to treat humanely. To do so is simply barbarous. It is seen that the facts stated in my narrative are fully substantiated, by rebel testimony, as well as by men who were in prison with me.

REFERENCES

Brown, Daniel Patrick. *The Tragedy of Libby and Andersonville Prison Camps.* Golden West Historical Publications, Ventura, CA. 1991.

Brown, Louis A. *The Salisbury Prison: A Case Study of Confederate Military Prisons 1861-1865.* Broadfoot Publishing Company, Wilmington, NC. 1992.

England, Otis Bryan. *A Short History of the Rock Island Prison Barracks.* Historical Office, U.S. Armament, Munitions and Chemical Command, Rock Island, IL. 1985.

Faust, Patricia L. *Historical Times Illustrated Encyclopedia of the Civil War.* Harper Collins Publishers. NY. 1991.

Graham, Harvey. *The War of the Rebellion: A Compilation of the Official Records of the Union and Confederate Armies.* Series I, Volume XLIII, Part I. Washington, Government Printing Office. 1888. pp. 337-339.

Griffith, Joseph E. "The Twenty-Second Iowa Infantry at Vicksburg." *Annals of Iowa.* July, 1868. pp. 215–219. State Historical Society of Iowa.

Hesseltine, William B. *Civil War Prisons.* The Kent State University Press, Kent, OH. 1962.

Historical Sketch: Twenty-second Regiment Iowa Volunteer Infantry. *Roster and Record of Iowa Soldiers.* Volume III. Des Moines: Emery H. English–State Printer, 1911. pp. 559-668.

Hotchkiss, Jed. *The War of the Rebellion: A Compilation of the Official Records of the Union and Confederate Armies.* Series I, Volume XLIII, Part I. Washington, Government Printing Office. 1888. pp. 581-582.

Marvel,William. *Andersonville: The Last Depot.* The University of North Carolina Press. 1994.

Mott, David C. *Abandoned Towns, Villages, and Post Offices of Iowa.* Reprinted from the Annals of Iowa. Vols. XVII and XVIII, 1930-32. J.W. Hoffman & S. L. Purlington Publishers. Council Bluffs, IA.

Twenty-Second Iowa Infantry Casualties at the Battle of Cedar Creek. *The War of the Rebellion: A Compilation of the Official Records of the Union and Confederate Armies.* Series I, Volume XLIII, Part I. Washington, Government Printing Office. 1888. pp. 133.

MORE CIVIL WAR BOOKS
FROM MEYER PUBLISHING

IOWA VALOR: A compilation of Civil War Combat Experiences from Soldiers of the State Distinguished As Most Patriotic of the Patriotic. By Steve Meyer. Tells the heroic involvement of Iowa's sons and fathers in the Civil War in their own words. Readers will experience the Civil War and learn of a state's involvement in the Civil War, of which little has been written but of which there is much to be proud. No state in the Union Army had a greater involvement than Iowa. From the first skirmish at Monroe Station, Missouri, through the last engagement at Horse Creek, Kansas, every major episode of the Civil War that Iowa troops were involved in is covered, using first-hand accounts from letters, diaries, battle reports, and war correspondence to newspapers. IOWA VALOR reveals the Civil War as seen and felt by soldiers and command officers who were actually there. IOWA VALOR also includes factual summaries about battles, Iowa Civil War Regiments and notable individuals. Clothbound, 528 pages, 150 period photos, 55 chapters, acid-free paper, indexed. Published in 1994. (ISBN 0-9630284-3-X)

IOWANS CALLED TO VALOR. By Steve Meyer. Paperback, 135 pages. The predecessor of, and companion to IOWA VALOR. A quick-reading book full of facts and stories about Iowa's entry into the Civil War. Included in the book are numerous citations from diaries and letters of Iowa Civil War soldiers which reveal their experiences in camp, and as they answered the Union's call. This book is full of information, quips, and anecdotes that anyone interested in Iowa history or the Civil War will enjoy. Published in 1993. (ISBN 0-9630284-2-1)

DISCOVERING YOUR IOWA CIVIL WAR ANCESTRY. A 64-page paperback "how to" book that helps you find out what your Civil War ancestor did. If you're curious about what your great-great-grandad Erastus did in the Civil War, "Discovering" is the book for you. It describes how to find out basic information about what regiment your ancestor served with and how to find detailed information about what battles and other significant events your long forgotten ancestor participated in. Most of these things you can find out without having to travel far, maybe not even out of your home town! Published in 1993. (ISBN 0-9630384-1-3)

Regimental histories and Civil War research. Author Steve Meyer has regimental histories for all Iowa Civil War regiments available. He also conducts special research on individual Civil War soldiers. For information on research and regimental histories, even a specially written history of your civil war ancestor(s), contact Steve Meyer at the above address.

WORLD WAR II BOOK
FROM MEYER PUBLISHING

SOUND RECALL: One Typical Midwestern Town Remembers the Events of World War II. By Bob D. Fahey. Life was going on in Fort Madison, Iowa, as unassuming as any other Midwestern community in December of 1941. Then came the eventful day of December 7. Not until four years later on August 15, 1945 could the people of Fort Madison begin to resume life as they had known it before the war. Fifty years later, the people of this quaint river town tell their story. It is one of desperation, patriotism, and comaraderie unparalleled in the Twentieth Century. And, it's a story that is representative of what people and communities all across the United States experienced during the trying times of World War II. This book is bound to bring back many memories to those who lived in these times, and it will serve as testimony to the generations that follow of the sacrifices made on our behalf. Published in 1995. Paperback, 192 pages, 85 photos. (ISBN 0-9630284-4-8)